Visitor's Gu
THE FRENCH

Visitor's Guide Series

This series of guide books gives, in each volume, the details and facts needed to make the most of a holiday in one of the tourist areas of Britain and Europe. Not only does the text describe the country-side, villages, and towns of each region, but there is also valuable information on where to go and what there is to see. Each book includes, where appropriate, stately homes, gardens and museums to visit, nature trails, archaeological sites, sporting events, steam railways, cycling, walking, sailing, fishing, country parks, useful addresses — everything to make your visit more worthwhile.

Other titles already published or planned include:
The Lake District (revised edition)
The Chilterns
The Cotswolds
North Wales
The Yorkshire Dales
Cornwall
Devon
East Anglia
Somerset and Dorset
Guernsey, Alderney and Sark
The Scottish Borders
    and Edinburgh
The Welsh Borders
Historic Places of Wales
The North York Moors, York and
    the Yorkshire Coast
Peak District (revised edition)
South and West Wales
Hampshire and the Isle of Wight
Kent
Sussex
Dordogne (France)
Brittany (France)
Black Forest (W Germany)
The South of France
Tyrol
Loire
French Coast
Iceland

The Visitor's Guide To

THE FRENCH COAST

Martin Collins

British Library Cataloguing in
Publication Data

Collins, M.
 The visitor's guide to the French
 Coast.
 1. Coasts - France
 2. France — Description and travel
 — Guide-books
 I. Title
 914.4'204838   DC601.3

Acknowledgements

Thanks are due to Mrs Pauline Hallam of the
French Government Tourist Office for
assistance in the preparation of this book.

 The black and white illustrations were
taken by the author, except for p15, 52 (top)
which were supplied by C.W. Footer and p57,
73, 115 which were supplied by the French
Government Tourist Office. All the colour
illustrations were taken by the author.

For Diana

© Martin Collins, 1985
ISBN 0 86190 136 3 (paperback)
ISBN 0 86190 137 1

Printed in the UK by
Butler and Tanner Ltd,
Frome, Somerset.
Published by
Moorland Publishing Co Ltd,
Station Street,
Ashbourne, Derbyshire,
DE6 1DE England.
Tel: (0335) 44486

Contents

	Introduction	7
1	The North, Pas de Calais, Picardy and Normandy	11
2	The Brittany Coast	34
3	The Coast of Pays de la Loire and Poitou-Charentes	63
4	The Aquitaine Coast	83
5	The Coast of Languedoc-Roussillon	96
6	Provence and the Côte d'Azur	113
	Further Information	137
	Index	154

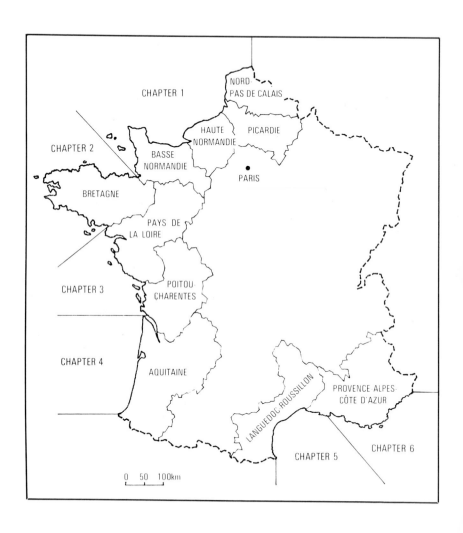

CHAPTER 1

NORD-
PAS DE CALAIS

CHAPTER 2

HAUTE
NORMANDIE

PICARDIE

BASSE
NORMANDIE

PARIS

BRETAGNE

PAYS DE
LA LOIRE

CHAPTER 3

POITOU-
CHARENTES

CHAPTER 4

AQUITAINE

LANGUEDOC-ROUSSILLON

PROVENCE-ALPES-
CÔTE D'AZUR

CHAPTER 6

CHAPTER 5

0   50   100km

Introduction

Each summer, tens of thousands of holidaymakers from all over Europe migrate to the coast of France, not least the French themselves for whom vacations are a national institution, a collective obsession. Without doubt, the majority of visitors seek the epicurean delights of warm sunshine and hospitable resorts in which to enjoy their hard-won leisure. It is equally true, however, that despite the blunt uniformity of mass tourism, holidays are capable of providing experiences as diverse as the individuals who take them, given a little forethought. No other coast in Europe can equal that of France for scenic contrasts, cultural and historic interest, and a wealth of amenity provision: there is truly something for everyone, which explains its universal appeal.

Man has settled on the coast since the dawn of civilisation — fishing, building fortifications and harbours, using the seaways for transport and communication. Seaside resorts as we know them, based on the discovery that sea air is good for body and soul, date back little more than a century. The era of sun-worship and widespread travel, promoted and served by a vast holiday industry, is a much more recent phenomenon; in France it has created new resorts and increased the prosperity of existing ones, while small unsuspecting communities and virgin coast have found themselves 'developed' to meet the increased demands for space and amenities.

By no means every coastal settlement preoccupies itself exclusively with the business of attracting holidaymakers, though the lure of revenue from tourism is clearly often hard to resist. Fishing is almost universal, while agriculture, wine-growing, the cultivation of shellfish and even salt-production impinge in their own ways on the coastal strip. Bleak industrialised stretches do exist, to be sure — witness Dunkerque and Marseille — but France's great ports rarely lack the kind of raw, colourful exuberance which makes visiting them so entertaining.

Innumerable locations are steeped in France's naval and military history, from sites of the earliest Roman occupation to the landing beaches of the last war. Religious buildings and monuments, domestic architecture too, stand like the movement of time congealed, vividly evoking the spirit and needs of their age, while the great festivals and processions held throughout the summer right round the coast keep alive religious and cultural traditions.

France's natural shoreline is a *pot-pourri* of topographical features: there are exquisite limestone cliffs and endless dune-backed Atlantic surf beaches, remote rocky headlands, intimate bays and a plethora of offshore islands, shallow coastal lagoons, reclaimed salt-marsh, forest, pebble banks and translucent waters rich in marine life. Natural forces themselves irresistibly conspire to shape and change the land, from raging forest fires in the south to storm damage and the inexorable march of wind-blown sand in the west and north.

By and large, these diverse environments and the wildlife they support are well respected. The establishment of national and regional parks and ornithological reserves simply underscores the need we all recognise, to protect areas of outstanding natural beauty and prevent the spoiling of important habitats.

Centres for marine biology research are dotted round the coast and numerous aquaria confront the visitor with an often astonishing array of marine life forms. Salt water and algae are used in *thalassotherapy* — the treatment of physical disorders and stress, with clinics at most major resorts.

While unspoilt and little-frequented stretches may be found readily enough, many parts of the French coast are densely settled, with recent demographic trends showing industry and population movements continuing to gravitate there. Increasing prosperity has produced a steady upward shuffle in holiday accommodation from tent to caravan, caravan to apartment, with one French family in nine now owning a second home, often on the coast. Other European nationals, particularly Germans, are joining in enthusiastically!

As a consequence of this, opportunistic and ugly building development, variously described as 'human rabbit hutches' and 'walls of concrete', blight parts of the Côte d'Azur, Vendée and Normandy, just as they blight the Spanish 'costas' and other holiday meccas. However, in its wisdom, the French government has imposed a policy of more moderate, low-rise building in regions like Aquitaine, currently undergoing tourist expansion, and past excesses seem unlikely to be repeated.

Interestingly, state sponsorship itself has spawned a chain of revolutionary new purpose-built resorts in Languedoc-Roussillon — the most ambitious project of its kind ever undertaken.

It is a great strength of the French coast that almost its entire length is accessible by road; yet that very advantage has generated acute problems of congestion and pollution in some areas, notably the Côte d'Azur. Until the 1980 Barcelona and Athens agreement to clean up the Mediterranean, industrial effluent and human sewage had threatened to overwhelm it, with wide-ranging implications for tourism. The crisis was averted, but elaborate pollution controls are still applied to French beaches.

North-west Brittany has fared little better, bearing the brunt of six major oil spills from tanker accidents between 1967 and 1980, including the well known *Amoco Cadiz* incident. Here too the visible traces of pollution have been removed, but these and other instances serve to highlight the vulnerability of a coastline to the effects of any human activity on a large scale, be it for profit or pleasure.

Visiting motorists will quickly discover that despite the French government's efforts to conserve oil and increase passenger traffic on its excellent railway system, 'car mania' persists. Coastal areas more than most suffer the consequences of their own attractiveness, drawing in cars by the thousand at peak season. Traffic jams, notorious on the Riviera, can sometimes be avoided by travelling during French mealtimes, but it is an uncertain strategy: better by far to cultivate patience and plan realistic itineraries. There are even parking discs for yachts on the Côte d'Azur!

The French enjoy a legal annual holiday entitlement of at least five weeks, and more public holidays than Britain. Though many choose to travel abroad, they are replaced in number by an influx from other European countries during the mass exodus to the coast in July and August — months when roads are most congested and accommodation is in greatest demand.

It has been suggested that the traditional holiday season is too short, but old habits die hard, and in less favoured areas resorts expect little trade before June or beyond the end of September. This consideration apart, late spring and early autumn bestow many advantages on those able to travel then.

Despite the growth in holiday apartments, the French coast is generously endowed with hotels, gîtes, holiday villages and campsites, many with an infrastructure of shops and entertainment catering for all tastes and pockets. Facilities for recreation vary according to the size of resort and the type of shoreline, as well as prevailing weather and sea conditions. In general, however, provision is excellent.

Yachting enjoys unrivalled popularity in Brittany and on the Mediterranean, where there are innumerable marinas, sailing schools and craft for hire. The Atlantic coast, from the Gironde to the Spanish frontier in particular, offers fine surfing, while scuba-diving and snorkelling are practised in more locations than it is possible to list. Windsurfing, like sea bathing, is possible anywhere that conditions allow. Seashore angling is unrestricted and opportunities for the sport abound in creeks, harbours, lagoons and river mouths. Practitioners of sand-yachting, water-skiing, hiking, tennis, golf, horseriding, swimming and much besides will find their requirements met by judicious use of this guide.

Few would question the significance of the beach itself to any coastal sojourn, since the majority of holidaymakers will count relaxation and a respectable tan high among their priorities. In search of a less capricious sun, many north Europeans migrate south and west where, in high summer, beaches often disappear beneath a tide of prostrate bodies! Fashions change, and while a decade ago women might have thought twice before removing a bikini top — something the French have come to regard as almost obligatory — naturism for both sexes is rapidly gaining momentum, especially on the coasts of Languedoc-Roussillon and Aquitaine where naturist communities are well established. There is, of course, no necessity to participate and more orthodox beach attire is equally prevalent: as someone once said, 'Nudism is a lot of fuss about nothing!'

Spanning nearly nine degrees of latitude and lapped by the southern North Sea, English Channel, Atlantic Ocean and the Mediterranean, climatic conditions on the French coast do vary considerably. Fortunately the sea moderates the sometimes excessive summer heat encountered inland and keeps north-western regions as mild as the Mediterranean in winter (Brest enjoys a higher average January temperature than Nice). Even parts of the English Channel are surprisingly equable, thanks to a finger of the beneficent Gulf Stream which caresses its shore, particularly the western Cotentin Peninsula of Normandy.

July sees temperatures generally at their highest values; even on the Mediterranean Côte d'Azur, however, where rainfall then is often negligible, low humidity keeps the heat bearable and nights are cool. Rainfall is highest everywhere in autumn, and more frequent throughout the year on the Atlantic and Channel coasts; drizzle and downpours there are not uncommon but in the west seldom persist all day.

During spring and autumn, more especially in late winter, Provence and the Riviera are chilled by that most unwelcome of northern visitors, the *mistral*. Cold dry continental air from the Massif Central is drawn south by low pressure in the Golfe du Lion for several days at a time: temperatures plummet and the countryside shivers, from the Rhône delta east along the Riviera. Cannes, Nice, Monaco and Menton, however, renowned for their balmy winter climate, shelter happily from the *mistral* behind coastal hills which take the final sting from its tail. By contrast, occasionally violent gusts of hot African air from the south — the *sirocco* — bring dry heat and airborne sand from the Sahara.

Sample weather statistics and sea temperatures appearing at the start of each chapter paint a broad picture of average conditions. However, uncharacteristic weather episodes invariably occur to upset the best laid plans. The author has encountered persistent cloudless heat on the Atlantic seaboard and tornadoes on the Côte d'Azur within the same month, while summer thunderstorms and sea mists have punctuated many a fine spell in most people's holiday experience.

Every attempt has been made to present a comprehensive and balanced portrayal of the French coast, but a guide of this size, encompassing so much, cannot claim to be exhaustive. The author's own choices and impressions have sometimes determined emphasis, though information throughout remains as objective and accurate as possible.

The book takes the form of a coastal journey, anti-clockwise from the Belgian border to Italy. Offshore islands have been included, with the exception of Corsica, considered too large and too distant from the mainland to receive comparable treatment. Every place and feature of note is considered with description and background. Sights or excursions are recommended, and an alphabetical entry in the 'Further Information' section lists water-sports and outdoor recreational facilities, along with a beach guide. Also listed there are the locations and opening times of public buildings, monuments, gardens, aquaria, nature reserves, lighthouses, etc, and important annual events.

Typical summer weather conditions on the North Coast of France						
	May	June	July	Aug	Sept	Oct
Average daytime air temperature °C	14.4	21	22.1	23	18.8	14.9
Typical daily sunshine hours	5.5	7	8.7	8.1	4.7	4.4
Days with some rainfall	23	20	9	5.5	16	16
Average sea temperature °C	10.5	14	15.5	17	16	14

1 The North, Pas de Calais, Picardy and Normandy:

BRAY-DUNES TO MONT-ST-MICHEL

The modest resort of Bray-Dunes stands barely 3km from the Belgian frontier, on the edge of an immense sweep of firm sand backed by dunes. It is France's northernmost settlement. At low tide there is an empty level of land and water, bisected by a line of surf, that stretches eastwards over the border to De Panne and westwards to Malo-les-Bains. The wind often scurries, unfettered, along these coastal flats, and sand-yachting — that curious hybrid sport of wheels and sail — is practised on the hard, open surface.

Malo-les-Bains, increasingly the residential quarter of Dunkerque, possesses more tangible attractions. Founded in 1870 by a local ship-owner, its pleasant boulevards and squares contain some fine shops and restaurants; entertainment is provided by a casino, a park and aquarium, a swimming pool

and skating rink.

Cranes and gantries on Dunkerque's dockside do nothing to enhance its westerly aspect, but Malo's amenities and the same expansive beach beneath a sea-wall promenade assure the town's popularity with local residents and visitors from nearby Lille. It was from these very sands that half a million troops of Britain's Expeditionary Force were evacuated during May and June 1940.

Since its birth in the ninth-century as a tiny fishing harbour close by a church (*kirk*) on the dunes, Dunkerque has suffered from a turbulent history and few old buildings remain: 80 per cent of the town was destroyed in World War II alone. It is, however, France's third largest port, with deep-water quays accommodating the most modern tankers and container vessels, extensive

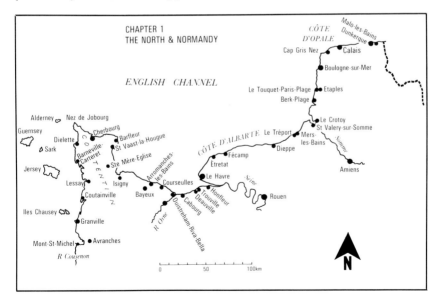

CHAPTER 1
THE NORTH & NORMANDY

ENGLISH CHANNEL

CÔTE D'OPALE
Malo-les-Bains
Dunkerque
Cap Gris Nez
Calais
Boulogne-sur-Mer
Le Touquet-Paris-Plage
Etaples
Berk-Plage
Le Crotoy
St Valery-sur-Somme
Mers-les-Bains
Le Tréport
Dieppe
Alderney
Nez de Jobourg
Guernsey
Cherbourg
Dielette
Barfleur
St Vaast-la-Hougue
Sark
Barneville
Carteret
Ste Mère-Eglise
CÔTE D'ALBÂTRE
Étretat
Fécamp
Amiens
Jersey
Arromanches-les-Bains
Le Havre
Lessay
Isigny
Courseulles
Coutainville
Bayeux
Honfleur
Deauville
Trouville
Rouen
Iles Chausey
Cabourg
Granville
Ouistreham-Riva-Bella
R Orne
Mont-St-Michel
Avranches
R Cousenon

0   50   100km

N

11

Rodin's 'The Burghers of Calais' and the town's Flemish-Renaissance Hôtel de Ville

shipyards, and a busy cross-channel ferry trade to Dover, Ramsgate and Folkestone. Boat trips round the harbour provide a graphic impression of this notable facility — Dunkerque's true *raison d'être*.

Clustered together in the town, the Musée des Beaux-Arts, Église St Eloi and Hôtel de Ville are worth a visit, as is the well appointed Codec supermarket. Elsewhere in the somewhat incohesive centre, one is unlikely to find much of interest, even less of beauty. As in so much faceless new urban development, traffic and crowds prevail, swamping the individual.

Although Dunkerque's ravaged past and fiercely industrial present have shaped the town and its surroundings, a steady flow of customers for shops, restaurants and hypermarkets is virtually guaranteed by its situation as a major passenger ferry terminal.

As if having to endure the worst

before being allowed to taste the delights and surprises ahead of us, Dunkerque's great petro-chemical complex must be passed. Only at Fos, near Marseille, does anything resemble it on the entire French coast: a surreal landscape of gleaming tanks, smoking chimneys, warehouses and heavy industrial installations. Knowing that such activity is vital to trade, jobs and the production of the commodities we all use hardly seems to diminish its impact, close as it is to beaches and sea and the port where our journey begins.

Petit Fort-Philippe is known for excellent fresh fish, while its busier neighbour, Gravelines, boasts a well preserved example of Vaubanesque ramparts. Neither is far from the ferry terminal: both stand closer still to the huge EDF nuclear power station, destined to become the most powerful in France by the late 1980s. With little oil and natural gas of their own, the French have pursued a vigorous nuclear energy programme and several power stations are situated on the coast.

With the industrial sprawl now left behind, more dunes run past Oye-Plage towards Calais. Behind them, cultivated fields and unpretentious villages are served by a maze of narrow lanes.

No other mainland European town or city handles more British holidaymakers than Calais, and the famous white cliffs of Kent lie a mere 38km away across the narrowest reaches of the English Channel. To consider Calais a starting point, to be passed through quickly en route for more exotic destinations, with scarcely a sideways glance, is understandable but slightly unfair. For what the town may lack in *chic* and guaranteed sunshine, it makes up for with sites of civic interest, a spirited French ambience and a splendid stretch of coastline south-west to Cap Gris-Nez.

Most of the shops, hotels, restaurants and amenities are found near the port area of Calais-Nord, rebuilt after World War II. A landmark from near or far, the Hôtel de Ville lifts its extravagant

fifteenth-century Flemish-Renaissance tower above the town and surrounding countryside: on successive visits it seems like an old friend! Before it, in the Place du Soldat-Inconnu, Rodin's celebrated sculpture 'The Burghers of Calais' stands on a raised plinth amongst lawns and flower-beds. It is an expressive statement of surrender; barefoot and dressed in tatters, six citizens handed over the town keys and themselves to Edward III in 1347, ending an eight-month-long siege. Calais was destined to remain in English hands for over two hundred years.

Commercial lace-making has been carried on here since the early nineteenth century, when the trade was brought over from Nottingham. Even today English names and terminology are still used, but the demand for lace is becoming less steady and Calais must rely upon her other industries — textiles, wood-pulp, chemicals, foodstuffs and tourism. A Musée des Beaux-Arts traces the town's artistic development, including the lace trade.

Quiet, shady parks are provided close

Cap Blanc-Nez, near Calais

to the town centre. One such — Parc St Pierre, opposite the Hôtel de Ville — contains the Musée de la Guerre. This diminutive bunker, an important German communications centre during World War II, now houses a simple but immensely evocative exhibition of wartime memorabilia: photographs, models, press cuttings, fragments of equipment. It is a grim reminder of the town's fate following the British withdrawal in 1940. Much of the dock area was destroyed but the fourteenth-century Église Notre-Dame, with a citadel on its north side built by Vauban, escaped and is being restored. For a panoramic view of Calais, visit the lighthouse, open during July and August.

Blériot's historic flight across the Channel in 1909 left from a beach just west of the town, and a monument there commemorates his achievement. Right along to Sangatte, picturesque and idiosynchratic wooden chalets line the dunes; there are old pill-boxes too, heralding many hundreds of kilometres of wartime coastal defences.

The Côte d'Opale takes its name from the milky colouring of inshore waters between Belgium and the Somme. Its most spectacular section lies from Calais to Boulogne, where high chalk promontories separate dry valleys. Here, rolling white cliffs and vast fields of limey soil, bearing a variety of crops, form an unforgettable patchwork of colours, pattern and texture, rising and dipping along the sea's edge. The area is a protected site with planned walking routes and nature trails. A vigorous south-to-north current undermines the great chalk headlands, causing substantial landslips; each century an estimated twenty-five metres of farmland is lost in this way.

The imposing grey monument at Cap Blanc-Nez is to Hubert Latham, whose attempts to fly the Channel during the same period as Blériot were doomed to failure, though he escaped unhurt from his exploits. In clear weather there are magnificent views from these cliffs to the English coast and it is easy to imagine how tantalising an air crossing must have seemed to those early aviators.

An almost boundless expanse of sand and dunes stretches for 10km to Cap Gris-Nez, providing some of the least frequented beaches in Europe. Bathing, however, can be dangerous due to the currents, and help may not always be close at hand. Only in Wissant's little bay, sheltered from easterly winds and the strong tidal drift, is swimming considered safe.

The lighthouse on Cap Gris-Nez, bristling with an impressive array of aerials and radar dishes, overlooks the Pas de Calais from Boulogne to Cap Blanc-Nez. Cornfields extend to old bunkers at the cliff edge, 45m above a fringe of boulders and angry surf. The cape is much visited. Inland, gaunt and weathered wartime buildings punctuate an agricultural landscape: one is surprised they are left standing until it is recalled that France was an occupied country in the not-so-distant past.

Audinghen's modern church, like that at Blériot-Plage, is incongruously graceless — an open, wire-braced tower surmounted by a twee cockerel, astride ceramic murals on exterior walls. What price contemporary substitutes for traditional ecclesiastical architecture when they result in such irreverent whimsy? Happily, of course, this is not always the outcome. Massive gun emplacements and another war museum near Cran-aux-Oeufs, offer more compelling distractions.

A waymarked footpath runs north from Audresselles' little harbour to Escalles, near Cap Blanc-Nez, along a switchback of chalk cliffs reminiscent of Dorset. 4km further south, Boulogne's port entrance is glimpsed from the broad beach and promenade at Ambleteuse, near the mouth of the River Slack.

High dunes lead to the splendid beach at orange-roofed Wimereux, a delightful fishing village at the seaward end of a picturesque valley renowned for its cider

Cathedral of Notre-
Dame de Boulogne,
from the Château,
Haute-Ville

and *crêpes* (pancakes with sweet or savoury fillings). This was the projected embarkation area for Napoleon's invasion of England, aborted after the Battle of Trafalgar.

Boulogne-sur-Mer, that mecca of day-trips, has a long history of association with the British, though now, like Calais, it is often only a port of call for the long-distance holidaymaker. Of Roman origin, today's town has two distinct faces. La Ville Haute, on a hill rising steeply behind tower-block offices and apartments, and threaded by cobbled streets, contains the Hôtel de Ville, a thirteenth-century château and the commanding dome of the Notre-Dame Basilica. A pathway round the ramparts combines a revealing tour of the old city with wide views over the port.

La Ville Basse, Boulogne's maritime and commercial centre, is a bustling modern town with numerous restaurants, hotels and cafés round the harbour catering for travellers in transit. (The locally caught sea-food is memorable!) This part was completely rebuilt after devastating air raids during World War II, and the high-rise flats ranked so conspicuously along the cliff tops derive from that period of redevelopment. In some contrast, colourful wooden beach huts line pleasant sands, much loved by Parisians, just north of the inner harbour.

This is continental Europe's largest fishing port and a major producer of

15

PLACES OF INTEREST IN CALAIS AND BOULOGNE

Calais
Lace-making and local history in the Musée des Beaux-Arts.
World War II mementos in old German communication bunker — photographs, weapons, uniforms, equipment, etc. Musée de la Guerre in Parc St Pierre.
Rodin's famous sculpture 'The Burghers of Calais' near the distinctive Hôtel de Ville.
Monument to Blériot's historic crossing of the English Channel by aircraft in 1909.

Boulogne
The hilltop Ville Haute, containing thirteenth-century château, impressive Basilica Notre-Dame and crypt, Hôtel de Ville — all in cobbled streets. Walk round the ramparts for views.
Seafood restaurants around the harbour in Ville Basse — views of shipping from the mole.
Climb to the top of the Colonne de la Grande Armée, 3km north off the N1 — commemorates Napoleon's intended invasion of England in 1803.

---

invasion of England, the slender marble tower tempts visitors up 263 steps to a height of 190m above sea level. It can be found off the N1, 3km north of the town centre.

Sand-dunes are a striking feature of the coast from Boulogne to the River Canche. Around the resort of Hardelot-Plage they are clothed extensively with birch, elsewhere with a scrubby mixture of gorse and pine.

Hardelot-Plage calls itself a 'Playground by the Sea', and the epithet fits. It offers a wealth of sporting facilities, including one of France's most beautiful golf courses, swimming pools, tennis courts, sand-yachting, cycling and horse-riding in the rugged dunes and on forest tracks, and waymarked walking trails. But any pretensions it may have had towards either village charm or smart elegance have been thwarted by a rash of modern apartment blocks and villas. Its beach, however, is above reproach — a truly magnificent acreage of fine, gently-shelving sand providing space for many outdoor activities.

South from the Canche estuary, dunes and sand have pushed the sea so far back that towns like Montreuil (once 'sur-Mer') and Rue are stranded kilometres inland. Le Touquet-Paris-Plage is liveliest of the resorts along this spreading coast and is well known to the English, whose wealthy nineteenth-century predecessors established an enclave of 'Englishness' here, endowing it with an air of refined luxury which still persists. Wooded outskirts conceal the really select residences — the mixed forest of sea-pine, birch, poplar and acacia was planted during the mid-1800s to shelter new property from wind and weather.

Within the town, and along the sea-front backing the double promenade, bizarre juxtapositions of gothic nineteenth-century villas and modern apartment blocks highlight the problems of integrating architectural styles when expansion or replacement of existing buildings is called for. Some stately old

processed fish products. (Try 'harengs saurs', a lightly cured Boulogne bloater, delicious with bread and potato salad.) Add to this trade an enormous volume of holiday traffic from Britain and a considerable import-export tonnage of timber, minerals, meat and fish, and the importance of Boulogne's extensive harbour becomes apparent.

For a literally breathtaking panorama over the port and the rolling wooded countryside inland, climb to the viewing balcony on the Colonne de la Grande Armée. Commemorating the massing of Bonaparte's forces at 'Camp du Boulogne' in 1803, prior to his intended

16

mansions are, indeed, empty and derelict, still grandiose in a faded, sorry way; it seems as if no-one has the heart to finally knock them down.

Le Touquet's street plan is open and symmetrical, its atmosphere lively but flavoured, perhaps, with a little English reserve. A lighthouse on the forest border affords superb views, and there is a pleasant covered market.

Like Hardelot-Plage, Le Touquet courts the sporting fraternity with quite enviable amenities, including a smart yacht harbour, a huge heated swimming pool, tennis courts, riding grounds, three golf courses, two casinos, a pony club, go-karting track, sand-yachting and a fine racecourse. If you prefer simpler pleasures, there is a beach of seemingly infinite dimensions stretching south past Stella-Plage and Merlimont-Plage to the Baie d'Authie; it is *char à voile* (sand-yachting) terrain par excellence! There are delightful walks, too, in the forest behind the town centre.

Upstream of Le Touquet, the little fishing port of Etaples struggles to stay open as the dunes extend. It boasts a new artificial lake for dinghy sailing, and a fascinating boatyard alongside the road, crammed with vessels undergoing repairs and laid up in storage. Could Etaples be anticipating its fate?

Tulip and gladioli nurseries, an airfield, and the 'Bagatelle' outdoor entertainment complex all lie north of Berk-Plage. Suburbs of this health resort sprawl well inland and the town, though sizeable, has few noteworthy features. But its seafront is popular and distinctive in a low-key way, lined with typically 1960s apartment blocks — a kind of 'old-fashioned modern'. Flowers and attractive hanging baskets abound. An immense pale sand beach with pastel-hued huts is backed by cafés and shops along a broad promenade and there are several campsites south of the town.

The countryside is low and windswept around the Baie d'Authie; trees and hedgerows have that bent-over, harassed look. Only two resorts — Fort-Mahon-Plage and the more mature Quend-Plage-les-Pins — interrupt a great sweep of empty dunes, rising in height to 36m and reaching down to the Somme estuary.

Due west of Rue, a thriving sea port in the Middle Ages, lie vegetated dunes, salt-marsh and meadows reclaimed from the sea. These vast tidal flats have long been an important staging post for over three hundred species of migratory birds, for many years hunted by wildfowlers. Some species became so endangered that conservation measures were introduced, and in 1968 a coastal strip 4km wide was designated as a reserve. The *Parc Ornithologique du Marquenterre,* which is open to the public, was created in 1973. There are waymarked paths through the dunes and hides for bird-watchers and photographers.

Neighbours le Crotoy and St Valery-sur-Somme face each other across the Somme estuary. They have long since lost their seasides and the intervening sandbanks are covered with verdant grass upon which sheep graze at low tide; for much of the time, seawater lurks in and out through serpentine muddy channels. Yet they are amiable places, full of shops selling *fruits de la mer.* Le Crotoy is a marvellous source of locally caught cockles, eels, prawns and crustacea, as well as containing the site of a castle wherein, we are told, the English temporarily imprisoned Joan of Arc before delivering her to Rouen.

St Valery's busy main street of stone setts leads to a pretty, tree-lined promenade and port. Tucked away in a courtyard is the historic little Chapelle St Pierre, its interior hung with model schooners and other full-rigged ships. William the Conqueror finally set sail from these quaysides for the invasion of England in 1066 after taking on reinforcements. In more recent times, St Valery was to become an important supply depot for the British army during World War I. Fishing for eels, shrimps and flatfish is possible from the seafront and in channels left by the tide — the whole Baie de Somme yields a rich harvest.

To the delight of enthusiasts, a steam railway, operating at summer weekends, connects St Valery with le Crotoy, via Noyelles-sur-Mer and Morlay. Out round Cap Hornu, the resorts of le Hourdel, Brighton and Cayeux-sur-Mer occupy the northern end of a pebbly strip bordering the extensive Hable d'Ault — lakes and marshland of an ancient bay. The pebbles are crushed and used in the manufacture of emery board and filtration systems.

Le Tréport, with its quieter twin Mers-les-Bains just across the River Bresle on the Normandy border, is a small fishing port and lively resort, well loved by Parisians for whom it is an easy drive. Old photographs show its harbour has changed little since the days of sail, though its maritime importance was considerably greater before the river mouth silted up. An unfortunate history of attack and destruction was not helped by the British who burned the town down repeatedly during the Hundred Years' War!

Many of le Tréport's houses, hotels, colourful shops and fish restaurants have been built distinctively tall and narrow, utilising a surprising variety of materials, from slate, brick and timber to concrete and flint; the rich textural surface of these Norman towns offsets a diversity of architectural style that can often jar. From le Tréport's animated quayside, walk out to the white lighthouse, or catch a cablecar from the beach to the Calvaire des Terrasses for wide views.

Long shingle beaches, sandy at low tide, stretch south to Criel-Plage but beware stonefalls from the cliffs and being stranded by the tide at Mesnil-Val. A precipitous wall of chalk cliffs characterises the 30km or so of coast to Dieppe; not an unrelieved grey-white like those farther north, but a soft intermingling of pale browns, creams, pinks and greens.

Above the shore, an unremarkable succession of hamlets and villages and the site of a nuclear power station lead on to Dieppe. This enterprising, multi-faceted port handles commercial cargo of fruit and vegetables as well as high grade fish. Varieties include turbot, bass and sole, the latter a Normandy speciality cooked in a rich cream sauce. Dieppe is also renowned for its scallops.

More than half a million passengers annually, two-thirds of them British, arrive here in cross-channel ferries. Ships dock close to the town centre, right alongside busy streets lined with arcaded shops, cafés and excellent fish restaurants. From the terminal buildings, it is but a short stroll to the pedestrianised Grande Rue, Dieppe's main shopping thoroughfare; Saturday mornings see it transformed into a huge, colourful open-air market — one of the very best in northern France. Nearby can be found the famous Café des Tribuneaux, and 200m away towards the harbour the cathedral-like Église St Jacques, much painted by Pissarro in his time.

Perched on a chalk crag, Dieppe's fifteenth-century castle houses a museum, with Impressionist paintings, prints and a unique collection of medieval carved ivories. High to the east of the port the fishermen's Chapelle Notre-Dame-de-Bon-Secours offers magnificent views. Between the two runs a broad esplanade, the Boulevard du Maréchal Foch, flanked by spacious, rather English lawns.

Good hotels, cafés and recreational amenities lend an air of vitality and animation to this popular resort. Car parking is mostly generous and free while a simple one-way system averts the congestion one might expect in such a bustling town.

In August 1942 the shingle beaches from Berneval to Ste Marguerite were the scene of the first Allied reconnaissance landings on Europe's coast, code-named 'Operation Jubilee'.

The abbey-church of Ste
Trinité, Fécamp

Although of the seven thousand
Canadian commandos deployed over a
thousand died, along with many
supporting troops, lessons learned from
this raid were to prove invaluable to the
Normandy landings two years later.
Dieppe remembers the fateful day with
numerous Canadian monuments and
flags and a dedicated museum 2km out
of town towards Pourville-sur-Mer.

Beautiful chalk cliffs, striated with
flints and yellow marl, undulate west
from Dieppe to Étretat — the Côte
d'Albarte (Alabaster Coast). A string of
small coastal resorts fringes the great
Caux plateau, a rolling plain of open
fields dotted with tree-sheltered
farmsteads. Beaches occupy the ends of
river valleys between shoulders of cliff
and are reached from ancient hanging
valleys — *valleuses* — left by a retreating
coastline.

Varengeville-sur-Mer (where the
cubist painter Georges Braques is

buried), Quiberville-Plage, St Aubin,
Sotterville-sur-Mer, Veules-les-Roses are
all variations on a theme of pebbly
beaches, breakwaters and beach huts,
caravans and chalets.

On opposite sides of St Valery-en-
Caux rise the twin limestone buttresses
of Falaise d'Aval and Falaise d'Amont,
both crowned by war memorials.
Veulettes-sur-Mer lies in a broad green
hollow, where the road, until now close
to the sea's edge, turns to approach
Fécamp. There is an exceptionally fine
viewpoint by the Notre-Dame-du-Salut
seamen's pilgrimage chapel, and from
the cliff edge beyond the beacon and
crucifix.

With the uncluttered, functional ethos
of a working town, Fécamp makes few
concessions to tourism. France's main
cod-fishing port, with trawlers ranging
as far afield as the Newfoundland
Banks, its economic stability depends
upon associated industries: canning and

19

fish-meal fertiliser production, rope and net manufacture, cod-drying and shipyards. The town is famous, however, on two counts — it is the home of Benedictine liqueur, with a distillery and museum housed in a nineteenth-century neo-Renaissance building (guided tours in English);and it is the birthplace of Guy de Maupassant.

The great abbey church of Ste Trinité is well worth a visit, its massive vaulted interior containing many interesting features, including recorded plainsong. Behind the high altar is the Sanctuary of the Precious Blood, attracting huge pilgrimages on the Tuesday and Thursday after Trinity Sunday.

Fécamp does have a pleasure-boat marina, but the beach is a rather bleak, uninviting place. Diving, however, is possible here and in many locations from Yport back to Dieppe, where waters are largely free from sediment.

Unlike its near neighbours, Étretat has star quality. Weathered limestone cliffs soar at either end of a long pebble bank. On the summit of the eastern Falaise d'Amont stands a monument and memorial museum to Charles Nungesser and Francois Coli, French aviators whose attempt to be first to fly the Atlantic ended in disaster on 8 May 1927.

Falaise d'Aval, an hour's return walk from the west end of the promenade, has a sensational arch and needle rock standing 70m above the sea. The shapely, striated erosion continues west past the Manneporte, another natural arch. These are some of Europe's most dramatic chalk cliffs, rivalling the best of Dorset and Kent. Swells breaking against the lofty, sculptured headlands present an unforgettable sight in heavy weather; equally memorable, when the light hangs like a curtain of luminescence down to a limpid sea, are stunning views and the delicate, changing hues of the rock itself.

Such intrinsic beauty has attracted writers and painters since the nineteenth century and a hint of Étretat's earlier dignified elegance remains, despite the postcards and ice-cream. The remarkable covered Market Hall is, disappointingly, a reconstruction. Backed by smart glass-screened cafés and restaurants, the pebble beach is justly popular.

Cap d'Antifer is a less welcoming spot. Visits to its severe, cream lighthouse are possible, but car parking is virtually non-existent. Although old gun emplacements dot the cape, land near the narrow lane from la Poterie is wired off for grazing and little visited.

Built less than a decade ago and clearly visible to the south-west, the long pier of the Havre-Antifer port receives oil tankers of up to half a million tons. From here to the outskirts of Le Havre, the cliff edge is rarely accessible, though the D940 runs parallel some 2km inland. Founded in the sixteenth century by Francois I to replace a silting-up Harfleur (now the old port), Le Havre suffered a total of 146 air raids during World War II and was all but obliterated; it took the French, with Allied help, over two years to clear the debris so that rebuilding could begin. From Europe's worst bomb-damaged port, a scene of abject devastation, Le Havre has recovered to become second in importance to Marseille in under forty years. The immense industrial complex on the north bank of the Seine is built mostly on alluvial land, with room for further expansion.

On the whole, Le Havre's face seems grey and vaguely forbidding, though such impressions are admittedly subjective. It was completely re-planned after the war by the pioneer of reinforced concrete construction, Auguste Perret. At one time hailed as the ideal twentieth-century town, with its architectural cohesion, living units imaginatively arranged over shops and offices, and an emphasis on wide, airy perspectives, today's evaluation has to be a more sceptical one. We are moving away from 'big is beautiful' towards design concepts that relate more to human scale: grandiose design, once built, must be lived with. While the motorist enjoys unlimited parking and free-flowing circulation, pedestrians often find the shopping centre too dispersed, and buildings (particularly in the Place de l'Hôtel de Ville) institutional and remote. However, it is all worth a look, preferably on foot. Among the sights are Perret's own Église St Joseph — a stark, conspicuous edifice on an unusual square plan — and a Musée des Beaux-Arts with works by Raoul Dufy, Eugène Boudin and some Impressionists and Fauves.

A splendid tunnel carrying road, cycle track and pavement leads to the heights of Montgeon Forest and a panorama of the harbour and sea, while smart villas and picturesque cafés in Ste Addresse, Le Havre's western suburb, look down a sweep of beach to the marina breakwater.

Until 1959, ferries were the only means of crossing the Seine downstream of Rouen. Now, the great Pont de Tancarville, one of the largest suspension bridges in Europe, saves motorists from that 125km inland detour to reach western Normandy. 1,400m in length, the bridge's considerable height above river level allows large vessels access to Rouen. For *aficionados* of bridges, there is a telescope and recorded commentary (in English) on the south bank, and floodlighting by night.

For long a favourite with the British, sailors and landlubbers alike, Honfleur is a gem. It was from here that the seventeenth-century French navigator Samuel Champlain set sail with orders to colonise the newly claimed territory of Canada and in 1608 founded Quebec. There are several quaint old cobbled streets, public gardens, a museum of local history and a quite extraordinary wooden church. Ste Catherine's all-timber construction, including its separate bell tower, is rare in western Europe and may have been intended as a temporary solution to rebuilding

---

PLACES TO VISIT BETWEEN THE SOMME AND THE SEINE ESTUARIES

Parc Ornithologique du Marquenterre
Wild bird sanctuary with pathways and hides for watching and photography.

Steam railway (weekends) from St Valery-sur-Somme to le Crotoy.

Le Tréport
Colourful harbour and seafood restaurants, cable car to cliffs and Calvaire des Terrasses viewpoint.

Dieppe
The Grande Rue shopping street and Saturday market, town-centre docks.

Côte d'Albarte (Alabaster Coast)
Beautiful limestone cliffs, especially at St Valery-en-Caux and Étretat.

Le Havre
Town centre rebuilt by Auguste Perret after extensive war damage.

Pont de Tancarville
One of Europe's great suspension bridges.

Honfleur
Bustling, picturesque Norman town with its lovely Vieux Bassin — an inner harbour surrounded by tall, slate-clad houses.

Deauville
The famous Promenade des Planches, a 2km board-walk at fashionable resort, renowned for sports, entertainment and horse-racing.

---

following the departure of the English after the Hundred Years' War.

This part of Normandy embracing the Caux, the Seine estuary, the Côte de Grace and Rouen, is associated with the emergence of Impressionism in the latter half of the last century. Honfleur became a focal point, with the artists reputed to have first met in the St Siméon inn at Mère Toutain's. The

Early morning,
Deauville

Musée Eugène Boudin contains works by Monet, Courbet, Huet, Corot and Boudin himself (a native of Honfleur), as well as works by 'foreigners' like Bonington and Jongkins. Writers and musicians were here too, among them Beaudelaire and Erik Satie, who was born at No 90, Rue Haute.

Honfleur's distinction as an artistic centre owes much to the creative energy and formal innovations of the late nineteenth century. Today's artists, with straw hats and quayside easels, go through the motions to please the tourists: mostly they have the act but no script.

Surrounding shopping streets may be narrow and crowded, and the western quay busy with traffic, but it is Honfleur's Vieux Bassin — the Old Harbour — which monopolises visitors' attention. Fishing boats and pleasure craft crowd the watersides, a dazzling kaleidoscope of colour and shimmering reflections. Beyond their masts and rigging rise terraces of slender, slate-faced houses up to seven storeys high, enhancing the sense of verticality and pattern against which life follows its everyday course.

There are many good cafés and restaurants, and stalls selling seafood, fruit and vegetables. You may find an exhibition of giant insects, a knife-grinder too, but Honfleur's rather unlovely estuary beach, reached by a little tunnel beneath the road west of the town, is a disappointment.

Gladioli grow on the ridges of thatched houses along the pretty D513 'Corniche Normande'. Busy and congested at times during the high season, it winds through an undulating landscape of orchards and farmland to Trouville, passing Criqueboeuf with its twelfth-century church, and the charming resort of Villerville dropping steeply to the sea.

Trouville is older than its classy neighbour, Deauville, and more picturesquely placed on high ground above the River Touques. Its unspoilt fishing harbour, wide sands, safe bathing and sporting facilities have earned it a reputation with French families who flock here in summer along the excellent access routes from northern cities. Shopping and eating places are many and varied, the quaysides and Norman-style fish market noteworthy, but the town's earlier opulence has disappeared.

Deauville boasts a riot of flags and gaily coloured beach tents; racehorses exercising on the sands, as if from a Degas painting; young boys scrubbing the boardwalk and watering potted shrubs outside expensive restaurants; and early beachgoers staking a claim in the gentle morning sunshine. At 9.30am the most celebrated promenade in Europe is deserted, but within an hour it will have sprung to life: 2km of wooden decking on which to sit or stroll in the knowledge that you will be scrutinised, and in turn are free to stare back! Such self-conscious parading is untypical of Normandy resorts, but Deauville does have an impeccable pedigree following long association with the rich and famous. One hotel chain advertises establishments in Deauville, La Baule and Cannes, and there is little doubt that they belong to the same exclusive league.

Built in the 1860s by the Duc de Morny, Deauville has retained much of its original character as northern Europe's most elegant watering-place; today it caters skilfully for a cosmopolitan clientele of all tastes and pockets. Its recreational amenities are legendary: La Touques racecourse, a sumptuous marina, a polo-ground, casino, tennis courts, golf courses, swimming pools and much more. During the season there are gala nights and a number of festivals.

New building development is refreshingly tasteful, while ostentatious neo-Gothic hotels and villas line the Boulevard Eugène Cornuché — relics from the days when the monied classes brought their families and servants to summer in this most fashionable of places.

Benerville and Blonville-sur-Mer form a single resort stretching west along the lush Côte Fleurie to the long promenade and casino at Villers-sur-Mer. The Falaise des Vaches Noires (literally 'Black Cows') take their name from large seaweed-covered blocks of fallen cliff below the Auberville plateau. The cliffs themselves are formed of dark clay, cut by ravines, in places crumbling and dangerous. It is a promising location for fossil-hunting, but must be reached on foot at low tide, a two-hour return walk from Houlgate or Villers.

Houlgate is a pretty, tree-shaded Normandy resort where both coast and a hinterland of wooded hills are equally appealing. Its magnificent sandy beach is backed by a sea-wall promenade extending to the foot of dark, brooding cliffs beneath which anglers and shellfish-hunters potter about amongst the rocks.

In 1066, Dives-sur-Mer was a sizeable port, enabling William the Conqueror's army to embark in a huge convoy of ships and smaller craft for the invasion of England. Reinforcements were collected en route from St Valery-sur-Somme before the fleet crossed the Channel and landed, three days later on 28 September, at Pevensey. The subsequent events of Duke William's conquest are graphically recorded on the Bayeaux Tapestry and in all our history books. The port at Dives is now completely silted up and given over to

Memorial to the capture of Pointe du Hoc in June 1944

industrial activity.

Despite a variety of holiday entertainments, an extended marina and a superb sandy beach, Cabourg slumbers on across the River Dives, waking intermittently to the twentieth century! Many visitors find this vaguely anachronistic air attractive and there are pleasant walks along wide shady avenues radiating out from the Casino and Grand Hotel, as well as a fine seafront and good town amenities.

Beaches between the River Orne and the Cotentin Peninsula, known as the Calvados Coast, were chosen for the great D-Day Landings of June 1944. Detailing these historic military undertakings lies outside the scope of this guide, but special reference is made to visible remains of wartime equipment and buildings, and in particular to the principal memorials and museums near the coast. The towns and villages involved are often eminently pleasing resorts in which to holiday: their connections with the landings, however, will be given precedence over descriptions of their amenity value.

Towards the mouth of the Orne, the sands at low tide are more extensive than ever — almost 2km wide at Merville-Franceville-Plage. Here is a unique collection of intact German fortifications, open to the public only since 1982 and well worth visiting.

Ouistreham is an international yachting centre at the end of the Caen canal. Its northern edge merges with Riva-Bella, a rather brash modern resort of funfairs and *frites*, but possessing an excellent beach. It was one of the first towns to be liberated in 1944, and a commemorative Museum of the Normandy Landings has been built here;

outside, all that remains of the war is a solitary blockhouse on the north shore.

Semi-urban ribbon development runs like a frieze above continuous sandy beaches to the huge white casino at Luc-sur-Mer. Just inland lie fields of wheat, and small British wartime cemeteries can be found at Douvres-la-Delivrande and Hermanville-sur-Mer. The skeleton of a whale washed up in 1885 is a local oddity in Luc-sur-Mer's Parc Municipal.

St Aubin-sur-Mer exudes an authentic, unspoilt charm which Courseulles-sur-Mer has lost. This once quiet resort is bearing the brunt of apartment block development. Lip-service is paid to the use of traditional materials — slate roofs and cladding, with muted colours — but the architecture is unmistakably 'tower block'. Even if the economics are right, the result is an eyesore, dwarfing nearby traditional buildings and most of the modern ones too.

Other than at Vers-sur-Mer, blessed with a charming cluster of wooden beach huts, the coast west to Arromanches is wilder and less frequented. Villas give way to caravans and chalets sheltering behind low dunes. There is a waymarked coastal footpath (Sentier de Littoral) and just inland, the lovely pastoral landscape of the Auge — old Norman manor houses and half-timbered farmsteads renowned for their Camembert and cider. This swath of countryside behind the beaches seems imbued with a kind of distilled tranquility, as if those dark days of war-time occupation and the bitter losses incurred during liberation have been absorbed, understood, and finally compensated for.

Arromanches-les-Bains was known only to a few discriminating French families who loved its spacious beach, before the invasion of 1944 put its name into history. Here, on 7 June of that year, the Allied armies landed from four thousand ships and a thousand smaller craft in the huge artificial 'Mulberry B' harbour (known to the French as Port

Winston). Remnants of the structure are best seen at low tide.

The principal Landings Museum, a severe concrete building behind the national flags of the Allies, is easily located at the east end of the town. It houses an impressive exhibition, with Royal Navy film, weapons, uniforms, photographs and plans, maps, autographs and dioramas. The public is admitted in guided groups and the museum is open all year round. In high season, milling crowds conspire against a thoughtful appreciation of the displays, but one should not be deterred.

Arromanches is heavily patronised during the summer and, as resorts go, can seem a little tawdry. The Landings Museum is confronted by car parks, bars, a busy shopping street and a popular beach; throngs of swimsuited holidaymakers in brilliant sunshine contrast uneasily with the relics of war. Some believe that the landings beaches as a whole are best seen outside the holiday period altogether.

Port-en-Bessin marks the eastern boundary of Omaha Beach, in the American sector. Planned as a naval base in the seventeenth century and almost hidden between tall marl cliffs, its lively fishing harbour is cradled by two semi-circular jetties. Farther west, between Colleville and St Laurent-sur-Mer, above Omaha Beach itself, lies the main American Military Cemetery.

Lawns, trees and borders along the approach walk are lovingly tended and, despite the passage of many thousands of visitors, a sense of caring reverence prevails. A huge central memorial bears maps of invasion strategy and the war's course further afield, while a massive, romanticised bronze figure stands above a simple pond, arms outstretched to the sky in an attitude of dignified supplication. Out beyond lie 9,386 graves, radiating in all directions across acres of mown grass. Each grave is marked by a white marble headstone. Every inscribed cross or Star of David represents a life lost, a family bereaved;

new building have obscured the battlefields themselves, the exception is Pointe du Hoc where shell-holes, gun emplacements and bunkers all remain untouched. Out near the point, a rough-hewn granite stele rises above twin plaques, in French and in English, remembering the courage of the American 2nd Rangers Batallion who scaled the great crumbling yellow cliffs to take this strategic German position. Beneath the stele, on a wall in the warren of underground rooms, a metal plate names some who perished, and there is a chilling view through the gun-slit at a strip of sea. Although access paths were improved for the Fortieth Anniversary celebrations, the site is undeveloped and unabused; even a steady scatter of fellow sightseers fails to diminish its impact.

8km south-east of Grandchamp-Maisy, a little fishing port near the Vire estuary, lies La Cambe German War Cemetery. It has the tragic distinction of containing more graves than any other in this region — almost 21,500.

Isigny-sur-Mer, with neighbouring Carentan, has long been a centre for dairy products. Like other towns on this coast, its seaside has silted up, yet flood-prone marshland around the converging Rivers Vire, Taute and Douve extends right to the centre of the Cotentin Peninsula — that square jut of France which points a finger at Lyme Bay. Cattle graze the flat alluvial pastures and their rich dairy produce goes to market at Isigny and Carentan, whose thirteenth-century Gothic church is visible from afar down the tree-lined waterway to the sea.

Ste Marie-du-Mont, to the north, has a fine landings museum sometimes hosted by local youngsters, and a monument to the 4th Division American Infantry who landed near here on Utah Beach, most westerly in the American sector. At la Madeleine stands a 'Liberty Way' milestone, several monuments and a memorial crypt, and there is a rose-granite stele in memory of the 2nd French Armoured Division at les-

perhaps more poignant still are the graves of those 'Known only to God'. It is a profoundly moving place.

There are more monuments to the landings at either end of the long sea-wall road at les Moulins and at Vierville-sur-Mer, where there is also a museum of American material in a Nissen hut. Another museum, containing exceptionally fine exhibits, can be found at Surrain, 5km due south of St Laurent.

If, as a rule, the passage of time and

American Military Cemetry, Omaha Beach

Dunes-de-Varreville. Yet a further museum exists at Ste Mère-Église, inland of Utah Beach on the N13, a town made famous by the film *The Longest Day*, and a venue for American war veterans on 6 June each year.

Except between les Gougins and Quineville, sand dunes block the view of beaches and sea from the coast road. Towns, villages and low hills inland from this marshy coastal fringe were thought by John Ruskin in the mid-nineteenth century to resemble Worcestershire. However, unlike that most English of counties, the Cotentin is surrounded on three sides by water. The region's north-eastern edge — the Val de Saire — is a granite plateau dipping gently beneath the waves, a rugged, slightly threatening coast of broken reefs and treacherous currents. The sea is held at bay behind walls and banks.

From the long jetty at St Vaast-la-Hougue, Vauban's squat seventeenth-century Fort de la Hougue stands beyond the sandy Grande Plage, its connecting isthmus. St Vaast possesses a sizeable marina but is unmistakably a working port too; fishing boats and colourful nets line the harbour quaysides and good, cheap oysters are plentiful. The white-painted apse of a tiny mariners' chapel near the jetty acts as a navigational aid for shipping.

Flat fields of carrots, cabbage and the covered heads of flax are separated from the sea by dykes — a touch of Flanders. Standing back from the D1 road farther north, the fortified and handsomely proportioned Manoire de la Crasvillerie is worth looking out for.

Sombre granite houses roofed with slate echo the phlegmatic, stolidly functional atmosphere that pervades the once-famous fishing port of Barfleur. Its Montfarville church repays a visit, and the Phare de la Pointe de Barfleur, 71m high, is one of the tallest in France.

Pretty coastal hamlets and small fields enclosed by hedge-covered walls characterise this northern perimeter of the Cotentin Peninsula; east of Cherbourg there are numerous market gardens.

Goury's octagonal lifeboat station, near the dangerous Alderney Race

To describe Cherbourg as grey and unyielding may be harsh, yet it is easy to be persuaded by the constant roar of heavy goods vehicles and by the uncompromising severity of its port architecture that the town is all industry and precious little else. Befitting its role as a major transatlantic port, long-standing naval base and cross-channel ferry terminal, water and quaysides predominate. But even away from the busy dock area, roads and pavements alike are often too congested for comfort.

For those with a few hours to spare, however, there are worthwhile sights to take in, including a new arts complex housing the extensive Thomas Henry collection; a Musée de la Libération in the hilltop Fort du Roule; the Parc Emmanuel-Liais with its tropical plants and, in summer, Anglo-French yacht racing offshore.

Rocky headlands, secluded shingly bays and a succession of tiny hamlets edge a landscape of field enclosures not unlike parts of Cornwall. Cap de la Hague, a flat tongue of land, pushes its bristling reefs defiantly out into the Channel; lighthouse towers, beacons and a few houses stand against an encompassing, bullying sea. Slipways radiate from Goury's octagonal lifeboat station, allowing a launch at any state of the tide. Its little sheltered anchorage provides refuge from the awesome Alderney Race, often running at over eight knots.

Past the wild Baie d'Ecalgrain, the Nez de Jobourg is reached along narrow lanes from Dannery hamlet. Barren, windswept and surrounded by reefs, it is nevertheless a well-visited headland, with cliff-top footpaths and telescopes for the extensive and very beautiful views of the Channel Islands and the Anse de Vauville. The 'Auberge des Grottes' tearoom-cum-restaurant is endearingly simple, if a little expensive, and parking is free. An amusing boat-shaped kiosk on wheels sells postcards and souvenirs but the cape is otherwise unexploited.

Dark moorland combes rear up behind the great sweep of the Anse de Vauville, as grand as any in south-west Britain. But on the granite spine above stands a man-made intrusion of monstrous proportions: a plutonium nuclear power plant, euphemistically called 'Usine de la Hague'. Already a futuristic complex of towers and faceless concrete, a programme of extension has festooned it with cranes and scaffolding. Three layers of security fence surround the vast site — two barbed-wire, one electric. Leaving aside the nuclear energy debate, one can only sympathise with local inhabitants whose wild and remote promontory has been irreversibly transformed; objectors have stencilled 'Radioactive-Danger' on walls and road signs as far away as Cherbourg.

Picturesque settlements dot the landscape farther south — a swarm of little '-villes'. Dielette, like much of northern Cotentin, is somewhat off the beaten track, a 'rough diamond' resort for locals. Sitting north of high granite cliffs at Cap de Flamanville, its long graceful curve of breakwater protects a small harbour and beach from the west, and there is a campsite right on the front.

Carteret, Barneville and Barneville-Plage have amalgamated to form a continuous settlement astride the shallow mouth of the Gerfleur, enjoying the climatic advantages of the Gulf Stream and commensurate popularity. A rocky headland to the north, near Normandy's largest dunes, carries a lighthouse and a cliff path (Sentier des Douaniers); it also shelters Carteret's beach and quayside, from which there

are regular sailings to Jersey and Guernsey, plainly visible to the west.

Extensive sands and many campsites stretch south beyond Portbail's harbour to Denneville, Surville, St Germain-Plage and the broad estuary of the River Ay. At its head lies the town of Lessay. The magnificent Romanesque abbey-church was repaired using original materials after serious damage during World War II. Founded in 1056, it is now one of Normandy's finest examples of Romanesque architecture.

Lessay's other attraction, its Holy Cross Fair, brings four days of trading and festivities from 9 September each year. Colourful tents fill the surrounding countryside and important horse and sheepdog sales are held each day. Sheep and geese are roasted on huge spits in the open, accompanied by music and dancing into the early hours.

A level wasteland of scrub and gorse, mildly reminiscent of the Camargue, stretches south towards Coutances; the Lande de Lessay. Along the sea's edge, enormous beaches figuratively swallow up all who visit them, with room to spare, while inland, onions and carrots flourish in the sandy soil. Compared with so much of the French coast, development north of Coutainville is modest and low-key, offering ample opportunity to 'get away from it all'. By the same token, sea bathing is not always safe or guarded and the big tides should be watched for, especially where there are sandbanks.

Coutainville, the peninsula's most forward-looking resort is flanked by 7km of these wild sandy beaches. Thanks to a branch of the Gulf Stream which washes this shore, sub-tropical vegetation clothes the hills behind the dunes, while pretty encircling countryside south of the Lande de Lessay holds secluded old manor houses in delightful valleys.

'South Sea Island' straw huts have replaced old bathing cabins — a sign of the times, for Coutainville is no slouch. In conjunction with neighbouring Agon,

the thrust of its development has been towards modern amenity provision and it boasts a casino, theatre, racecourse, swimming pool, golf-course, boating facilities (including water-skiing and diving), tennis, horse-riding, cycles for hire and angling.

Campsites are in good supply down much of this coast (though less so in the north) and from Coutainville to Granville is no exception. Past the broad, marshy outlet of the River Vanlee, crossed by a causeway at low tide, Granville's old town rises ahead on a granite promontory.

Its citadel was built by the English in 1439 to consolidate their position against the threat from French-held Mont-St-Michel, but it fell nevertheless two years later. A circuit of the ramparts may be made, with superb views in clear conditions extending to Brittany, from the large Place de l'Isthme. Within its protecting walls, the Haute Ville is a warren of narrow streets and arches, its west end dominated by the massive Église Notre-Dame.

Like barracks the world over, Granville's is a cheerless hulk of a building out on the Pointe du Roc. Its assault course ends near wartime gun emplacements: a lone gun barrel mounted on concrete plinths still stands sentinel over the northern approaches. Nearby is a delightful aquarium, and a path leads past the red-topped lighthouse round the rocky point itself — a spectacular walk in stormy weather.

Granville has been wistfully dubbed 'Monaco of the North', after its casino and headland rock. Busy and varied in character, the lower town has lively shops and cafés, and a 'Historial granvillais' waxworks museum. It is also a centre for *thalassotherapy* (sea-water cures). There are pleasant walks in the Jardin-Publique Christian-Dior, of coutourier fame, giving access along a cliff path to Douville's immense beach. Granville's own is a narrower affair beneath shaley cliffs, but enjoys the added bonus of a swimming pool.

Scalloped concrete breakwaters shelter Granville's important harbour complex. In addition to handling commercial cargo and ferry services to Jersey and the Iles Chausey (a popular day-trip), it provides generous moorings for pleasure craft. Large crowds are drawn to the quaysides in early August for a Breton-like 'Pardon of the Sea'.

Beaches of shaley sand run south through St Pair and Jullouville to the smart pine-shaded bars and villas of Carolles-Plage. The Baie du Mont-St-Michel unfolds ahead but cliffs hold back views of the island itself until St Jean-le-Thomas is reached; even then, poor visibility can intervene. Although a veritable paradise for children around Carolles, the attractiveness of the beaches diminishes towards Genets and bathing becomes more hazardous. Each July, a pilgrimage is made right across the sands to Mont-St-Michel, but at other times a guide is essential for this 8-9km walk. (Apply to the Place des Halles, Genets.)

Perched 100m above the See estuary, Avranches offers unsurpassed views of Mont-St-Michel from its immaculate Jardin des Plantes. The eighth-century bishop of this charming old town founded the famous abbey so, as one would expect, there are significant historical connections. For a sight of some important eighth to fifteenth-century manuscripts, visit the Musée d'Avranchin.

Topographical links are most plainly

Wartime relic on Granville's Pointe du Roc

PLACES TO VISIT ON THE COTENTIN
PENINSULA

St Vaast-la-Hougue
Colourful fishing harbour, Vauban's
seventeenth-century Fort-la-Hougue.

Barfleur
Large, quiet harbour and one of
France's tallest lighthouses.

Cherbourg
The hilltop Fort du Roule contains
the Musée de la Libération. Port
complex, cargo vessels, cross-channel
and transatlantic liners.

Cap de la Hague
Remote rocky cape near the Alderney
Race.

**Baie d'Ecalgrain and the Nez de
Jobourg**
Windswept, wild bay and headland.

Barneville-Carteret
Washed by Gulf-Stream — cliff
paths, lighthouse, sailings to Channel
Islands.

Coutainville
Sub-tropical vegetation, vast beaches
and a wealth of modern amenities.

Granville
Ramparts surrounding Haute Ville,
views of Brittany from this 'Monaco
of the North'.

Mont-St-Michel
Great abbey-church with museum
and guided tours; shops and
restaurants in the Grande Rue; the
highest tides in Europe.

seen from the air and flights round the
bay operate from an aerodrome south-
west of the town. Avranches has a lively
centre, an imposing Basilica, and a
monument to General Patton's crucial
advance from here on 31 July 1944.

Rounding the head of the Selme
estuary, Mont-St-Michel is half-
glimpsed across fields of maze and in
breaks between apple orchards and old

Normandy farmhouses. Village churches
are still heavily built, with slate, wedge-
shaped roofs atop square towers. Before
long on our journey west, a remarkable
metamorphosis in church architecture
unfolds.

Mont-St-Michel needs few
introductions: for most of us it has
become a visual cliché as familiar as the
Matterhorn or the Eiffel Tower. But as
coachload upon coachload of visitors
are skilfully shepherded round its abbey-
church and museums, and left to join the
press of bodies already souvenir-hunting
in the Grande Rue, thoughts turn to the
years before organised tourism, to the
origins of this quite astonishing place.

During the eighth-century, a series of
tidal waves are thought to have
inundated the forest surrounding two
granite outcrops in the Cousenon
estuary. Huge deposits of mud and
quicksand so altered the pattern of tidal
flow that the rocks became permanently
isolated features. Tombelaine, 4km out
in the bay, remained a true rock island,
but access to the nearer one was possible
at low tide, and a tiny chapel was put up
on its summit (known then as Mont
Tombe) in AD709.

Not until the twelfth century was the
great abbey begun. Three hundred years
later, fortifications were added,
rendering it inviolate despite years of
sporadic harassment by the English.
During the Hundred Years' War,
however, pilgrims were granted entry
and a sort of Middle Ages equivalent to
the commercial exploitation of our own
time sprang up, with craftsmen and
hoteliers prospering. With the French
Revolution, the monks were dispersed,
the buildings looted and in the late 1700s
Napoleon turned the Mount into a
prison. These were years of decadence
and decline, which prevailed until a
century ago when the State took over
and commenced restoration.

Today, close on 750,000 sightseers
arrive annually, and a little town of
hotels, restaurants and shops has
developed, leading up from the main

The Vieux Bassin, Honfleur

St Vaast-la-Hougue

Golfe du Morbihan

Porte du Roi entrance. Space here does not allow for a detailed description of the intricate cluster of historic buildings, but frequent guided tours in several languages are laid on for visitors. The Festival of the Archangel Michael is especially worth attending in late September.

While it is possible to walk round the almost circular base of the Mount (barefoot or in wellington boots), an eye must be constantly kept on the phenomenal tides, the highest in Europe, which surge in at up to 60m a minute; they even wash over the causeway car park during spring and autumn equinoxes.

From the banks of the River Cousenon on Normandy's border with Brittany, Mont-St-Michel is a remote, ethereal pyramid. Seen thus from afar, across tidal flats, it is perhaps at its most impressive. Even today, in an age accustomed to large man-made structures in the landscape, it presents a uniquely thrilling sight.

2 The Brittany Coast:

MONT-ST-MICHEL TO LA ROCHE BERNARD

After the great tidal inundations which left Mont-St-Michel an island, the sea-level fell back, uncovering vast salt-water marshes extending up to 10km inland from the present coast. Drainage and cultivation have continued since the twelfth century, slowly consolidating the Marais de Dol and encouraging settlements between the Normandy border and Cancale. In the east, near the canalised River Cousenon, a network of ditches, dykes and *polders* enables extensive tidal flats to be successfully grazed by sheep. Mont Dol, a prehistoric granite mound farther west near Dol-de-

Bretagne, overlooks this perfectly horizontal landscape, chequered with crops and lines of poplar and willow.

Villages along the littoral, such as Cherrueix, le Vivier-sur-Mer with its mussel beds, and St Benoît-des-Ondes, are suspended between the *marais* and an almost infinite desert of mudflats. Tides here are immense. An impetuous sea rises and sinks, never resting to catch its breath, its entire cycle spent sliding from horizon to foreshore.

Cancale's long-standing reputation for oysters lives on, despite a disease setback twenty years ago which wiped

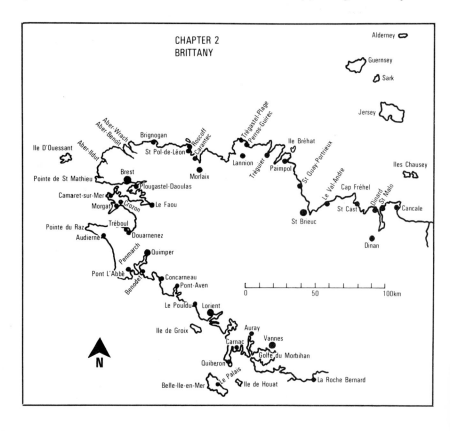

Typical summer weather conditions on the Brittany Coast						
	May	June	July	Aug	Sept	Oct
Average daytime air temperature °C	16	22.7	25.1	24.1	21.2	16.5
Typical daily sunshine hours	6.1	6	9.5	8.2	4.7	4
Days with some rainfall	27	19	9	7	17	17
Average sea temperature °C	12	14	16	17.5	16.5	14.5

out the native spat; from the long Fenetre jetty there are good views over the oyster beds at low tide.

As well as instruction in sailing, scuba-diving and water-skiing, the resort offers a selection of colourful restaurants and hotels. Granville and Mont-St-Michel are often visible from the clock tower of St Meen church, but there are 189 steps to reach it! Other excellent panoramas over Cancale and the bay may be gained from the War Memorial above the little port, and from the Pointe du Hock, reached along the cliff-top Sentier des Douaniers.

At the Pointe du Grouin, Brittany sticks out a rocky finger and turns its back on the Baie du Mont-St-Michel. Cap Fréhel is seen faintly in the west, beyond a succession of headland reefs and islands in a clear turquoise sea — the Côte d'Emeraud.

Rothéneuf Cove, roundly embraced by cliffs, dunes and pines, is a popular location for water sports, while out near the point are some sculpted rocks, twenty-five years of obsessive work by a local priest. From here, 3km of white sand sweep round past Paramé to the ramparts and cathedral spire of St Malo.

Magnificently situated on a former island at the mouth of the River Rance, St Malo still looks for all the world like a fortified coastal town of the Middle Ages. In its heyday during the sixteenth to eighteenth centuries it produced many illustrious ship-owners and mariners:

men as diverse as Jacques Cartier who was to discover Canada in 1535; and the notorious French slaver and privateer of the late 1700s, Robert Surçouf, whose legal piracy was so successful that he retired at twenty-eight! St Malo is still remembered for its corsairs — privateers who were given official status.

Although its ramparts date back to the thirteenth and fourteenth centuries, the Old Town is not quite what it appears to be: in the course of bitter fighting between German and American forces in August 1944, it was burned to the ground. What we see today is neither restoration nor piecemeal modern substitution, but wholesale reconstruction. By numbering blocks of masonry in the ruined buildings, and lovingly copying the medieval stonemason's craft, St Malo was skilfully and uncompromisingly re-created.

Over the years, new stone has weathered and darkened to match the remaining sixteenth-century fragments, and there are some pleasant alleyways and corners. However, the grid of dour, grey-brown granite buildings of uniform age and surface can sometimes seem oppressive — an echo of mourning, perhaps, for the loss of its original heritage.

For the visitor, St Malo is hung with fairy-lights, its streets lined with restaurants, brasseries and bistros by the score, especially round the main square,

The Bassin Vauban, St
Malo

Place Châteaubriand. A tour of the
massive ramparts — so solid that they
were little damaged by bombs or
shellfire during World War II — is
strongly recommended, principally for
views of Intra Muros, the enclosed
walled town. Still wider coastal
panoramas open up from the castle
watch-towers, and there is a local history
museum with wax figures in the keep's
south-west wing. An unusual aquarium
in the ramparts near the Porte St
Thomas, contains a range of salt and
fresh-water life.

Outside the old walls, a twenty-minute
walk across low-tide shallows brings
visitors to the Ile du Grande Bé, the last
resting place of the poet and adventurer
François-René Châteaubriand. To the
north, and also at low tide, Vauban's
seventeenth-century Fort National may
be reached from the Plage de l'Eventail.

St Malo's port handles commercial
freight, passenger traffic from England
and the Channel Islands, and supports a
fleet of deep-sea trawlers. Local boat
trips also run regularly to Dinard, and
up the River Rance to Dinan. The
pleasure-boat harbour in the Bassin
Vauban is a colourful crush of yachts
and cruisers, its little port office
providing comprehensive information
on tides and weather.

Less picturesque by far is St Malo's
immediate industrial hinterland, but the
beaches and flowery gardens of St

with natural advantages, one being its
sheltered position, another the influence
of the Gulf Stream which maintains a
more than equable climate. The Grande
Plage is fringed with cafés and shops and
can become crowded, but there are two
other extensive beaches, as well as
innumerable sandy coves among rocks
facing the Channel.

Eight kilometres of level cliff-top
paths link a series of headlands and
unsuspected little bays to the west; a
good bus service runs parallel to the
coast from Dinard to St Briac and
Lancieux for those wishing to walk one
way. Take the terraced path up round
the Pointe du Moulinet for stunning
views of a translucent green sea and the
long profile of St Malo across the Rance.
The walk continues south-west along the
sea-wall Promenade du Clair de Lune,
floodlit at night and the venue for open-
air concerts of recorded music during
the summer.

With its baroque villas and a lingering
flavour of 'La Belle Epoque', Dinard
might have been accused of staid
pretensiousness were it not for many
forms of modern entertainment and
recreational facilities, very much of the
1980s. There is a fine Musée de la Mer, a
casino, a yacht marina with summer
regattas, golf tournaments, an Olympic-
size swimming pool and a large tennis
club; all this in addition to numerous
local boat trips and flights to the
Channel Islands. Individually as
different as chalk and cheese, Dinard
and St Malo combine to form a resort
area as popular as any in Brittany.

St Lunaire's Pointe du Décollé is
reached by a natural rock bridge known
as the 'Saut du Chat' (Cat's Leap), and
nearby Pointe de la Garde-Guérin offers
outstanding panoramic views. St Briac-
sur-Mer is a personable little resort with
a lively harbour and several pine-fringed
sandy beaches. A 300m long bridge
spans the River Frémur from here to
Lancieux's vast sands, as the coastline
turns in then out to the slender Pointe du
Chevet.

Servan-sur-Mer are quickly reached.
Apart from its Musée de Cap Horniers
(Cape Horn vessels) in the Tour Solidor,
and the Parc des Corbieres viewpoint, St
Servan is known for its Corniche
d'Aleth, a fascinating 1km-long walk
round a rocky fist of land in the wide
Rance estuary.

Before 1967, crossing the river to
Dinard entailed the use of ferries or a
substantial detour to the bridge at
Châteauneuf. Now the D168 runs
straight across 750m of dam, housing
the world's first tidal-power electricity
generating station — the 'Usine
marémotrice de la Rance'. Though
technically interesting, the scheme has
not proved as profitable as was hoped,
and as yet there is no sequel to it.
Nonetheless, an absorbing half-hour
may be spent studying the explanatory
displays and walking along the dam.

Known variously as 'Queen of
Brittany' and 'Gem of the Emerald
Coast', Dinard is, indeed, a cut above
the average. Founded as a resort by a
rich American in the mid-nineteenth
century, when it was still a small fishing
hamlet, it attracted a genteel, well-to-do
clientele, mostly American and British,
who still come here in strength.

As a seaside resort, Dinard is blessed

At the northern extremity of the Baie d'Arguenon, St Cast-le-Guildo boasts one of Brittany's largest beaches — some of its best views too, principally from Pointe de la Garde and Pointe de St Cast, both reached by cliff paths. The town is very busy in season and comprises four quarters: Les Mielles, the main hotel and shopping centre; L'Isle, the fishing and yacht harbour to the north; Le Bourg, the administrative centre to the west, including an interesting modern church; and La Garde, a wooded residential area, the so-called 'garden suburb'.

Built in the thirteenth and fourteenth centuries and restored 300 years ago, the massive silhouette of Forte la Latte looms across the Baie de la Frênaye.

This imposing fortification, hugging the crest of a rugged rock islet, is connected to the mainland by two drawbridges. Guided visits reveal a cannon-ball foundry, lookout posts and a walled keep.

Cap Fréhel has the flavour of Land's End, but access is free. A bookstall on Breton wildlife, a pony ride, and caravans selling *crêpes* and souvenirs are its only concessions to tourism. It is not so much developed as over-visited, so that the same problems of erosion exist here as in Cornwall — unsightly tracts of bare, dusty soil snaking out round the cliff edges. In fact, it is a well-established tourist spot, within easy reach of numerous campsites and apartments, and on a fine summer's day is thronged

The cliffs of Cap Fréhel, an ornithological reserve; Forte la Latte in the distance

with thoroughly cosmopolitan sightseers.

In the 'Fauconniere' restaurant (a circular structure oddly reminiscent of the 'Ptarmigan' near Cairngorm's summit), you can sit with a plate of mussels or a drink and look out across guano-plastered rock and boundless ocean.

This is an ornithological reserve, heavily populated by gulls and cormorants. Paths encircling the cape provide spectacular coastal views in good weather; even in poor visibility, seabirds and the remarkably clear blue-green water flooding over rocks the colour of wine, 70m below, are visually rewarding.

Some say that Cap Fréhel is at its most impressive viewed from the sea and boat trips run out from Dinard. During storms however, clouds of spray rise well above cliff level and it is for such conditions, among others, that a lighthouse exists. Entry is by 'voluntary contribution' and the climb is eminently worth making, less to see the lantern than the Cotentin Peninsula, Jersey, and to the west Bréhat, provided you are favoured with clear air.

Small coves are reached down steepish paths along the Lande de Fréhel cliff-top moors. Extensive dunes and a large sandy beach at la Ville-Men give way inland to cliffs supporting bracken and richly scented pine forest. Sables-d'Or-les-Pins has a curious selection of elaborate houses, popular sands and a main street as wide as an airstrip! Pleasant forest walks and marvellous pine-backed beaches with steep access lead round to Erquy, a thriving little shellfish port nestling inside the protective arm of its sandstone cape.

A tour of the Pointe de Pléneuf and the Promenade de la Guette at le Val-André, both half-hour strolls, offers viewpoints galore of the Baie de St Brieuc and the splendid golden sands of le Val-André itself. Most westerly of the Côte d'Emeraud resorts, it caters for many sports and outdoor activities, as well as other holiday needs, and attracts large numbers of summer visitors. A tumulus, dolmen and cromlechs can be found at neighbouring Pléneuf-Val-André — a mere *soupçon* of what lies ahead in this land of prehistoric megaliths.

St Brieuc, the busy commercial and administrative capital of Côtes-du-Nord department, lies 3km from the coast, on a plateau between the Gouédic and Gouet rivers. It is a city in all senses, with wide boulevards and a high-rise skyline; but its spirit is still tenaciously 'market town' and there is a fascinating old quarter grouped round a rare example of a twelfth-century fortified cathedral.

Unlikely though it may be as a main holiday destination, the authorities of St Brieuc have done much to popularise it as a resort. As well as hotels, restaurants and entertainment, there are water sports, walks and beaches out at St Laurent-de-la-Mer, Pointe du Roselier and les Rosaires.

Fish and early vegetables leave St Quay-Portrieux for England and, though no longer a deep-sea fishing base, its boats still catch lobster round the Roches de St Quay. Like many resorts of its size on this coast, it is well patronised: of four beaches, the liveliest is Plage de St Quay which has a casino and sea-water swimming pool.

A string of modest little harbours, headlands and coves stretch north-west to the Anse de Paimpol. Large-scale oyster cultivation is replacing some of the prosperity Paimpol enjoyed in the days when its deep-sea fleet could fish for cod on the Icelandic banks. Inshore fishing and pleasure-boating, along with a market for early vegetables, play their part too, and there are some undeniably pleasant water-side locations. However, an approach by land, past railway sidings, jumbled industrial development and unprepossessing streets, leaves an impression of sour decline.

Pointe de l'Arcouest is the picturesque embarkation point for a ten minute crossing to the Ile de Bréhat, two pink-granite islands joined by a neck of land. Surprisingly well visited, there is ample scope for walks in a landscape of tiny walled fields and villas. Rainfall is scanty and the climate exceptionally mild, allowing fig trees, oleander, myrtle and mimosa to flourish outdoors.

Lézardrieux lies 10km from the open sea up the Trieux estuary and has a fine little harbour. Tréguier's situation at the confluence of the rivers Guindy and Jaudy is not dissimilar but its anchorage can accommodate larger vessels.

Tréguier's heart — Place du Martray — is dominated by a beautiful granite cathedral and cloisters dating from the thirteenth century. St Tugdual is one of - Brittany's finest church buildings and well rewards an hour or two's exploration; the cloisters are particularly lovely, containing several recumbent stone effigies. Through the delicate arched traceries of Breton granite, one looks out across the bleached blues and pinks of hydrangeas to a quiet lawned courtyard dominated by the great complex of Gothic roofs, towers and arches. Outside, in the Place du Martray, stands a statue commemorating France's greatest rationalist writer, Ernest Renan; his home, the seventeenth-century Maison de Renan, is now a museum.

The nearby village of Minihy-Tréguier is the birthplace of St Yves, patron saint of lawyers. On 19 May each year it is the scene of a specially colourful 'Pardon'. Many thousands of pilgrims, including celebrated lawyers, take part in traditional costume, with bagpipes and bombards, candles and banners and

The Cathedral of St Tugdual at Tréguier

Plage de Trestrignel at Perros-Guirec

dancing into the night.

The Breton *pardons*, time-honoured expressions of religious fervour, have changed little down the centuries. Church ceremonies are followed by processions during which banners, candles and effigies of saints are carried through the streets to the accompaniment of hymn singing. The social components ensue; festive gatherings with music, dancing and occasionally Breton wrestling. Some large and stage-managed, others intimately local, *pardons* are held throughout Brittany, providing visitors from France and abroad with an authentic folk spectacle in traditional costume. It is well worth planning an itinerary to include one.

As an ideal base from which to explore western Brittany, Perros-Guirec is immensely popular, and its topography tends to disperse holidaymakers thus preventing any sense of overcrowding. The resort occupies a broad wooded headland, with its best bathing beaches facing north. There is a well sheltered marina and an artificial lake provides extra safe conditions for children.

Sea-sculpted pink granite rocks at Trégastel-Plage

Lined by large hotels, a casino and a conference centre, the wide, curving Trestraou beach — a half-moon of gently shelving white sand — looks out towards the Sept Iles. This group of seven islands (to which frequent boat trips run) is an offshore nature reserve, a sanctuary for cormorants, gannets, puffins, gulls and oyster-catchers.

A cliff path (Sentier des Douaniers) encircles the whole Ploumanach peninsula, taking in Pointe du Squewel's square-cut lighthouse and the first of many unusual granite rock formations. Ploumanach has its own delightful little beach, but the harbour has succumbed to rather vulgar tourist exploitation.

From the Table d'Orientation on Perros-Guirec's headland, to Trébeurden, 22km west, the Corniche Bretonne winds along the 'Pink Granite Coast' — an absorbing stretch of creeks and sandy bays, of pools, caves, lagoons and fantastic sea-sculpted rocks.

Around Ploumanach and Trégastel-Plage, the weathering of the granite

shoreline reaches its zenith and the rocks alone are an enthralling attraction. Their great bulbous, pink forms rise from the sea, scalloped and smoothed by the action of rain and waves. Some are hugely undercut, others perch in unlikely equilibrium, as exposed as gritstone tors; others still are heaped together like giant, slumbering reptiles. Man's propensity for finding the recognisable in the random has endowed individual rocks with names: the Witch, the Corkscrew, Napoleon's Hat and many others. Caves beneath an enormous cluster known as the Tortoises, near Coz-Pors beach, contain a small museum and aquarium. Altogether, it is a phenomenon not to be missed.

Trébeurden's two family beaches are separated by an isthmus leading to the rocky mound of le Castel, and from Pointe de Bihit the sea is dotted with islets, some grassy-topped and wooded.

Set back on the River Léguer, the busy, rose-granite market town of

Locquirec, small harbour, lots sandy beaches

Lannion lies at a hub of roads radiating to the coast and to many historical sites inland. Its Église Brélévenez was founded on an outlying spur by the Knights Templar in the twelfth century and is reached by a long flight of steps. Elsewhere in the town are numerous old Breton houses and pedestrianised alleyways.

Unlike the Cornich Bretonne, the Corniche Armorique from St Michel-en-Grève to Poul Rodon provides only intermittent glimpses of the sea's edge. At first, however, it skirts the Lieu de Grève, a superb 4km of golden sand (muddy at low tide). Halfway along rears the Grand Rocher, climbed by a steep path and offering fine views of the bay, once a vast forest; fossilized remains are revealed at exceptionally low tides.

Following a heavily indented coast, the Corniche passes the little fishing and sailing resort of Locquirec, and ends 5km beyond. Here the road leaves the department of Côtes-du-Nord and enters Finistère, France's most westerly outpost.

Cycle-touring is a popular way to see Brittany and laden machines being stoically pedalled uphill or joyously freewheeled down are a common sight on its roads. The French nation is unequivocally car-orientated, but its penchant for *velos* (mopeds) is equally passionate among the less well-off. Elderly citizens bearing sticks of French bread ride them sedately enough, but youths are inclined to travel at full throttle, knees up, relying on the sound like that of a demented lawnmower to clear the road ahead! On the whole, cycling is at its best on endless kilometres of country lanes away from busy highways, though lack of signposting demands good maps of a scale no less than 1:100,000.

Small harbours, diminutive resorts and more eroded pink granite continue round the Pointe de Primel to Morlaix, huddled in the gorge of the River Dossen. Its clean white houses are

SOME NATURAL FEATURES OF INTEREST ON THE NORTH BRITTANY COAST

Cap Fréhel
Seabird colonies, red cliffs and a clear green sea.

Sept Iles
A seven-island nature reserve reached by frequent boat trips from Perros-Guirec.

Ploumanach and Trégastel-Plage
Fantastic pink granite rocks sculpted by waves and rain.

The *abers* — shallow inlets in the far west, extremely picturesque at high tide.

overshadowed by a two-storey viaduct almost 60m high, carrying the main Brest-Rennes-Paris railway. Morlaix's town centre is often congested, but under the viaduct and towards the estuary there is a broadening out, with many pleasant shops and cafés alongside the yacht basin. Sitting between the estuary of the Penzé and Morlaix, the family seaside resort of Carantec is the setting for two summer *pardons*. Ile Callot, just offshore to the north, may be reached on foot at mid to low tide.

The twin-spired thirteenth-century Ancienne Cathédrale at St Pol-de-Léon presents a magnificent sight rising above a fringe of flower beds in the afternoon sunshine. Its striking beauty relies on supremely graceful proportions and a façade of warm brown granite, rather than on great size. Another architectural wonder stands at the intersection of Rue Verderel and Rue Général Leclerc: the high belfry tower of the Kreisker Chapel — its slender fifteenth-century Gothic steeple set the pattern for many a Breton church tower.

At times during the summer season, 'muzak' pervades the town, blaring forth from loudspeakers on every street corner: an incomprehensible indulgence by the local authorities (though it has to be said, one not unique to St Pol). Were the music Breton, or softer, fewer of us would feel beseiged by it, as if caught in a perpetual supermarket!

This is vegetable country. Hardly a field is to be seen without its tractor, or a little army of figures working the land. Cauliflowers, onions, artichokes, potatoes and cabbages are sent through St Pol-de-Lion's market and thence to Plymouth, using Roscoff's indispensable deep-water port. No other non-tidal facility existed west of St Malo until six million francs were allocated for its construction. North Finistère is now one of the EEC's major food-exporting zones, with Britain a major consumer.

Roscoff, unexpectedly for a cross-channel port, is a close-knit agricultural community, its old buildings appropriately homogeneous. Notre-Dame-de-Kroaz-Baz has a Renaissance belfry as astonishing as its name, with carved ships-and-cannon embellishment. Close by is the excellent Charles Pérez Aquarium.

Roscoff boasts a marine biology research laboratory and a *thalassotherapy* centre (sea-water cures), but an irresistable lure for many a visitor is the wild and rocky coastline. At ebb tide below the shingle beaches, rock pools and beds of kelp provide a haven for casual fishing of all kinds. A long jetty on concrete pillars, of recent construction, spans these rocky shallows out to the deep water channel near Ile de Batz. By the time you reach the end, the remaining crossing is a very short one indeed! The island's theme echoes the mainland's: market gardens, fishing, seaweed collection and beaches.

Here and there along this north-west edge of Brittany, diversions to the shore are worthwhile, but for the most part the cultivation of crops takes precedence. Villages see few tourists from one week to the next, their shops and bars seeming content with local business.

Since Normandy was left behind, architectural styles have changed and now the metamorphosis is complete. Hamlets and villages announce themselves from a distance with conspicuous chapels or belfry towers. Each is an extraordinary marriage of ornamentation and strength — intricate Gothic needles of stone, often built around with tiered balconies bearing calvaries and crosses at each corner. They seem too fragile to survive a single storm, let alone five hundred years of Atlantic weather and human history: until, that is, one remembers that they are hewn from Breton granite.

Dunes of the palest sand drift round the Baie de Kernic and the Grève de Goulven. Served from the south by a very good road (D770), Brignogan-Plage must rank as the busiest resort on this quiet stretch of coast and is well loved by local families. Kermarguel and Guisseny overlook another river mouth, and in the west can soon be spotted France's tallest lighthouse. On an offshore island, Phare de la Vierge stands 75m above the sea, 30m higher, for example, than the Bishop Rock light.

Shallow inlets called *abers* characterise north-west Finistère. Scenically delectable at high tide, these flooded river mouths narrow and twist inland until they form tidal creeks between steep wooded banks. Hamlets dot the patchwork of fields which the *abers* dissect. Lannilis is the largest: a few shops, a thin scatter of hotels and houses, and many boats. These places, half rural, half seaside, are for those who enjoy pottering, peace and quiet, and where the pace of life can be slowed to a leisurely crawl.

L'Aber-Wrach's small yachting anchorage lies on a peninsula with views of the Baie des Anges and a plethora of islands. Beyond Aber-Benoît, Portsall has a good sheltered beach and moorings, and from Trémazan, across the little bay, the Roches de Portsall and the Roches d'Argenton run south, picturesquely menacing, parallel to the coast.

There follows a succession of low

Aber-Wrac'h

headlands separating sandy coves, while
offshore beacons warn shipping of reefs.
The coast road is stunningly beautiful,
threading through hamlets of old Breton
houses, and tiny ports, down to Aber-
Ildut. Yet beneath the apparent Arcadia
of remotest Brittany runs an
undercurrent of grievance, an urge to re-
assert the Breton identity and traditions.

The majority of Brittany's 2½ million
inhabitants are not so passionately
nationalistic as to flaunt the law by
advocating independence: cultural
renewal — rekindling the old Breton
language, crafts and literature — is
action enough. But for a hard core of
extremists, resistance to centralised
government and to unification with the
rest of France generates more direct,
sometimes violent, acts. In between lies a
range of options capable of drawing
attention to the issues. The power of the
brush is easily resorted to which,

perhaps, explains why French signposts
in this sleepy backwater have been
daubed with paint.

Good sailors should take a boat trip
from le Conquet to the Ile d'Ouessant,
though sea conditions can be rough. The
island's traditional character has been
preserved under the auspices of the Parc
Régional d'Armorique, and a modest
living is gleaned by the islanders from a
few crops, sheep and fishing. Colonies of
seabirds are especially numerous in the
autumn, and although summertime on
Ouessant can be extremely pleasant, the
island bears the brunt of severe winter
gales. Its Phare de Créac'h is reputedly
the most powerful in the world.

Pointe de St Mathieu, compared to
most of Brittany's major headlands, is
refreshingly quiet. An old plan of its
abbey-church, whose monastery ruins
date back to the sixth century, shows it
occupying the entire point, and today's

The lighthouse and ruins
of an old abbey-church,
Pointe St Mathieu

remains are correspondingly extensive.
Unfortunately, they are brutally
juxtaposed, not to say trodden upon, by
the shining striped tower of St Mathieu's
lighthouse. At the top is a light of
prodigious candle-power and a view to
match.

The Crozon Peninsula splays an open
hand and shields Brest from the
Atlantic, creating one of the world's
most beautiful roadsteads. Ninety per
cent of Brest lay in ruins after the last
war, but its recovery has been complete.

From the south it is a well wooded
city — only the yellow dockside cranes,
standing like marshbirds, betray a busy
port and naval arsenal. Clean, wide
boulevards lined with shops and
businesses stride down in ruled grid-
lines, each pale grey building resembling

the next, all stylistically rather dated
now.

What Brest may lack in colourful bar
and café life is made up for in its superb
setting. If you are spared a sea fog,
splendid views may be gained from
Cours Dajot on the old ramparts, while
the remarkable Château and Tour
Tanguy, both housing museums, face
each other across the River Penfeld. The
adjacent Pont de Recouvrance offers
good views of the docks, and happens to
be Europe's highest lifting bridge. (Note:
only French nationals are allowed to
visit the arsenal and naval base).

There is a good range of quality
hotels, moderately priced for the
discerning French, and the city forms a
convenient base for excursions by land
and sea. It is worth noting that the Palais

Calvary at Plougastel-Daoulas

des Arts et de la Culture puts on a variety of exhibitions, entertainment and events throughout the year.

Two thousand acres of strawberries are cultivated on the Plougastel Peninsula; part of this prodigious crop is sent to Britain. Hedgebound roads wind between isolated hamlets to tiny settlements on the deeply dissected, shingly coast. It is an area impervious to change. For the most part, old Breton customs and dress prevail and the appurtenances of twentieth-century tourism seem to count for little.

The village of Plougastel-Daoulas contains one of Brittany's finest calvaries, built in 1602-4 to celebrate the end of the Plague. These granite monuments, usually the work of local masons, depict scenes from the Passion and, sometimes, the story of Catell-Gollet (Catherine the Lost), condemned to eternal hellfire for concealing her amorous exploits from confession. Figures, sixteenth-century costume,

facial expressions and all, radiate a vitality and animation rarely surpassed by other forms of religious sculpture.

When tides flood the estuary, le Faou's sixteenth-century church peers at its own reflection from a terrace above the inlet, and tranquil water stretches west from the old quayside, out beyond Landévennec towards the Rade de Brest.

Le Faou is a pretty village, its main street overhung by the upper storeys of old, slate-clad houses; from here a corniche road (D791) crosses the River Aulne to the Crozon Peninsula, well known for its spectacular coastal scenery. Regular ferries run from le Fret to Brest, and the Pointe des Espagnols provides a viewpoint *par excellence* over the Goulet (Sound) de Brest.

Camaret-sur-Mer, a little farther west, is a modest resort and France's premier lobster port. Neither quaint nor starkly functional, it is a hotch-potch of unpretentious bars and restaurants,

47

Naval museum in Vauban's 'castle' at Cameret-sur-Mer

stalls selling sticks of rock and waffles, an old ship from the days of sail moored at the quayside.

The walk along a natural sea-dyke (the Sillon), passes abandoned trawlers and looks down to a beach of perfectly round pebbles and silver sand. Beyond the lighthouse are jetties where yachts berth and divers leave for local underwater expeditions. The somewhat down-at-heel Chapelle Notre-Dame-de-Rocamadour, at the end of the Sillon, contains model ships in a colourful interior, while Vauban's tower is now a Musée de la Marine.

But those lovers of the sea with a romantic sense of history and a keen imagination will find themselves drawn, with incredulous disbelief, to several beached sailing vessels of considerable size and antiquity, lying where the tides last pushed them up. Decades of erosion

have washed away their superstructures, but the great timber hulls are intensely evocative.

Cars drive without restriction over the Pointe de Penhir, reducing the delicate turf to a stony wasteland: it is nevertheless a magnificent viewpoint above 70m-high cliffs. The thick double cross is a memorial to Bretons of the Free French forces in World War II. 2km inland, about a hundred megaliths form the impressive and compact Alignements de Lagatjar.

The Anse de Dinan is a pretty sweep of sand and cliff near a natural rock arch, but farther south a more exposed, austere landscape leads out to Cap de la Chèvre. Morgat's fine beach and harbour are, by contrast, well protected, with moorings for up to 400 pleasure craft. As well as small caves between Morgat and le Portzic, large sea caverns beyond Beg ar Gador — les Grandes Grottes — are reached by boat trips. Crozon itself is a bustling little town, partly pedestrianised, with an uncharacteristically modern church.

From the brown, grassy whaleback of Ménez-Hom, surrounded by open moorland at the heart of the Parc Régional d'Armorique and crossed by the GR34 long-distance footpath from St Brieuc to Douarnenez, are some of the most extensive views in all Brittany. On the adjacent coast, hamlets and sands lead down the Baie de Douarnenez to Ste Anne-la-Palud, whose *pardon* on the last Sunday in August is exceptionally rich. The village contains a sixteenth-century painted granite statue of its saint.

Douarnenez and Tréboul sit astride the Port-Rhu estuary. An artists' colony sprang up here in the 1870s but today Douarnenez is a busy port and canning centre, handling sardine, tuna, mackerel and crustacea. Below the narrow streets of the old quarter, cafés and restaurants along the Quai du Rosmeur look pleasantly out over jetties where fresh fish is auctioned each morning. Elderly Breton ladies wearing the traditional black dress and scarf, or high lace *coiffes*, are in evidence here, as in much of western Brittany. Outnumbering their menfolk, they are often seen at markets, or simply sat in the shade watching the world go by. Starched *coiffes* have become a popular symbol of essential 'Breton-ness', much as the kilt is used to epitomise Scotland: both actually represent regional rather than national dress.

Douarnenez's upper town is nowhere quite free of a working ethos, with building sites, trading activity and heavy traffic, but to the north its Plage des Dames and the pretty Ile Tristan reflect the holiday face of neighbouring Tréboul. Tréboul is a yachting centre of some note and an appealing family resort. Rock pools abound in the estuary at low tide, and a pleasant path connects the Mole du Biron with Plage des Sables

---

PLACES TO VISIT IN WEST FINISTÈRE

Ile d'Ouessant
Part of the Parc Régional d'Armorique — seabirds, crops, the most powerful lighthouse in the world. Reached from le Conquet. (Crossings can be rough!)

Brest
Docks and naval arsenal rebuilt after World War II. Ramparts and high lifting bridge (Pont de Recouvrance).

Plougastel-Daoulas
Village with one of Brittany's best seventeenth-century calvaries.

Crozon Peninsula
Rugged coastal scenery, beached old sailing ships, Grande Grottes sea caverns, the Pointe de Penhir viewpoint, France's premier lobster port.

Douarnenez
Busy fishing port with old quarter, women wearing traditional lace *coiffes* of region.

Pointe du Raz
Sensational 'Land's End' of France — spectacular in rough weather.

Blancs, near the sea-water cures clinic.

Pointe du Raz is the sensational tip of a rather featureless peninsula, site for another EDF nuclear power station. The journey out to it is worth making. From the Sémaphore, a rugged path over barren, shaley slopes, follows a precipitous cliff edge and the final viewpoints over the Phare de la Vieille to the Ile de Sein are spectacular. Fishing vessels sometimes work the Raz de Sein, a tidal race between offshore reefs, but in stormy weather it is a fearful place.

St Tugen, Pont-Croix and Plozévet have interesting fifteenth- and sixteenth-century churches, and the large lobster and crayfish port of Audierne, with its quayside main square, is well worth visiting. Boat trips leave for the Ile de

Tréboul from across the
Port-Rhu estuary at
Douarnanez

Sein and a *pardon* is held here on the last Sunday in August.

An immense, unbroken sweep of beaches down the Baie d'Audierne is backed by dunes and a wind-scoured hinterland. Numerous streams flow to the coast, only to become blocked to form *étangs* (lagoons). Quite unlike Raz and Penhir to the north, the entire Penmarch Peninsula scarcely stands above sea level, so that waves breaking over the reefs during storms assume their true, eye-level proportions.

Outside Notre-Dame-de-Tronoën stands Brittany's oldest calvary, badly eroded but still magnificent. Unfortunately it is not easy to locate in the sand-swept landscape. The area is criss-crossed by minor roads and tracks, largely unmapped, and greater priority has been given to signposting campsites than settlements and important buildings!

Up to the end of the sixteenth century, cod-fishing brought prosperity to the inhabitants of Penmarch. However, disaster was to follow disaster: the fish left, tidal inundations devastated the land and an anarchic rebel leader, La Fontanelle, massacred thousands, burning down houses and plundering what was left. Even today, preoccupied with market gardening and somewhat off the tourist track, Penmarch can appear introverted and lack-lustre.

St Guénolé's fine museum of Finistère Prehistory is surrounded by artfully reconstructed dolmens. Not far away at the port's north-west corner and conspicuously higher than adjacent

reefs, rise great blisters of igneous rock upon which surf beats incessantly.

St Pierre, on the Pointe de Penmarch, is utterly dominated by the powerful Phare d'Eckmühl, an enormous structure of grey-brown granite. No less than 307 steps need climbing to reach the gallery and a predictably wide-ranging panorama. Two smaller outlying towers and numerous beacons, some striped, others coloured, decorate acres of rocky shore at low tide; their function is clear to see, as saw-toothed reefs jut out in menacing rows, especially to the east.

France's defiant thrust against the Atlantic ends here, replaced by a great inward arc down the Bay of Biscay to the Spanish frontier. Small resorts — Guilvinec, Lechiagat, Lesconil and

Loctudy — mark this turning point and lead east to the Anse de Bénodet.

Traditional 'Bigouden' costume is worn extensively at markets and fairs in the region; round Pont-l'Abbé, starched lace *coiffes* are exceptionally tall and are often worn regularly throughout the week. The town makes dolls in French provincial costume and has a museum of Bigouden dress and furniture.

Occupying a delightful wooded position at the mouth of the Odet estuary, Bénodet's small port is popular with sailors. The resort caters admirably for beachgoers too, with vast south-facing stretches of sand between Ile-Tudy and Beg-Meil. For those with a penchant for exploration by water, boat trips run to Loctudy, the Iles de Glénan, and up the pretty River Odet to Quimper.

Though well inland, Quimper deserves more than a passing mention. Capital of Finistère and archetypically Breton, it lies in a small valley at the tidal limit of the River Odet. Its huge Gothic cathedral was built during the thirteenth to fifteenth centuries but its two towers were not added until 1856.

West from the cathedral's soaring façade, streets in the old quarter are perilously overhung by half-timbered buildings. They are both charming and paradoxical, for beneath their original subsided upper storeys, smart new shops sell expensive jewellery and high-technology merchandise behind smoked plate-glass.

The town's range of shops is complemented by an excellent indoor food market selling all manner of local produce. Outside, streets are filled with the liquid melodies and tripping grace-notes of the wooden whistle. These tiny round instruments are played and sold by travelling musicians in local towns during the holiday season.

Quimper's Musée des Beaux-Arts contains one of the finest collections of sixteenth- to twentieth-century paintings in north-west France, including works by Corot, Fragonard, Boudin,

Traditional Breton lace head-dresses called 'coiffes'

Traditional costume in Quimper's indoor market

Rue Kéréon, Quimper

Velasquez, Rubens, Boucher and Carriere; it also carries a rotating selection of seventeenth- and eighteenth-century drawings and engravings.

The Musée Breton is housed in the former Bishop's Palace and exhibits Gallo-Roman remains, Breton costume, regional folklore and history, and Quimper pottery. 'Quimper-ware', dating back to 1690, may be seen first-hand at the working pottery, and modern ideas compared with the longer-standing designs based on blue glazes and human figure motifs. But be warned — the pottery is closed during the last three weeks in August!

For three days ending on the fourth Sunday in August, Quimper hosts one of Europe's most spectacular gatherings: the Great Festival of Cornouaille. Needless to say, accommodation is at a premium as processions, traditional music, dancing and craft fairs attract many thousands of visitors.

Giant Breton cut-out figures straddle the road into Concarneau; it needs no such introductions, being both unequivocally Breton and an established tourist destination. The exciting Fête des Filets Bleus, during the middle weekend of August, generates an extravaganza of dances and processions in costume, with some of the best bagpipe music to be heard in Brittany. The fête's origin lies in providing help for sardine fishermen and their families, and even today the famous blue nets are taken aboard each morning before the trawlers leave.

Concarneau is a major tuna-fish and canning centre, but its deep-sea fishing industry has been badly hit by rising costs and falling prices. Foreign

The entrance to Ville-
Close, Concarneau

competition and over-fishing in the
Atlantic have also contributed to its
demise, yet the wide, busy harbour still
provides interesting sights for the visitor.
The impressive Musée de la Pêche, in
Ville Close, explains and illustrates
Concarneau's history, as well as many
aspects of fishing in general.

Ville Close is the ancient fortified
island town wherein the English were
besieged during the fourteenth-century
wars with France. From outside, the
massive ramparts appear inscrutable,
plainly built to defend rather than please
the eye. Inside, however, are myriad
shops, galleries, cafés and restaurants,
occupying a total area no larger than
350m by 100m; groups of street
musicians often play in the triangular

entrance courtyard.

Much of the craftwork on sale — the
dessins, aquarelles and *poterie* — exploits
a regional motif but subscribes to an
almost universal European craft *genre*.
Even so, the best is of a high standard,
while the mediocre is skilfully marketed.
Have a peek at the curious little
exhibition of pictures, flowers and
figures made from shells, near the end of
Rue Vauban.

For a small fee payable at the clocktower, a walk round most of the
ramparts may be taken, 3-4m above
busy streets. As you pass long sequences
of arrow-slits in the fortifications,
images of the colourful harbour beyond
form themselves together like frames in
a cine film, and there are wide views

54

from the turrets.

Boat crossings to the Iles de Glénan may be made from the town quay. The nearby bathing beaches of les Sables Blancs lie in a sheltered, pretty area with villas fringing the sand.

Downstream of Pont-Aven, the river becomes a wide estuary with many bays and inlets; small fishing ports, like Kerdruc and Port-Manech, lie well off the beaten track and are worth a detour. Pont-Aven itself has attracted painters ever since its association with the Post-Impressionist Paul Gaugin in the 1880s. His colourful style lives on, blatantly plagiarised in exhibitions and shop window displays. There is a wooded walk, 'Chemin Forestière', overlooking the town's old mills; and a curious traditional chapel at Trémalo, both reached up shady lanes off the D24.

In common with much of coastal Brittany, domestic architecture away from towns hereabouts is simple, even austere: solid, square dwellings with steep-pitched roofs, whose gable-ends fill the landscape like white circumflex accents.

The coastline abounds with delightful places, from Bélon's oyster beds and pretty Kerfany-les-Pins, to Doëlan's deep estuarine inlet and the well established little harbour resort of le Pouldu at the mouth of the River Laïta, on the border between Finistère and Morbihan. With a richly varied coastal configuration and a mild climate which escapes the heavier rainfall of north Brittany, Morbihan lends itself admirably to the practice of water sports and associated activities, from sailing and sand-yachting to fishing and diving.

Another great French city devastated by wartime bombing, Lorient, too, has risen like a phoenix. Its name derives from the India Companies of the seventeenth and eighteenth centuries which brought prosperity through trade with the East (*l'Orient*). Among its spacious boulevards and gleaming new buildings are the Notre-Dame-de-Victoire, the Hôtel de Ville and the

---

WHAT TO SEE IN AND AROUND QUIMPER

Quimper
Fourteenth-century Gothic cathedral and half-timbered houses.
Musée des Beaux-Arts for an outstanding collection of sixteenth-to twentieth-century painting.
Working pottery making 'Quimper-ware'.
The Great Festival of Cornouaille in August with traditional music, dancing, art and craft fairs.
Boat trips down the pretty River Odet to the coast at Bénodet, holiday and yachting centre.

Concarneau
Ville Close is old walled town in harbour, with ramparts and a maze of shops and restaurants. The Fête des Filets Bleues in August.

Penmarch Peninsula
Wild and rocky.

Palais de Congrés.

The World War II German submarine base adjacent to the port was built of such substantial concrete that it withstood aerial attacks and was captured intact by the French at Liberation. It is still used as a submarine base by the French navy, but is not open to foreign visitors. Keroman fishing port itself, purpose-built sixty years ago, is surpassed in size only by Boulogne, and has modern facilities backing directly onto the railway.

Like Concarneau, Lorient's fishing industry has fallen on hard times, with unemployment well above France's national average: the picture at Brest is similar. Attracting tourist revenue (the salvation of many large towns) is a problem for a commercial city whose visible heritage spans only forty years. However, Lorient is in easy reach of splendid sandy beaches and picturesque fishing harbours, with a spreading rash

Minihy-Tréguier
Pardon of St Yves — 19 May.

Perros-Guirec
Pardon of Notre-Dame-de-la-Clarté
— 15 August.

Carantec
Pardon of Notre-Dame-de-Callot —
Whit Sunday.
Pardon of St Carantec — third
Sunday in July (10am)
Pardon of Notre-Dame-de-Callot —
Sunday after 15 August.

Plouguerneau
Pardon of St Peter and St Paul — last
Sunday in June.
Pardon of St Michael — last Sunday
in September.

Camaret-sur-Mer
Pardon of Notre-Dame-de-
Rocamadour and Blessing of the Sea
— first Sunday in September.

Ste Anne-la-Palud
Grand Pardon — Sunday after 15
August.

Locronan
Petite Troménie — second Sunday in
July.

Douarnanez
Festival Mouez ar mor (Voice of the
Sea) — third Sunday in July and
preceding week.

St Tugen
Pardon — Sunday before St John's
Day (3pm).

Notre-Dame-de-Tronoën
Pardon — third Sunday in
September.

Quimper
Great Festival of Cornouaille —
fourth Sunday in August and
preceding three days.

Concarneau
Fête des Filets Bleus — Sunday after
15 August.

Pont-Aven
Festival of the Golden Gorse — third
Sunday in July.

Carnac
Pardon of St Cornély — second
Sunday in September.

Ste Anne-d'Auray
Grand Pardon — 26 July.

Vannes
Festival of Arvor (in front of
ramparts) — 15 August.

of neat new hotels and villas indicating
peripheral tourist growth, even if the city
itself faces a less than certain future.

Port-Louis is 'seaside' for many in
Lorient. Away from its beach facing the
Ile de Groix, colourfully painted house
frontages line quiet streets. There is a
Musée de la Marine in the old citadel,
and a number of fairs and markets are
held during the summer. The
seventeenth-century town ramparts were
built in the reign of Louis XIII to fortify
the headquarters of the first India
Company, which failed (Lorient,

instead, was to receive subsequent
companies, and Port-Louis declined).
Walking along the walls is not without
some risk where the footway becomes
narrow above a considerable drop to
stone paving below.

For 14km south-east from Pointe de
Gâvres, a military firing range occupies
the coastal strip, before it is cut through
by a deep channel running out from the
vast, shallow Rivière d'Etel.

St Cado is a tiny road-end settlement
off the D16, resembling a thousand
other sleepy backwaters in Brittany

Le Palais, Belle-Ile

---

where dogs slumber in the sunshine and fishermen mend nets waiting for the tide. Except, that is, for an exceptionally charming Romanesque Templar's chapel with primitive stained glass, an ornate gallery and a model sailing ship. Outside, across a courtyard, steps lead to a simple stone calvary, and there are many lovely islets out in the basin, some bearing fishermen's cottages.

Joined to the mainland by an isthmus of sand which at one point is barely wide enough to accommodate road and railway, the Presqu'ile de Quiberon, once an island, juts 15km out to sea. In so doing, it acts as a natural breakwater against Atlantic swells, providing an immense area of sheltered seaway, the Baie de Quiberon.

The peninsula's 'Côte Sauvage'

confronts the ocean, bearing the worst of waves and weather. Low, rocky promontories, reefs and caves are lashed by an often malevolent sea, so that where there are sandy coves, bathing can be extremely dangerous. It is possible to drive along this coast from Quiberon to Port-Pigeon, but walking will provide more stimulating impressions and there are good tracks all the way to Portivy.

Old military buildings still dot the peninsula, which is predominantly an open, airy flatness of small fields west of the main settlements. Quiberon itself is hugely popular with families, but other good beaches, backed by pine woods, exist all along the east coast. Port Maria, which cans and distributes sardines, is the embarkation point for car ferries to Belle-Ile, and for boats to the Iles de Houat and Hoedic.

Belle-Ile is Brittany's largest island, ringed with great cliffs, sandy beaches, inlets and ports. It is good walking country and excursions round the island are also available by boat and coach. The seventeenth-century museum at le Palais elucidates Belle-Ile's turbulent history, though in more recent times it has attracted poets, painters, philosophers and actors, among them Sarah Bernhardt.

In close proximity to each other on the west coast are three dramatic features: The Aiguilles de Port Coton, the Grand Phare, and fjord-like Port Goulphar. The east coast can boast safer bathing, the lobster and sardine port of Sauzon and the lively harbour at le Palais. Bangor, the island's oldest settlement, with an eleventh-century parish church, lies inland.

Carnac is a name familiar to archaeologists and students of antiquity the world over. The town stands at the centre of a vast concentration of more than 3,000 megaliths, stretching 25km along the coast.

The standing stones (*menhirs*) are of great interest; estimates of their age vary between 3,000 and 7,000 years, but a definitive explanation for their existence is not forthcoming. Symbolic and mystical components of an ancient civilisation, the stones are aligned accurately to compass points or sunrise and sunset, suggesting links with sun or moon worship. Other monuments — tumuli, burial chambers and covered passages — are mainly communal tombs.

North-east of Carnac town centre the conspicuous Tumulus St Michel contains several burial chambers and galleries, round which guided tours are conducted during the summer. Atop the mound are a chapel, a small calvary and a *table d'orientation*. Most of the remains and artefacts from the tumulus, in addition to innumerable prehistoric specimens excavated in the locality, can be found in the prestigious Musée Miln-Le Rouzic in Carnac. The town's seventeenth-century Église St Cornély is dedicated to the patron saint of horned cattle (!) and on the second Sunday of September a *pardon* is held in his honour.

There are no signs to help pedestrians find the Tumulus St Michel, but take the D781 towards La Trinité, and the D119 towards Auray for the alignments; both are reached in half a kilometre.

The principal alignments at Carnac

THE MAIN PREHISTORIC SITES AROUND CARNAC

Tumulus St Michel
Burial chambers and galleries, off D781.

Ménec, Kermario and Kerlescan
Alignments of standing stones, off D119.

Mané-Lud, Grand Menhir and Table des Marchands
At Locmariaquer, east of Carnac on shores of Golfe du Morbihan.

Musée Miln-le Rouzic
This museum at Carnac contains many excavated finds.

The Alignements du Ménec, Carnac

are those of Ménec, Kermario and Kerlescan. More immediately compelling than the stones themselves on a busy day will be fellow sightseers strolling round them, climbing over them, cycling past them and being photographed in front of them! Perhaps the alignments are best seen out of season when, free of bright T-shirts and picnickers, the imaginative leap required to ponder their origins is rather easier to make!

Nearby Carnac-Plage is an expanding modern resort with an exceptionally fine sandy beach over 2km in length, leading round to the hillside village of la Trinité-sur-Mer. From the Kerisper bridge there are lovely views of the Crach estuary and la Trinité's marina.

The last significant coastal feature before Brittany gives way to Pays de la Loire is an immense, island-dotted inland sea — the Golfe du Morbihan. Swift tidal currents prevent silting-up of the narrow channel at Port-Navalo, and the sheltered Morbihan itself is used extensively by oyster fishermen and pleasure craft.

There is really no substitute for exploration by boat, though roads do encircle the gulf; excursions of varying length start from Port-Navalo, Locmariaquer, Auray and Vannes. Space does not permit a comprehensive guide to the islands, over forty of which are inhabited, nor to the many shoreline settlements, but a day or longer spent in the region would be well rewarded.

At the tip of Morbihan's north-west enclosing arm lies little Locmariaquer and its famous dolmens. The dark chamber and capstone of Mané-Lud

Romanesque Templar's Chapel at St Cado, Rivière d'Etel

hide unceremoniously behind a cottage; the Grand Menhir and Table des Marchands are found a little nearer the village, by a cemetery. A lad in shorts and sandals will recite a descriptive text like a tape-recorder, but the site is shabby and neglected by British standards. When the Grand Menhir, once 30m high, fell and broke into four pieces, the very earth must have trembled: it is reckoned to weigh 350 tons!

The Promenade du Loch, a pleasant tree-lined stroll, provides views across Auray's riverside quays and oyster beds to its fifteenth-century St Goustan quarter. North of the town, Breton religious fervour reaches its height on 26 July when pilgrims by the thousand converge on Ste Anne-d'Auray for its Grand Pardon, preceded by a nocturnal torchlit procession. The Renaissance-style basilica, replacing a seventeenth-century chapel commemorating the miraculous unearthing of a statue of Ste Anne by the peasant Yves Nicolazic, is part of an ensemble of hallowed buildings which includes a moving memorial to Breton casualties of World War I.

Vannes remains a medieval town in character, but today is a thriving agricultural and industrial centre. It escaped major war damage, retaining a robust vitality and evidence of its distinguished past for all to see. Old buildings rise in tiers, forming an amphitheatre above the ramparts, moat and floodlit gardens, while gabled houses in Place Henri IV, Rue des Halles and Rue Noë are lavishly decorated with human and animal motifs.

Overhanging, half-timbered dwellings dating back over three hundred years, protrude, like those of Quimper, above sophisticated shop fronts in narrow cobbled streets. 'Muzac' pours forth from successive loudspeakers during the high season, detracting from the town's ambience; there is, alas, no escape!

Sights to see from the ramparts include a quaint row of wash-houses alongside the moat — one of the town's most picturesque corners — and the Cathédrale St Pierre. This great edifice is well worth visiting for its unusual Italian Renaissance chapel and fine tapestries depicting miraculous cures made by St Vincent Ferrier, whose tomb lies in the Chapel of the Holy Sacrement.

Vannes is well endowed with historic

PLACES OF INTEREST IN AND AROUND VANNES

Vannes
Old buildings, gabled houses lavishly decorated, ramparts, moat and floodlit gardens.
Cathédrale St Pierre with tapestries and unusual Italian Renaissance chapel.
Museum of Prehistory; Museum of the Oyster.

Ste Anne d'Auray
Celebrated for its 'Grand Pardon', religious pilgrimage on 26 July, nocturnal torchlight procession.

Golfe du Morbihan
Huge inland sea, dotted with islands. Boat trips run from Vannes, Port-Navalo, Locmariaquer, Auray.

Old wash-houses alongside the moat and ramparts, Vannes

Vannes and the
Cathédrale St Pierre

buildings and museums. Fascinating
finds from Morbihan's first megalithic
excavations can be seen in the Château
Gaillard and there is a Musée de
l'Huitre, devoted to the oyster.
Motorists will find the town less well
endowed with road direction signs!

Small ports on oyster-rich estuaries
fringe the Presqu'ile de Rhuys, among
them le Tour-du-Parc, Damgan and
Billiers. Just beyond the mouth of the
Villaine, downstream of la Roche
Bernard, we cross Brittany's border,
though holiday brochures, eager to
exploit the attractions of the Guérande
Peninsula and La Baule, often stretch
Brittany's fabric, as it were, to fit over
this extra bulge of coast to the Loire.

Good Beaches in Morbihan
Quiberon peninsular
Carnac
Benodet
Eral, west of Auray
Locmariaquer

3 The Coast of Pays de la Loire and Poitou-Charentes:_____

LA ROCHE BERNARD TO THE GIRONDE

The marshy centre of the Parc Régional de Brière occupies 38,000 acres between the Villaine and Loire rivers. Once an undulating forest, it was transformed into swamp and peat bog following a temporary rise in sea level; since then it has been systematically drained and its natural resources tapped. Local *Brièrons* have fished it, thatched with its reeds, grazed stock on it and cut its peat. However, the development of a canal and road network has opened up the area, and visitors can observe wild-life and enjoy recreational pursuits on or around the stretches of water.

The same sea-level fluctuations, culminating in a permanent drop of 15m, left vast tracts of salt-marsh and mudflats on the coast between Guérande and the Ile de Batz where before a sizeable bay had existed. Batz became joined to the mainland by subsequent accumulations of sand — they have all but encircled the former gulf, leaving one narrow channel at Pointe de Pen Bron, through which the tides ebb and flow.

Piriac-sur-Mer and its brasher neighbour la Turballe, both fishing and sailing ports, lie on more open coast to the north; Guérande, which gives its name to the peninsula, stands on an edge of land 50m above the heart of the Marais Salants.

Guérande is a supremely well preserved medieval fortified town, its fifteenth-century gateways and ramparts intact, though the moat is now an engirdling boulevard. Salt commanded high prices as the principal food preservative during the Middle Ages, and until the Revolution Guérande's salt-pans brought considerable prosperity to the region. A museum in the St Michel gatehouse contains material on the industry and the people who work in it.

The Marais Salants is an extraordinary matrix of canals and low clay banks, channelling the rising tide into shallow rectangular reservoirs called '*oeillets*'. Evaporation takes place and the crystalline sea-salt is gathered, dried and heaped into '*mulons*' — shining pyramids which line the marsh edge. Each *oeillet* yields as much as 3,000kg of salt in a good hot summer.

Out on the mudflats of the Grand and Petit Traict lagoons, clams, mussels, winkles and oysters are cultivated — le Croisic is an important centre. This small, white town, once surrounded by

Typical summer weather conditions on the North Atlantic Coast						
	May	June	July	Aug	Sept	Oct
Average daytime air temperature °C	16.5	22.8	25.5	24.6	21.9	17.6
Typical daily sunshine hours	7.3	8	10.8	7.6	7.4	5.8
Days with some rainfall	23	18	6	13	13	9
Average sea temperature °C	13	15	17	18	17	15

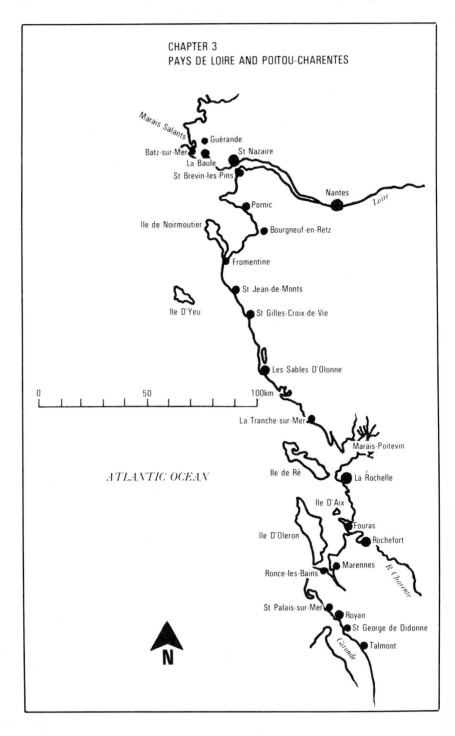

CHAPTER 3
PAYS DE LOIRE AND POITOU-CHARENTES

Marais Salants

Guérande

Batz-sur-Mer

La Baule

St Nazaire

St Brevin-les-Pins

Nantes

Loire

Pornic

Ile de Noirmoutier

Bourgneuf-en-Retz

Fromentine

St Jean-de-Monts

Ile D'Yeu

St Gilles-Croix-de-Vie

Les Sables D'Olonne

0   50   100km

La Tranche-sur-Mer

Marais-Poitevin

ATLANTIC OCEAN

Ile de Ré

La Rochelle

Ile D'Aix

Fouras

Ile D'Oleron

Rochefort

Marennes

Ronce-les-Bains

R. Charente

St Palais-sur-Mer

Royan

St George de Didonne

Talmont

Gironde

N

La Baule

La Rochelle

The 'Cote Sauvage', north of Royan

Atlantic surf near Biarritz

Salt-marshes of the Guérande Peninsula

sea, faces north-east across the salt-marsh shallows. It is lively and crowded in season, being both a sailing and fishing port, with a handsome seventeenth-century harbour frontage.

Fishing is year-round for sardine and crustacea, including prawns during the winter months. Not surprisingly, there is a daily fish auction (*poissonerie*) and seafood restaurants are plentiful. Bathing beaches are situated a kilometre away on the south shore at Port-Lin.

A Musée Naval is housed in the Hôtel de Ville, while the Aquarium Côte d'Amour, near Quai du Port Ciguet, contains a great diversity of specimens. The little sixteenth-century Notre-Dame-de-Pitié has an interesting high lantern tower worth looking at.

The Grande Côte, a succession of rocky coves, whitewashed villas and holiday homes, is balding beneath the onslaught of holidaymakers' feet. From

the granite belfry of Église St Guénolé in the little town of Batz-sur-Mer, one-time home of Balzac, there is a breathtaking panorama from the Presqu'ile du Rhuys in the north, right down to the mouth of the Loire, and, closer at hand, over the Marais Salants. Adjacent to the church are the Gothic ruins of Notre-Dame-du-Murié, and due south, a Sentier des Douaniers leading from the Pierre-Longue *menhir* to some impressive sea rocks.

La Baule is approached through the old fishing port of le Pouliguen where the Guérande Peninsula has anchored itself to the mainland. Pretty quaysides are backed by a wooded suburb of substantial ivy-clad residences exuding an almost tangible confidence in their own immutability: real estate at its most palpable!

La Baule — poised, stylish and well-bred — is one of Europe's great coastal

The Château Pornic

attractions, on a par with Cannes and Deauville. In addition to parks, fashionable shops and a wide variety of entertainment and accommodation, the immense south-facing beach is legendary. From the Port de Plaisance at le Pouliguen, 8km of imperceptibly shelving golden sand, freshly raked and levelled each day, extends south-east in a gentle curve to Pornichet. Opportunities for water and beach sports are legion.

For once, seafront high-rise blocks are tastefully cohesive; even the very light itself seems scrubbed clean. There are scores of hotels ranging from the luxurious to the modest, as well as chalets, flats, and studio apartments;

many French move to this resort themselves during the summer period. Fish dishes are an outstanding speciality of local restaurants.

Until the late 1700s, wind-blown sand from the Loire estuary pressed in on the little village of Escoublac, eventually forcing its inhabitants to rebuild 3km inland. However, the troublesome dunes were stabilised in 1840 by the planting of a thousand acres of maritime pines and the forest now acts as a windbreak to the north, contributing to an equable micro-climate within the Baie d'Amour.

La Baule-les-Pins, a twentieth-century urban extension, leads east to the former salt-workers' village of Pornichet,

PLACES TO VISIT AROUND LA BAULE

Parc Régional de Brière
Wildlife and recreational pursuits in an area reclaimed from sea.

The Marais Salants
Salt-pans in production during summer.

Le Croisic and Batz-sur-Mer
Small resorts, the former an important shellfish centre.

Guérande
Well-preserved fortified medieval town, salt-town.

La Baule
Stylish, lively, superbly appointed resort.

St Nazaire
Ship-building city, impressive shipyards at mouth of the Loire.

already a popular resort by 1860. Around Pointe de Chémoulin, the mighty Loire ends its 1,000km journey from the Massif Central to the ocean with a flourish of industrial and maritime activity at St Nazaire.

With all the advantages of a deep-water harbour, St Nazaire has been a major ship-building centre since the mid-nineteenth century, and its dockyards will be of special interest for the two huge basins in which France's largest passenger ships were built. The Forme-écluse Louis Joubert (entrance lock) and the old German wartime submarine base, virtually intact like the one at Lorient but now a civilian industrial site, are both intriguing. Sadly, the vast shipyards — 'Chantiers de l'Atlantique' — from which emerged great liners like *France* and *Normandie*, as well as a host of naval and merchant vessels, are suffering even more severely from the world recession in shipbuilding than Nantes, St Nazaire's sister port upstream.

Much of the town was reconstructed following war damage, the residential quarter a familiar grid of broad avenues and pleasant boulevards leading south to the beaches between the avant-port and Pointe ville-es-Martin. There is a shady Jardin des Plantes with an extensive southerly outlook. Factories and gravel-workings towards the airport are relieved by the spectacular hump (and equally spectacular prices!) of the Mindin toll bridge, obviating a lengthy detour to Nantes to cross the Loire.

Between them, the wooded resorts of St Brevin-les-Pins and St Brevin-l'Ocean possess a wealth of amenities, including pleasure-boat moorings, swimming pools, water-skiing, scuba-diving,

Harbour and Château at Pornic

waymarked footpaths, cycling, horse-
riding and tennis courts. Farther south,
beyond Tharon-Plage, the less
hospitable Pointe de St Gildas pushes a
reef-ringed finger seaward. It was here
that the steamship *St Philibert*
foundered on 14 June 1931 and 500

passengers returning from the Ile de
Noirmoutier were drowned.
    The D751 road leaves south-east from
this rugged point, along the Côte de
Jade to Pornic. Between Préfailles and
Ste Marie, however, lie 8km of splendid
cliff-top path (another Sentier des

Douaniers) overlooking irridescent green inshore waters, after which the coast is named.

Pornic has grown at the head of a south-facing natural creek, whose steep little cliffs shelter a good-sized fishing fleet, though the struggle against silting-up is unremitting. The Vieille Ville, genteel and pastel coloured, looks over the harbour from a pleasant slope and is flanked on the west by the Jardin de Retz valley.

Pornic's *piece de resistance* is a fourteenth-century granite château, standing aloof amidst trees midway between the inner harbour and the huge new *port de plaisance*. Its commanding presence is best viewed from the south, opposite le Mole or on the Corniche de Gourmalon. There are several sandy beaches nearby along the wooded coast, with walks out to the ocean on the Corniche de la Noéveillard and Corniche de Gourmalon. Boat trips run regularly to the Ile de Noirmoutier.

The villages of la Bernerie-en-Retz and les Moutiers form a continuous settlement down the Baie de Bourgneuf. Bourgneuf-en-Retz has a small museum devoted to the whole Pays de Retz area and includes displays of ancient farm tools, archaeology, natural history and regional folklore.

With the crossing of the Etier du Sud comes a notable change in the countryside. The Ile de Bouin and the Marais de Machecoul form flat grazing lands thousands of acres in extent. There are isolated thatched huts with gable-ends curved to windward, and scattered single-storey farmsteads sheltering behind windbreaks of hedging, reminiscent of the Camargue. Wooden shacks and net-hoists dot the banks of canals which intersect this region right to the sea's edge, and above the level plane of earth, space is measured by telegraph poles — thin vertical indices against an empty sky.

An elegant modern toll bridge carries the D38 across to the Ile de Noirmoutier, but for the adventurous

there is an alternative: at low water, take the D948 'Passage du Grois', a nineteenth-century causeway, at high tide 4m beneath the waves! Comprehensive information (in English) is displayed on boards at nearby Beauvoir-sur-Mer.

Market gardening and fishing constitute the islanders' main livelihood, though the Ile de Noirmoutier's gentle climate favours holidaymakers too, and there are opportunities for riding, sailing and tennis. East of the tiny capital, Bois de la Chaise provides a popular diversion from the otherwise rather featureless low relief; here are stands of mimosa, maritime pines and oak, not far from several sandy beaches, notably Plage des Dames.

The west is dominated by *marais salants* (salt marsh), featured in Guériniere's Musée d'Art et de Tradition. Good views of the island and adjacent coastline may be gained from the château, which also houses an interesting museum.

Car ferries ply between Fromentine and the diminutive Ile d'Yeu, 20km out to sea, but tides do not always allow return the same day. Unlike Noirmoutier, Ile d'Yeu is sterner, more Breton in character, bringing to mind Belle-Ile, much farther north. Port-Joinville, on its north coast, is an important tuna-fishing centre — a small but lively place with a memorial museum to Marshal Pétain, incarcerated in the Fort de la Pierre-Levée during World War II. There is a Festival of the Sea in May.

The southern 'Côte Sauvage' is a magnificent sight in rough weather; picturesque Port-de-la-Meule huddles there in the shelter of a cove, providing refuge for its lobster-fishing fleet. From here a rugged cliff path leads 2km north-west to the remarkable Vieux Château; built in the eleventh century on a rocky shoulder separated from the main cliff by a deep chasm, its profile is pure story-book romantic. The original drawbridge has been replaced, but a pathway gives

High season at les Sables
d'Olonne

access to the keep, from the top of which
are marvellous ocean views.

Inland, the *marais* pushes a level hand
south to the River Vie, but pine-clad
dunes, running past Notre-Dame-de-
Monts through campsite country, form a
much frequented coastal strip nearly
2km wide.

Great leaning slabs of concrete
announce St Jean-de-Monts — more
attempts at seafront modernism, set in a
veritable maze of minor roads. A smart
resort of gleaming white towers and
entertainments galore, its beach is on a
truly grand scale: the beach huts, pier,

swimming pool and other accroutements
seem dwarfed by it. 3km of promenade
with spacious car parking link Plage St
Jean with Plage des Desmoiselles, but
beaches stretch way beyond the town
limits, from Fromentine to Sion-sur-
l'Ocean — an almost uninterrupted
26km.

From here to Croix-de-Vie there is
little of intrinsic interest. A rash of
'*Colonies de Vacances*' and anonymous
new building provide the essential
ingredients of holidaymaking:
accommodation, beaches and shops.
The effect may be inoffensive and

point for the Ile d'Yeu. From the dunes out towards the Pointe de Grosse Terre is an armchair view of all shipping activity.

The Forêt d'Olonne, a spine of land between the watery Marais de la Vertonne and the ocean, runs for 15km down the coast to la Chaume. Pines interspersed with occasional stands of oak densely cover the dunes, providing innumerable forest walks, and a habitat for deer which may, with luck, be observed from the warren of footpaths transecting the area.

Les Sables-d'Olonne is an enduringly popular resort and in high season the sands of its immense beach all but vanish beneath a dark brown veneer of solid suntan! Its great attraction lies in its diversity. No-one would deny the seafront a five-star rating — there are sheltered waters east of the mole, a Casino de la Plage and an elegant swimming pool nearby. Sands stretch, too, past Le Remblai, a popular eighteenth-century promenade with excellent shops, to la Rudelière and the start of the Corniche coast road.

On days of inclement weather (and they can never be ruled out on the Atlantic seaboard!) the active fishing and cargo port, famous for its catches of sardine and tuna, offers endless diversion, as do the town's many shops and restaurants. Early-risers will catch the morning fish market, and locally caught seafood, not surprisingly, appears on most menus.

Fascinating displays of regional prehistory, folklore and contemporary art can be found in the Musée de l'Abbaye-Ste Croix, a restored Benedictine abbey to the east of the centre, while the late-Gothic Église Notre-Dame-de-Bon-Port repays a visit. Children will enjoy the Marine Zoo and Aquarium.

Heavily patronised by the French themselves, les Sables-d'Olonne can become very congested, and car-parking a headache. One solution (and a recommended excursion anyway) is to

eminently forgettable, but hosts of joggers, cyclists and beachgoers bear witness to the fundamental simplicity of recreational pleasure.

Low rocky cliffs and a sprawl of hotels and villas lead along the Corniche Vendéene to St Gilles-Croix-de-Vie, two towns in one that embrace a big, snaking bend near the mouth of the River Vie. There is a busy market in the old café-lined streets, but attention is likely to be monopolised by the port, containing up to 200 fishing vessels. Pleasure boats come and go from the new '*Port de Plaisance*' and there is an embarkation drive round the docks to la Chaume. This picturesque quarter across the port's channel contains some old fishermen's cottages near the Tour d'Arundel, and is generally quieter. A passenger ferry plies the 200m back to the main town from flower-decked quaysides.

La Chaume possesses its own complement of bars and eating places, as well as a small summer fairground and little sheltered beaches. Much fished from and offering wide views of the Sables-d'Olonne bay, a long jetty leads out a considerable distance beyond the seventeenth-century Fort St Nicolas, providing excellent vantage points from which to watch the flotillas of fishing and pleasure craft returning to harbour on the afternoon tide.

· Crowded camping grounds at Château d'Olonne dominate the Corniche for a while as it winds south-east above low cliffs and tiny pebble beaches towards Puits d'Enfer. Just inland is an interesting zoo, an airfield, and, nearer Talmont-St Hilaire on the

D949, the Musée automobile de Vendée, an inscrutable white warehouse in which over a hundred vintage cars are on show.

The coast becomes an indistinct graduation from water to land, spread with oyster beds and inlets round the River Payré. Minor roads branch south-west off the D21, providing access to small settlements, among them St Vincent-sur-Jard, where George Clemenceau spent the last three years before his death in 1929. His home, Maison de Clemenceau, is open to the public.

More afforested dunes dotted with campsites, the Forêt de Longeville, lead south round Pointe du Grouin du Cou, to la Tranche-sur-Mer. Beaches on this exposed coast are susceptible to heavy seas, and bathers should be cautious if a swell is running.

La Tranche is a floral town, a centre since the 1950s for tulips and gladioli. Eastwards from here, a holidaymaking fringe with its miscellany of clubs and campsites, stalls and supermarkets, rubs elbows with a thriving market garden

Fishing in the rising tide at l'Aiguillon-sur-Mer

Traditional transport on Ile de Ré

industry producing potatoes, garlic and tempting bunches of onions. During the summer months, the two manage to co-exist. Tractors vie uneasily with impatient motorists on the coast road, the topographical boundary between agriculture and the narrow margin of land conceded to holidaymaking.

As in much of rural France, cameos from the nineteenth century appear unexpectedly round a bend in the road: a frail old lady in blue-printed frock and headscarf incongruously loading wood onto a cart; or an elderly peasant swathed in black and grey against the sun, walking slowly amidst the T-shirts and tans of holiday crowds, perplexed for a month or two, perhaps, by the tide of hedonism.

Behind the Pointe d'Arcay, an ornithological reserve, the Lay estuary points a narrowing tongue of water up to la Faute and l'Aiguillon-sur-Mer. From a bridge connecting the two towns, young and old together lower large, wire-braced nets into the rising tide for shrimps, small fish, or whatever is there for the catching. Luck, rather than skill, is the name of the game, and weed the commonest catch, but it is an animated and amusing spectacle. Wooden piers reach out over low-tide mud banks in the river mouth, for fishing and shellfish cultivation, along with flowers, are important livelihoods.

We are at the brink of the Anse de l'Aiguillon, all that remains of an immense sea gulf which once extended inland as far as Niort. Rivers and sea currents deposited a black clay mud called *bri*, progressively silting up the bay and creating a vast *marais*, yet it was not until the thirteenth century that drainage began with the construction of the Cinq-Abbe canal. Reclamation work continued intermittently, so that by the nineteenth century a system of dykes and polders had succeeded in invigorating the region and human settlements were well established.

Arcaded shopping street,
La Rochelle

Today, the Parc Régional du Marais-Poitevin is the undisputed Camargue of the Atlantic coast, a 'Green Venice' of waterways in which everything moves by boat. Former limestone islands are now hilly outcrops bearing villages such as Maillezais, St Michel-en-l'Herm, Champagné, Marans and Elle, and the gulf's former shoreline can still be traced along the edge of the northern plain.

Measuring 40km by 30km, the region from ground level seems limitless — an infinity of rough pasture grazed by pale cattle, lined here and there with poplar and willow. The coastal *marais desséché* (dry marsh) presents an open, airy surface, criss-crossed by canals and dykes, its heavy soil worked to yield beans, barley, corn and sunflowers. Sheep and cattle feed in the salt-meadows and the local butter is renowned for its flavour. Inland, the *marais mouillé* (wet marsh) is prettier

and more intensively cultivated, in summer a sanctuary of cool water and overhanging foliage.

The inhabitants of the Marais-Poitevin — *maraichins* — live in low, whitewashed houses built above the level of sea floods on hillocks or dykes. There are few roads that lead anywhere, so people, crops and stock move about in punts called *yoles* or *plattes*. This same form of transportation provides the tourist with a more authentic experience of the Marais-Poitevin than motoring does, and is to be recommended. Boat excursions are arranged from villages west of Niort: Courçon, St Hilaire-le-Palud, Sansais, Arçais, Damvix, La Garette and Maillezais. Topographically not unlike Holland (some of its waterways were excavated by the Dutch themselves), the Marais-Poitevin also lends itself well to cycling.

Right on the border of Poitou-

Charentes, where the River Vendée ends its serpentine wanderings and flows into the Anse de l'Aiguillon, a ribbon of tarmac runs west across flatlands and marsh to low-water level. Port-du-Pave is an unremarkable backwater of squat dwellings, as unlikely a destination for large lorries as one could wish to find. Yet they arrive here from Bordeaux and other cities, lumbering down to the road end, technological intrusions in a landscape that is all straight horizons and sky. Here, too, are the vans, trailers and tractors of the mussel and oyster fishermen who supply them. Traceries of wooden stakes and platforms pattern the mud banks, while boats glide up creeks, unseen but for their mastheads at ebb tide.

La Rochelle's claim to being the Atlantic coast's most stylish resort will be contested by the likes of La Baule or Biarritz. And yet for many, La Rochelle does indeed have an edge over its rivals, if not for its seafront amenities, then for its exquisitely elegant architecture, an historic old quarter, a fascinating port complex, and delightfully arcaded shopping streets. Modern commercial and industrial development occupies a peripheral zone, leaving the old town intact and unsullied. It is a place to wander in — cosmopolitan, vibrant, full of charm and character.

None of the principal sights is far from the Vieux Port, itself a considerable tourist attraction. Three great towers guard the entrance: the fortress-like, pentagonal Tour St Nicolas, dating back to the fourteenth century; Tour de la Chaine, once the anchor point for a massive chain raised nightly to secure the port; and Tour de la Lanterne, the original lighthouse and one-time prison, with 300-year-old graffiti on the cell walls and a magnificent panorama of the town from a second-floor platform.

La Rochelle's fishing fleet works both inshore and as far afield as the coasts of Britain and Portugal; its vessels moor in the main Vieux Port and in a larger

---

MAIN SIGHTS IN LA ROCHELLE

The Vieux Port
Three towers: Tour St Nicolas, Tour de la Chaîne, Tour de la Lanterne. Fishing and pleasure craft, quayside cafés and stalls.

Rue du Palais
Arcaded shopping street with street theatre and musicians.

Hôtel de Ville
Italian Renaissance façade and ornate interior. Markets in Place du Marché, pleasant shady Parc Charruyer and the popular Promenade du Mail. Numerous museums, from local history to Asian Art. Eighteenth-century Jardin des Plantes.

La Pallice
Old German wartime submarine base 5km west. Boat excursions to the islands.

Parc Régional du Marais-Poitevin
To the north of la Rochelle. 'Green Venice' of waterways and dykes, everything moving in punts (*plattes*). Excursions from villages west of Niort.

---

bassin a flot beyond Tour St Nicolas which also accommodates cargo ships. The smaller *bassin* is an important pleasure craft marina.

Many a pleasant hour is spent by visitors at cafés on Quai Duperré overlooking the harbour, flanked by seafood stalls, artists and craft vendors: the privilege, of course, is paid for with the drink!

Bounded by the Grande-Rue des Merciers and Rue du Palais, the *quartier commerçant* reflects its trading and military origins in a rectilinear grid of paved streets and connecting passages, often vaulted for shelter in bad weather. The huge Hôtel de Ville, with its Italian Renaissance façade, is an extraordinary

Fruit market, La Rochelle

confection of fluted columns, decorated ceilings, pillars, crests and statuettes, including the mark of Henry IV and Marie de Médicis under whose patronage the building was created.

Elsewhere in the Grande-Rue are sixteenth- and seventeenth-century timber houses faced with slate, and in Rue du Palais, one of the principal shopping streets, stand the Hôtel de la Bourse and Palais de Justice. Farther up near Place de Verdun (spacious, but expensive parking) is found the rather austere Cathédrale St Louis, and Café de la Paix, a surviving example of nineteenth-century opulence. 200m east, in Place du Marché, colourful indoor and outdoor markets sell seafood, fruit, vegetables, meats, cheeses and other produce against a background of half-timbered houses.

Laid out on the remains of ancient fortifications, Parc Charruyer forms a swath of grass, trees and water down to the popular Promenade du Mail which leads out through more gardens, past a casino, towards the sea beaches.

Almost the whole of La Rochelle lends itself to absorbing exploration. If time allows, there are several museums from which to choose: Musée Lafaille, in an eighteenth-century Jardin des Plantes, houses a curious miscellany, from carved coral and antique furniture to scientific instruments and a stuffed giraffe! Local history, including the famous siege of La Rochelle in 1627-8, some unusual ceramics, and examples of Asian art, appear in the Musée Orbigny. The Musée des Beaux-Arts has a collection of paintings and drawings from the seventeenth century to the early 1900s. Maps, engravings and displays in the Musée du Nouveau Monde trace the development of La Rochelle's relationships with the Americans since the Renaissance.

La Pallice, 5km to the west, was an important German submarine base during World War II. Its deep-water port facilities now handle large seagoing cargo ships as well as car ferries to the

THE MAIN OFFSHORE ISLANDS

Belle-Ile
Cliffs, sandy beaches, inlets and ports — good walking country. Aiguilles de Port Coton, impressive sea rocks. Fjord-like Port Goulphar. Lobster and sardine port of Sauzon, lively le Palais harbour. Ferries from Quiberon.

Ile de Noirmoutier
Reached by low-tide causeway or modern toll-bridge. Market gardening and fishing. Museums and Bois de Chaise woods. Good beaches.

Ile d'Yeu
More rugged. Port-Joinville important tuna-fishing centre. Côte Sauvage cliff path to eleventh-century Vieux Château. Ferries from Fromentine.

Ile de Ré
Chain of limestone islets, scarcely above sea level. Renowned for asparagus. Beautiful fortified town of St Martin-de-Ré. Phare des Baleines viewpoint.

Ile d'Aix
Napoleon's last stay before deportation — museum with fascinating exhibition of relics. No cars allowed. Mother-of-pearl craft workshops. Vineyards.

Ile d'Oléron
France's second largest island, after - Corsica. 3km-long Pont-Viaduc toll bridge. Ostreiculture, vineyards. Fine beaches, especially St Trojan-les-Bains area. Sand dunes and pine forest. Very popular.

Ile de Ré. Boat excursions to the Ile de Ré, Ile d'Aix and Ile d'Oléron also leave from La Rochelle's Vieux Port in the summer. Every alternate year the resort receives competitors in the Plymouth to La Rochelle yacht race.

Essentially a chain of flat limestone islets precariously joined by narrow rocky fingers, the Ile de Ré stands just 19m above sea level at its highest point. Early vegetables, especially the asparagus for which it is renowned, are cultivated in tiny plots, alternating with vineyards and a scatter of woods on the fertile eastern section; the *marais salants* around Ars-en-Ré in the west have fallen into disuse.

Ré is an island of long beaches and intense reflected light. A cowl-like *coiffe* called a 'quichenotte' is still worn occasionally by women against the sun's penetrating brilliance, though the custom is rapidly dying out.

Several small villages of low, white dwellings dot the island, but its capital, St Martin-de-Ré, should not be missed. Scene of a siege during the Hundred Years' War in which the English were eventually routed, the town is encircled by Vauban's great fortified walls. Charming narrow streets lead down to an island of houses surrounded by a wet dock busy with fishing and pleasure craft.

From here, the D735 road runs out past la Couarde-sur-Mer and pine forest to the Phare des Baleines, with its spiral staircase of 257 steps and a panorama as far-ranging as one would expect it to be. The island is served by a number of hotels and many campsites.

With a climate and flora more reminiscent of the Mediterranean than the Atlantic, the tiny Ile d'Aix is reached by launch from La Rochelle and from la Fumee, near Fouras. Here in 1815, Napoleon spent his final hours on French soil before his deportation to St Helena. The Maison de l'Empereur (Musée Napoléonien) devotes ten rooms to a comprehensive and fascinating exposition of this great historical figure, his family and entourage. Uniforms and costumes, signed documents, portraits, weapons, furnishings and works of art all conspire to leave a lasting impression. Nearby, a collection of ethnological and zoological material from Africa may be viewed in the Musée africain.

Even in season, the island is quiet since no cars are allowed. Salt production has been replaced by the cultivation of oysters and mother-of-pearl craftwork in workshops opposite the church. Vineyards flourish here, too, producing a pleasant dry white wine.

Fouras is a local resort; when it is busy, the chances are that Rochefort will be deserted. It is frequented by the inelegant, the untanned, a cross-section of ordinary men and women, as well as by the ubiquitous young and *chic*, all of whom come out to enjoy its leafy seafront and join the animated crowds.

Four sandy beaches facing different directions provide a choice if shelter is required, Plage du Sémaphore, beneath the elevated Promenade des Sapinettes, being generally the most populous. In the Anse de Port-Sud, children have the time of their lives on a beached fishing boat — a kind of marine adventure playground. On the adjacent sands below a slipway, often obscured by sunbathers, stands a monument commemorating Napoleon's embarkation for the Ile d'Aix.

Defending the mouth of the Charente, Fouras' fifteenth-century château dominates the western seaboard. Within are a dusty courtyard and a small museum of local history, while from its two *tables d'orientation* 40m above the sea, one looks across to offshore islands, distant Rochefort, and the town's patchwork of orange roofs.

Rochefort has played a major part in French naval history since it was chosen for the strategic defence of the Atlantic coast against threatened British invasion during the mid-1600s. Its Musée Naval contains much explanatory information on the arsenal and dockyards, and some unusual model ships.

Built on a great loop in the River Charente, the town conforms to a tight grid of right-angles, alleviated by flowery avenues, trees and lawns. Despite a *Port de Plaisance*, a racecourse and a busy shopping centre, Rochefort is pre-eminently a working town with few real concessions to tourism. For all that, the museum to the author Pierre Loti (Maison de Loti), the well-endowed Musée municipal des Beaux-Arts, with its superb Polynesian masks, and the Église St Louis, are all interesting ports of call.

If sightseeing is bringing you to your knees, the Hôpital Maritime is near at hand, applying deep spring water to the treatment of rheumatism, joint and skin disorders!

Ile d'Oléron, 30km long and 6km wide, is France's second largest island, after Corsica. It has been connected to the mainland since 1966 by the country's longest bridge, the graceful Pont-Viaduc d'Oléron, spanning over 3km. Pedestrians go free, and use of the cycle track is moderately priced, but motorists pay a stiff toll.

Le Château d'Oléron is chief port and a major location for the cultivation of oysters, while at the island's watery heart, St Pierre d'Oléron handles commercial and administrative business, being also a focus for the local wine trade. An exceptionally mild climate and fine bathing beaches, especially around St Trojan-les-Bains, attract thousands of holidaymakers during July and August and although hotel accommodation is limited, campsites are in good supply, particularly along the western 'Côte Sauvage'.

High sand dunes and pine forest, common coastal features which have been interrupted since la Tranche-sur-Mer by low lying *marais*, re-emerge on Oléron, providing a foretaste of what is to come on our journey south.

More marshy flatlands, sub-divided by irrigation channels and the Seudre-Charente canal, sweep north to Rochefort. Herds of cattle and isolated hamlets are lost amongst endless straw-coloured reeds and grasses and a radiant paling of reflected skylight over water.

Marenne's conspicuous English-style church faces la Tremblade across a maze of oyster beds at the mouth of the River Seudre. Fifty per cent of France's oyster production originates from Charente-Maritime: up to a staggering 45,000 tonnes in a single year.

It is a vulnerable harvest, easily damaged by disease, excessive mud or salinity, storm, cold, and even attack by crabs and starfish. Young wild oysters (*naissain*), at the mercy of sea currents, are fixed to tiles and stakes during the summer. At about nine months, they are collected and placed in artificial ponds called *claires* and allowed to mature for another year, before purification and marketing. Adult oysters in the Marennes *claires* are fed on a microscopic seaweed ('*naviscule bleue*') which imparts the distinctive greenish tinge and delicate fragrance of '*l'huitre verte*'.

Ronce-les-Bains overlooks a large body of shallow sea, almost enclosed by Ile d'Oléron's southernmost tip. Low tides reveal extensive mudflats and a forest of oyster stakes, but the sandy fringes of this great natural basin, where they exist, make for uncrowded beaches and sheltered swimming: at Plage d'Embellie, for example, bathing is supervised and there is ample car parking space. Trails abound in the Forêt de la Tremblade; many are waymarked and timed, to facilitate planned itineraries, while horse-riding is a popular alternative to walking.

The French inclination to call their exposed ocean shoreline 'Côte Sauvage' (Wild Coast) is not as consistent an indicator of 'wildness' as one might imagine: it is often applied equally to rocky foreshore near roads and settlements, and to remote beaches far from habitation. Language, after all, is not an exact science and the intention is undoubtedly to evoke rather than to define. However, the 'Côte Sauvage' from the Pertuis de Maumusson to Pointe de la Coubre is *sauvage* in spirit as well as in word.

Largely unfrequented, and reached by forest tracks from the D25, its dunes and beaches bear the full brunt of Atlantic

Phare St George and the beach at St George-de-Didonne

swells: bathing, as notices warn, is extremely dangerous throughout its 12km-length. Salt-spray and the thunder of surf drift inland, but the Forêt de la Coubre, through which the coast is reached, was badly damaged by fire in the drought of 1976.

At the neck of a curved arm of sand, Phare de la Coubre rears a red and white tower 60m high — with Phare d'Eckmühl in Brittany, France's most powerful mainland lighthouse. To the south, Phare de Corduan and Pointe de Grave join forces in demarcating the mouth of the mighty Gironde estuary.

La Palmyre has a zoo containing many species of birds and animals and occupies 20 acres of mixed wooded terrain just inland of the D25. Pink flamingoes by the perimeter wall ensure passing motorists are tempted to stop, and the zoo advertises itself as far away as Royan! Many thousands flock here during the high season and are catered for with a café, souvenir shop and Western-style village.

Inside Pointe de la Coubre's protective sand-bar, Bonne Anse provides safe anchorage for boats. The lovely Palmyre and Grande Côte beaches, however, are unsafe for bathing in some sea conditions, with strong currents at high and low tide. They are hugely popular nonetheless.

A staggering volume of holidaymakers congregates along the Grande Côte, visiting the zoo and beaches, picnicking at the forest edge.

For much of July and August, parked cars line the verges of the D25 for many kilometres and road signs warn against leaving between 5pm and 7pm during the evening rush to campsite or hotel for dinner!

From St Palais-sur-Mer, a waymarked footpath ('Sentier de la Corniche') winds through oak woods, across a small ravine to the oddly-shaped Roche du Moine, the Pont du Diable and les Pierrières, a leisurely hour there and back.

We are at the northern end of 12km of mostly built-up resorts, abundantly well endowed with amenities and attractions — a favourite holiday destination for both French and British families and known as the Côte de Beauté. A succession of pretty, shielded bays called *conches*, served by a scenic coast road, connects St Palais with Nauzan and Pontaillac, Royan's old quarter. These intimate resorts, backed by shops, cafés and nearby campsites, epitomise the qualities for which this coast is famous: safe sandy beaches fringed with rocks and pine trees — an idyllic environment for all ages.

Royan itself was severely damaged by aerial bombardment in 1945 and has seen extensive rebuilding, though some elegant old villas and hotels on its outskirts survive. It is a smart, modern town which shuns garishness, extravagance or exclusivity, perhaps explaining its appeal to the discerning visitor. There is no shortage of fine restaurants and shops, car parks are plentiful, the environment clean and spacious.

A system of piers and moles encloses Royan's port, from which car ferries (Bac) sail at frequent intervals for Pointe de Grave, saving travellers who wish to reach the Gironde's west bank from the longest inland detour on the entire French coast — some 120km to Bordeaux (though another ferry does cross at Blaye). Boat trips also run out to the Phare de Cordouan, built on the site of the Black Prince's fourteenth-century lighthouse.

No account of Royan's centre, however brief, should omit the Église Notre-Dame, whose slabby modern belfry rises 65m and dominates the skyline. Designed and constructed in the late 1950s, the church is worth perusing for its impressive nave, pyramidal baptistry and a bronze Joan of Arc.

Two kilometres of golden sands and a tamarisk-lined promenade curve round la Grande Conche, Royan's famous 'Front de Mer'. In addition to beach and water sports, a marine centre, a swimming pool and tennis courts, alternative entertainment is offered by a 'Toboggan Aquatique' and the Royaland Amusement Park.

Round built-up Pointe de Vallières, the small town of St George-de-Didonne overlooks another splendid sweep of gently-shelving beach, ideal for youngsters; large, well-appointed campsites are situated nearby. Footpaths lead out to Pointe de Suzac above warm limestone cliffs; at Fort Suzac there are wartime gun emplacements and immense views across the silt-brown waters of the Gironde estuary.

It is quite possible to continue on footpaths (*sentiers cotiers*) through intermittent woods parallel to the D25, right along past Plage de Suzac (also called 'Plage d'Anglais'), Plage des Vergnes and Conche des Nonnes to emerge at Meschers-sur-Gironde. At low tide a beach route may be used.

Hollowed out and embellished with shells by prehistoric man, the 'Trous de Meschers' (caves) have provided refuge through the centuries for fishermen, religious fugitives, smugglers and pirates. Each cave possesses a small spring and hearth, some have been transformed into homes or restaurants. Large caves at the cliff base are the remains of ancient quarrying.

Talmont, like Meschers, is a sightseer's delight: curious, evocative, unique. Summertime crowds have to be expected and tolerated, but fortunately

Côte Sauvage and Phare de la Coubre
Reached through forest off D25.

La Palmyre Zoo
Many species of birds and animals,
'Wild-west' village.

Grande Côte
Beaches, sand, ocean, pine forest —
hugely popular.

Côte de Beauté
Pleasant, well-appointed little resorts
north of Royan.

Royan
Excellent beaches, restaurants, shops.

Modern Église Notre-Dame.
Frequent car ferries across Gironde
to Pointe de Grave.

St George-de-Didonne
More good beaches.

Meschers-sur-Gironde
Reached by cliff paths — inhabited
caves.

Talmont
Église St Radegonde perched above
estuary for twelve centuries. Fishing
jetties and fields of sunflowers.

Cognac
Excursion inland, home of brandy.

---

nearby parking and picnic places are
generous so that the diminutive, quaint
old village, its alleyways a riot of
flowers, remains pedestrianised and
tranquil.

Vulnerable to undermining by the
estuary's strong currents, the twelfth-
century Église St Radegonde sits
precariously atop a limestone cliff. The
nave of this fine Renaissance church was
claimed by the sea several centuries ago,
but work has been carried out to
consolidate the exposed supporting rock
and prevent further damage. There are
multi-lingual recorded commentaries on
its history and architecture, and few who

visit Talmont will wish to miss seeing the
building at close quarters. The site is a
very pretty one indeed, but perhaps the
best views of all are from the little rocky
beach to the east, or from fields of
sunflowers near la Caillaud, above the
long wooden jetties of local fishermen.

Though still maritime by nature for
several tens of kilometres upstream, the
Gironde beyond Talmont can hardly be
included in a guide primarily concerned
with the coast. And so we cross back to
the Pointe de Grave, at the
northernmost tip of the Médoc on the
estuary's left bank.

4 The Aquitaine Coast:

THE GIRONDE TO HENDAYE

Jellyfish float past the ferry like pale moons in the brown estuary water between Royan and Pointe de Grave, but rarely venture inshore. Just south of where we put in at Port Bloc stands le Verdon, effectively Bordeaux's port, all crane gantries and oil storage tanks. It provides deep-water access for large oil tankers and container ships and a matching infrastructure of modern equipment, vast storage facilities and an expanding industrial estate. Oil is taken upstream in smaller vessels to the refineries at Ambès while the railway and N215, running through the heart of the wine-growing Médoc, carry their share of Bordeaux's commercial trade with the rest of the world.

The Basilica Notre-Dame-de-la-Fin-des-Terres, at Soulac-sur-Mer, had been all but engulfed by drifting sand when it was dug out and restored during the 1800s; a worse fate befell the ancient town of Noviomagus, overrun by the sea here in the sixth century. Such examples serve only to underline the vulnerability of coastal settlements to changes wrought by the elements: erosion here is balanced by deposition there in a slow, perpetually shifting play for supremacy by land and ocean.

Man's influence is plain to see, and he is by no means always the loser: reclamation of salt-marsh to arable land is as dramatically to his advantage as the undermining of buildings or farmland is his loss. Nowhere on the French coast has there been a more telling and far-sighted act, however, than the transformation of the Landes.

Up to the beginning of the nineteenth century, that long, ruled edge of France from the Gironde to the Adour rivers was an immense, inhospitable wasteland of dunes, sand and scrub. Unrelieved by bays and headlands, except at Arcachon, and facing the uninterrupted force of the Atlantic Ocean, the ravages suffered by this coast can well be imagined. Sand was continually deposited, forming extensive dunes reached by only the highest tides. Their dry tops were blown up to 25m a year inland by prevailing westerlies, choking vegetation and, in turn, spawning new accumulations. Human habitation was unthinkable in such locations. Land and ocean, both moved by the unremitting power of the wind, merged along a wild, desolate shore whose presence was felt tens of kilometres away to the east.

In 1788, a civil engineer by the name

Typical summer weather conditions on the Aquitaine Coast						
	May	June	July	Aug	Sept	Oct
Average daytime air temperature °C	18	23.7	27.2	25.7	24.2	19.7
Typical daily sunshine hours	6.1	6.3	9.8	6.6	7.4	6.6
Days with some rainfall	21	15	8	19	9	8
Average sea temperature °C	14	16	18	19	19	17

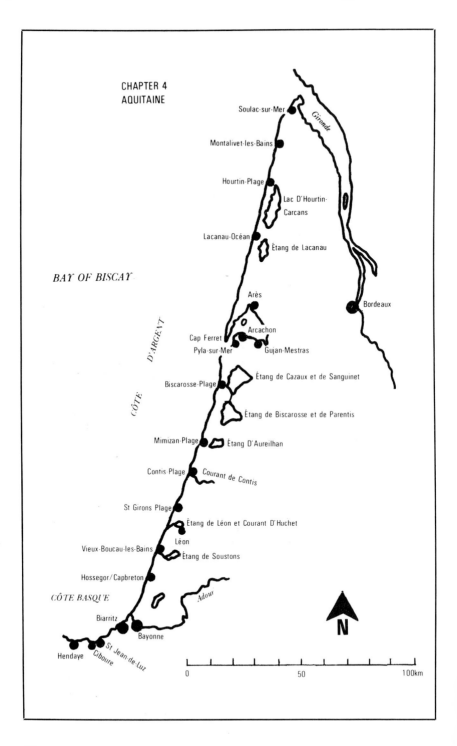

CHAPTER 4
AQUITAINE

Soulac-sur-Mer

Gironde

Montalivet-les-Bains

Hourtin-Plage

Lac D'Hourtin-
Carcans

Lacanau-Océan

Étang de Lacanau

BAY OF BISCAY

Arès

Arcachon

Cap Ferret

Bordeaux

Pyla-sur-Mer

Gujan-Mestras

D'ARGENT

Étang de Cazaux et de Sanguinet

Biscarosse-Plage

CÔTE

Étang de Biscarosse et de Parentis

Mimizan-Plage

Étang D'Aureilhan

Contis-Plage

Courant de Contis

St Girons Plage

Étang de Léon et Courant D'Huchet

Léon

Vieux-Boucau-les-Bains

Étang de Soustons

Hossegor/Capbreton

CÔTE BASQUE

Adour

Biarritz

N

Bayonne

Hendaye

St Jean-de-Luz

Ciboure

0   50   100km

of Brémontier set in motion an ambitious plan to stabilise the dunes. Fences were systematically erected, well away from highest tide limits, to create an artificial barrier of drifted sand and discourage further migration inland. It was fixed by planting *gourbet*, a species of marram grass with especially quick-growing matted roots. The work was to last over eighty years but has been conspicuously successful.

Despite the planting of pine trees for consolidation, the hinterland was still poorly drained and the impoverished soil resisted efforts to establish agriculture. In the mid-1800s, another enterprising engineer, Monsieur Chambrelent, initiated wide-scale drainage and afforestation with maritime pine, oak and cork-oak. It was an inspired decision.

Today, the reformation is complete and the Department des Landes possesses an immeasurably rich resource: almost $2\frac{1}{4}$ million acres of pine forest. It will colour the next 230km of our journey — a pervasive, encompassing presence, as mysterious and atmospheric for some as it is claustrophobic and repetitive for others.

As for the dunes: although they still stretch up to 5km inland, the highest and most extensive in Europe, they are for the most part static — a benevolent windbreak for the plantations which in turn provide shelter for human habitation.

In the absence of large towns, again excepting Arcachon, and without an established tradition of resort amenity, the Landes was ripe for development when France's increasingly prosperous population spilled over from customary holidaymaking areas like the Riviera and north-west coast. It has proved more than equal to the challenge, accommodating visitors from other European nations too, not least the Germans, Dutch and British.

The mighty sweep of ocean beach reaching from Soulac almost to Biarritz is known as the Côte d'Argent (Silver Coast), an epithet inspired, no doubt, by its infinite pale sand and dazzling light. In places, amenity provision is extraordinarily varied, bringing people from all walks of life into a region ideally suited to an outdoor 'sun-and-sea' vacation.

Near St Vivien-de-Médoc are apartments, campsites, bungalows, shops, a cinema and prolific sporting facilities, including tennis, golf, riding, archery and sailing. At nearby Grayan-et-l'Hopital, a 'Euronat' naturist village, one of many on this coast where seclusion is easily found, nestles in 1,000 acres of pine forest. Ranged alongside the coastal roads are yet more holiday centres, and at Montelivet-les-Bains a self-contained holiday village offers horse-riding and cycle-touring on surfaced forest tracks, in addition to its other attractions.

Streams flowing seaward from the inner Landes find their exits barred by impregnable dunes and for centuries have accumulated into *étangs* (lagoons) surrounded by unusable marsh. Drainage channels have dried out the *marais*, but the *étangs* remain, a necklace of them strung out south to Hossegor, with Arcachon's great basin a central pearl.

First to be encountered is Lac d'Hourtin-Carcans, 19km long by 4km wide, alone in not bearing the name *étang*. This miniature inland sea lies between forest and *marais*, remote and thinly frequented in its middle reaches. The long-distance footpath from Soulac to Biscarosse-Plage (GR8) threads the Landes coast, takes a line through the high dunes on Lac d'Hourtin's west shore, and passes on through Lacanau-Océan, Arès and Arcachon.

Just north of Maubisson, at the lake's southern end, stands the 'Base de plein air de Bombannes', affirming the French predeliction for sport and fresh air: there are facilities for water sports and swimming, gymnastics, tennis, archery, and even picnicking.

Lacanau-Océan receives the big

Atlantic swells onto its wide sandy beach and is the venue for a summer surfing fête. Otherwise the resort is a rather undistinguished jumble of shops, stalls, bars and villas, some stark new apartment blocks and a concrete promenade. Chalet development to the north, almost a suburb, reflects its proximity to Bordeaux, for whose inhabitants this is the handiest of seasides.

New buildings sprout along this coast like a planted crop. Thanks to government policy, however, the unsightly tower blocks which spoil parts of the Riviera, Vendée and Normandy have given way here to the 'more human kind of growth' advocated in 1975 by France's equivalent to Britain's National Trust — the Conservatoire de l'Espace littoral.

The French have not been alone in progressing from camping and caravans to owning holiday apartments,for the Côte d'Argent is popular with Germans.

Lest the wrong impression be given, camping is still a great French institution and is on the increase. But while campsites are sometimes an eyesore, prejudicial to the local ecostructure for about three months of the year, apartment complexes, whatever their merits, become permanent fixtures on the coastscape. Ironically, the boom in second-home ownership is already showing signs of decline as the effects of recession are felt.

Étang de Lacanau is altogether prettier than Lac d'Hourtins — a tranquil body of open water ringed by a reedy, tree-shaded shore with several points of access. There is much sailing, water-skiing and wind-surfing, while fishing yields perch, pike and eel.

Arès lies at the apex of a vast tidal triangle — the Bassin d'Arcachon. Reedy mud-banks exposed right across the bay at low tide are dotted with poles and stakes, for, along with fishing and tourism, oyster cultivation is a major

The seafront at Lacanau-Océan, Côte d'Argent

industry, employing many thousands of local people.

The basin's eastern edge is a continuum of modest villages lined with plane trees and low houses, each distinguished by an imposing town hall. Andernos-les-Bains, an ancient settlement with the remains of a fourth-century basilica near the tiny Église St Éloi, is an important oyster centre and holiday spa-resort, with a casino and summer fair. South-east stretch Taussat, le Renal, Lanton, Audenge and Biganos, every bar and restaurant in this oyster economy offering shellfish for the visitor's delectation.

At peak season, events are staged for holidaymakers on this busy shoreline, from oyster fêtes to cycle races, circuses to regattas. And all round the basin are innumerable small, waveless, sandy beaches with attendant campsites.

The Parc ornithologique du Teich occupies 300 acres of marshy delta at the outflow of the River Eyre. *Résevoirs à Poissons* — a kind of natural fish farm — have been established to sustain bird life and encourage migratory species. Herons, storks, wild geese, ducks and swans live well in this favourable habitat, and there are special viewing stations as well as an Environment Centre.

Gujan-Mestras is the south shore's main town, other than Arcachon itself; more a merging, perhaps, of several tiny oyster ports characterised by picturesque tiled cottages, shops, stalls and restaurants dedicated to oyster-worship!

The arrival of the railway during the mid-nineteenth century gave rise first to la Teste then to Arcachon, as the inhabitants of Bordeaux discovered the attractions of a coast only 60km distant. By then an oyster industry was already springing up, in the bay and on the Ile aux Oiseaux; despite problems with disease, Arcachon became, and remains, a major European producer.

There are facilities for many sports in and around the resort, including bowls,

---

PLACES TO VISIT ON THE CÔTE D'ARGENT

A string of large fresh-water lagoons (*étangs*), providing opportunities for sailing, canoeing, wind-surfing, water-skiing, fishing, bathing: Lac d'Hourtins-Carcans, Étang de Lacanau, Étang de Cazaux, Étang de Biscarosse, Étang de Léon, Étang de Pinsolle.

The great Landes pine forest — footpaths, tracks and minor roads linking small villages, ideal for cycling, walking, riding. Endless Atlantic beaches and Europe's biggest sand dunes. Innumerable campsites.

Courant d'Huchet
Boat trips on one of three waterways reaching the ocean through lush vegetation.

Bassin d'Arcachon
Oyster and shellfish centre, smart resort and oyster villages, bird reserve, boat trips to Ile aux Oiseaux and Cap Ferret.

---

tennis, skating, swimming, water-skiing, diving, walking and fishing. An Aquarium and Musée contain both living and static exhibits of local marine life. The busy town offers a modern shopping centre, two casinos and walks along the seafront Boulevard de la Mer.

Tidal constraints apart, the Bassin d'Arcachon is a haven for pleasure boats, and moorings exist for some 1,800 craft. Regular trips run to Cap-Ferret, the Ile aux Oiseaux and round the bay.

Jetties, moorings and a sheltered beach at Pyla-sur-Mer face across to the long tongue of Cap Ferret; its southern tip ends at the great Toulinguet and Arguin sandbanks, falling only narrowly short of closing Arcachon's seaway altogether. From Belisaire, north of Cap-Ferret's conspicuous lighthouse (open to the public), little trains commute across the isthmus to ocean beaches during the summer months.

Dune du Pilat is an astonishing sight: a mountain of sand 4km long, reared against the sky 114m high, the largest in continental Europe. Slowly nudging its way onto campsites and forest behind it, this immense crest of sand, too hot for bare feet after mid-morning on a sunny day, is mounted by a stairway at one point but may be climbed almost anywhere — a strenuous 'two-steps-up, one-down' scramble.

Views from the Saharan summit are tremendous: east over the canopy of forest, north-west to the sand islands and Cap Ferret, south down the glittering Atlantic seaboard beyond Pointe d'Arcachon into a blue and white infinity. Bathing on the beach beneath the dune requires caution as tides funnel through the Bassin d'Arcachon's constricted entrance.

Buses serve the coastal campsites along D218; beaches are gained via forest tracks. While tree cover may be dense, individual plantations vary considerably in age and texture, from bright green youngsters to the slender, mature curves of 20m-high giants. Fire is an ever-present threat, and a network of firefighters (*sapeurs-pompiers forestiers*) has been set up to detect and extinguish outbreaks. Forest rides and firebreaks allow teams to reach any location quickly, while activities likely to cause fire, such as camping and excessive public access, are strictly controlled.

Many pines are felled after fifteen to twenty years for timber and paper-making; trees thirty to forty years in age, however, are periodically tapped for their resin. A traditional ceramic pot, wired to each trunk below an incision, collects the viscous, milky syrup for about three weeks. It is coaxed out by the use of sulphuric acid (hence warnings not to touch), significantly reducing the size of cut required, before being taken to distilleries and used in various industrial processes.

Bathing at Biscarosse-Plage,

Mature pine trees in the Landes tapped for resin

geographical centre of the Côte d'Argent, is rendered safer by conscientious lifeguard surveillance from towers, a roving jeep and even an occasional helicopter! Typically, the beach assumes virtually infinite proportions, with some holidaymakers prepared to walk several kilometres in search of privacy and solitude, or the naturist locations which, officially and otherwise, flank the main, easy-to-reach sands.

To north and south, beach and ocean converge, and in the farthest distance, at the limit of vision, a luminescent glow radiates from sunshine on sea spray. Tides ebb and flow quickly, altering

Traditional Landes homestead near Mimizan

beach topography so that warm lagoons behind sandbars can become treacherous channels within a short space of time. Considering this tidal restlessness, water temperatures in July and August are pleasantly high.

The Étang de Cazaux et de Sanguinet is linked to the Étang de Biscarosse et de Parentis by a navigable canal. Both lagoons provide water sport, though oil pipelines from wells around Parentis-en-Born, and a firing range to the north, are apt to impinge on a holidaymaking reverie — unless one sticks, ostrich-like, to the coast! Even that is denied us here, for a military testing ground (Centre d'Essais des Landes) sprawls over 20km south and 6km inland. There are tank-tracks and signs of shell holes.

Mimizan, site of an ancient settlement just south of the delightful Étang d'Aureilhan, was rescued from the easterly march of sand in the eighteenth century and at the leading edge of the dunes, fixed by the first plantings of *gourbet*, stands the belfry of a thirteenth-century Benedictine abbey-church. A little farther on, the D626 reaches Mimizan-Plage, with a monument at its northern end to the aviators Lotti,

Lefevre and Assolant who landed here on 16 June 1929, after an audacious crossing of the North Atlantic.

The D652 connects a succession of Landes villages, quiet in winter but surprisingly animated during the summer season. This entire stretch of coastline is peppered with campsites, from grandly-appointed 'canvas towns' to the humblest *camping à la ferme*. With so many self-catering holidaymakers around, small wonder the village shops do well! Lit-et-Mixe, with its own campsite, is a representative centre, and its imposing church is worthy of investigation.

The low-slung houses of the Landes are built in forest clearings, traditionally surrounded by a kitchen garden and perhaps a patch of corn. Of timber construction under a broad tiled roof, accommodation is often limited to the ground floor, with verandas under the eaves and an attic; many are extremely picturesque.

Other roadside attractions include sales of pottery, ambitious affairs by British standards, and one can often find a visiting circus if a diet of sun, sea and sand needs spicing; bars and cafés do a

volleyball; how different in a winter
storm!

An impressive campsite laid out in
forest, with shops, swimming pool and
tennis courts, introduces St Girons-
Plage. The beach approaches have take-
away food stalls, a supermarket and
bar/restaurant, with adequate car
parking. Other than from the
lifeguarded sector, however, bathing can
be dangerous in the heavy surf;
comprehensive information on tides and
the disposition of currents is posted at
the main beach entrance. A string of
holiday homes lines the dune tops; like
silted-up boat hulls, they seem scarcely
able to resist the inexorable ingress of
drifting sand, but nevertheless are well
used.

The Étang de Léon debouches into the
Atlantic via the Courant d'Huchet, most
impressive of the trio. Boat excursions
depart from the lagoon's south shore,
off the D142 from Léon, taking four
hours for a round trip along the *courant*,
through profuse foliage, past vines and
wild hibiscus to the ocean dunes.

Farther south, the last of the *courants*
meanders between Étang de Soustons
and the diminutive Étang de Pinsolle, to
form another body of water before
reaching the sea — lac de Port-d'Albret.
This provides bathing, wind-surfing,
pedalos and a beach at the small resort
of Vieux-Boucau-les-Bains.

Built around a salt-water lagoon
linked to the sea by canal and girdled by
pine forest, Hossegor presents a
cheerful, mildly fashionable face. It
offers visitors horse-riding, surfing, golf,
an open-air cinema, motor museum and
watching the Basque sport of *pelota*.

The lagoon (Lac d'Hossegor) was
once an arm of the River Adour, which
now wanders inland to join the Gave
before flowing west through Bayonne.
Landes-style villas crowd the lagoon's
shoreline and more new development is
in evidence as far north as les Estagnots.
There is an excellent beach of fine sand,
but sea bathing is largely unsupervised
and cannot be said to be wholly safe.

brisk evening trade.

Three watercourses in the southern
Landes, unlike the rest of their
frustrated number, do find an exit
through the dunes. At the confluence of
a myriad of streams, the Courant de
Contis, first to be encountered, passes
through dense and unusually varied
vegetation to enter the ocean at Contis-
Plage.

Cap-de-l'Homy-Plage, another road-
end, has its obligatory bar/restaurant
and campsite. The dunes are still lofty
and continuous, their seaward face
scoured steep by wave action. On a
benign summer evening, the beach is a
place for strolling or a gentle game of

Grande-Plage, Biarritz

An unremarkable harbour, breakwater and lighthouse belie Capbreton's former maritime importance — its seamen sailed to Newfoundland as long ago as 1392. Connected to Hossegor by ferry, it, too, is a popular bathing resort, with immense sands to the south.

At the contiguous urban centres of Bayonne, Anglet and Biarritz, we leave the Landes and Côte d'Argent for the Pays Basque, that fiercely independent-spirited region straddling the western frontier between France and Spain. The separatist movement, like that of the Bretons, is an active one and political graffiti on walls and buildings not uncommon. Should holidaymakers on the popular Basque coast choose to ignore it, however, they are unlikely to be reminded in any other way of the issues and activities generated by separatist extremists. Whether this immunity is permanent remains to be seen.

Bayonne, chief town and spiritual capital of the Basque country, lies several kilometres inland, its port recently improved by the construction of a 1,200m-long breakwater to prevent silting-up of the Adour. The massive town walls and remains of Gallo-Roman fortifications are seen amidst shady gardens, and there are good views from the citadel.

One of France's finest church buildings and a great landmark, the Cathédrale Ste Marie contains much of interest, including fourteenth-century cloisters, sixteenth-century stained glass and an 80m-high spire. In addition, the city has two museums well worth visiting: the Musée Basque, dealing with the region's history, its seafaring, costumes, sports, arts and crafts; and the Musée Bonnat (in Rue Jacques Lafitte) with its wonderful collection of paintings and drawings, the latter including priceless works by Rembrandt, Michelangelo, Botticelli and Durer.

Bayonne goes wild during the first week of August — *grandes fêtes* time —

Port des Pêcheurs, on Biarritz's rocky headland

with an extravaganza of Basque sports, bullfights, traditional singing and dancing, and night-long merrymaking.

Biarritz, regal seaside resort and large, sophisticated city, is smart, cosmopolitan and a little expensive. It became fashionable after Empress Eugenie persuaded husband Napoleon III to holiday there; even today 'La Belle Epoque' lingers on in the old-fashioned elegance of beautifully kept gardens and grand hotels. Biarritz remains fashionable in the 1980s: the emphasis has simply shifted to the provision of modern amenities and it boasts several heated swimming pools, four golf courses, two casinos, riding stables, tennis courts and equipment for most water sports. Brine springs and a mild climate have also earned the city a reputation for salt-water cures.

For surfers and lovers of the Atlantic, the surf beaches, unchangingly magnificent, are the real magnet. This, after all, is the surfing mecca of the French coast, some would say of Europe. Lifeguards supervise the Grande Plage, and for some twenty francs a day you can occupy one of the colourful striped beach tents. Other long reaches of firm sand, open to ocean swells, extend north beyond Pointe St Martin's lighthouse along the 'Chambre d'Amour' and, more exposed, to the south along the Côte des Basques.

Biarritz's rocky headland forms a natural harbour, Port des Pêcheurs, and shelters a tiny inlet beach, Plage du Port-Vieux. A footbridge leads across to the Rocher de la Vierge, the most westerly outcrop and a marvellous veiwpoint; on this same promontory stands an excellent Musée de la Mer, housing France's reputedly largest aquarium, a sealion pool and an aviary, as well as many natural science displays relating principally to the North Atlantic.

Ilbarritz, at the northern extremity of the Côte Basque, provides an alternative if Biarritz is congested, and has a pleasant little beach café. 3km further south there is a panoramic coastal viewpoint from the Chapelle St Madeleine, on the cliff-top corniche road at Bidart. Car parking, not easy hereabouts in season, is less fraught around the Plage de Parlementia and at nearby Guéthary, an ancient fishing port on a natural inlet.

Near the foothills of the Pyrenees, St Jean-de-Luz, the most Basque in character of all towns north of the border, is a charming and fascinating resort. Whaling had been an important livelihood for local fishermen, and those from Biarritz, until the British and Dutch imposed access restrictions on the Arctic coast 300 years ago.

Today, St Jean-de-Luz is France's premier tuna-fish and anchovy port, and its harbour, separated from neighbouring Ciboure's by a fish-wharf, is as animated and industrious as any on the entire coast. Much of the catch is frozen, but a proportion enters the 'Saupiquet' dockside canning factory, finding its way into those delectably spiced tuna and vegetable recipes.

Quaysides are invariably bustling with activity: the comings and goings of divers and yachtsmen, crew from the deep-sea fleet repairing their nets, catches being off-loaded, artists at easels, and a colourful array of absorbed onlookers. For a good general view of the port against an almost Venetian backcloth of seventeenth-century houses in the Quartier de la Barre, make for the road bridge (N10) across the River Nivelle.

Largest and most celebrated of the Basque churches, Église St Jean-Baptiste is vaguely forbidding from the outside. Within, however, awaits a feast of intricate features and ornamentation, including three-tiered galleries built of oak and reached by an iron staircase, paintings, statuettes, model ships, and a wealth of architectural embellishment. It should not be missed! The Maison Louis XIV Château on Quai de l'Enfant is also worth visiting.

Both harbour mouth and a delightful arc of sandy beach are protected from big Atlantic swells by a mid-bay breakwater. In 1749 high seas breached the old quarter, destroying 200 houses; to prevent a recurrence of this catastrophe, a deep, paved drainage channel has been constructed between the sea-wall promenade and the half-timbered seafront residences, to take overspill from waves during storms and very high tides. Little footbridges cross the drain from each front door.

St Jean-de-Luz stages a number of Basque festivals during the summer, with *pelota* tournaments, bullfights and traditional music. A Festival of St John is held in June, a Tuna Festival in July.

For stunning views of the whole region (in good weather), take a 10km-trip inland: beyond Ascain (off the D918), the narrow D4 climbs to Col St Ignace, from where a mountain railway leaves for the 900m-summit of la Rhune, right on the Spanish border. The panorama extends from the Pyrenees to the coast and, on the distant northern horizon, the forest of the Landes.

Ciboure, the composer Ravel's birthplace, is picturesquely situated at the back of the bay below clusters of orange-roofed villas. Altogether quieter than St Jean-de-Luz, there is a diving school, boating and fishing from the harbour, backed by a warren of half-timbered houses along narrow streets. The Église St Vincent, like an echo of St Jean-Baptiste a kilometre distant, is no less worthy an edifice, with a thematically identical, though plainer, interior. It is reached via a paved courtyard past an eighteenth-century stone cross.

Socoa's interesting fortress, built by Henry IV and later remodelled by Vauban, guards the bay's entrance, but unfortunately is not open to the public. Another offshore breakwater serves to

Diving-school launch leaving St Jean-de-Luz

Hendaye's busy frontier with Spain

Repairing nets on the quayside at St Jean-de-Luz

protect the exposed shoreline.

Food stalls, a go-kart track and informal cliff-top parking are pointers to the heavy use received by the Corniche Basque. Rugged coastal scenery and green, rolling countryside are reminiscent of Cornwall and, despite evident popularity, this stretch to the frontier town of Hendaye somehow manages to retain freshness and charm.

The cliffs of Cabo Higuer, seen from the white villas at Hendaye-Plage, constitute our first firm sighting of Spanish soil. Surroundings here, away from frontier traffic, are dignified and graceful; nineteenth-century hotels behind the beach give way to avenues and gardens filled with mimosa, tamarisk, palms, magnolia and a host of other luxuriant plants. Like Biarritz,

Hendaye-Plage also caters for the modern holidaymaker with facilities for most sports and activities.

A noticeable Spanish flavour pervades Hendaye-ville: frontiers are seldom as clear as the line on a map and there is an intermingling of customs and appearances, like the liquid merging of watercolour.

The vast frontier complex of customs posts for road, railway and airport extends inland to the A63 Autoroute, but Hendaye-ville itself sits on a bend in the River Bidassoa — prosperous, lively, with more than its share of banks! From one of the flowery gardens above yacht moorings on the river, we can contemplate the ochre town of Fuenterrabia, a kilometre away in another country.

5 The Coast of Languedoc-Roussillon:

CAP CERBÈRE TO THE RHÔNE

Beyond Cap Cerbère, the brown dissected hills of Spain roll into a shimmering, villa-encrusted distance along the Costa Brava. Cliffs rise steeply around the cape, with its inauspicious stony pull-in and odd lighthouse, 2km from the Spanish frontier.

Cerbère itself, a cramped, unpretty place, dominated by a viaduct and new road, its buildings grey and rather unkempt, is France's southernmost town. It is also the border railway station; years of use by tourists passing through have imbued the place with an almost tangible world-weariness. Even so, some waterfront attractions exist: a small beach and marina, scuba-diving, and wide views from the ancient Tour de Ker'Roig.

The N114 corniche snakes tortuously along the Côte Vermeille, named after the reddish soil, and is frequently choked with traffic at peak times. Cap Réderis affords one of the best viewpoints, extensive both to north and south, though that from Cap l'Abeille is hardly less fine.

Hillsides have been elaborately irrigated for viticulture; barrel-shaped stalls at the roadside offer tastings of the slightly sweet local wines for which

Banyuls-sur-Mer is especially noted. This small fishing port and resort nestles in two bays separated by a promontory and is dominated to the west by high ridges thrown down to the sea by the great Pyrenees chain of mountains. A long-distance footpath, GR10, traverses their entire length from here to Hendaye on the Atlantic coast.

The *port nouveau* at Banyuls is popular with yachtsmen and there is bathing from the pebbly beach, backed by restaurants and a promenade. The coastal waters to Cerbère — clear, deep and rich in marine life — are a designated reserve and a paradise for divers. Marine biology laboratories, associated with the University of Paris, are established in the town, and there is a good aquarium.

The sculptor Aristide Maillol lived and worked at Banyuls: his memorial to the war-dead can be found on Ile Grosse, reached by a causeway. (Another of his works, 'Three Nymphs' is housed in the Tate Gallery, London.)

Vineyards and cork-oaks lead on past Cap Béar to Port-Vendres, the *Portus Veneris* of the Romans, fortified as a military port by Vauban in the seventeeth century. Today, fishing and

Typical summer weather conditions on the Languedoc-Roussillon Coast						
	May	June	July	Aug	Sept	Oct
Average daytime air temperature °C	20.1	26.5	28.4	28.1	26.1	21.1
Typical daily sunshine hours	7.9	9.2	11.6	8.6	7.9	7.5
Days with some rainfall	7.5	8	1	9.5	3.5	6.5
Average sea temperature °C	15	20	19	21	17	18

St Jean-de-Luz

Collioure

Futuristic apartment blocks at La Grande Motte

Stes Maries-de-la-Mer

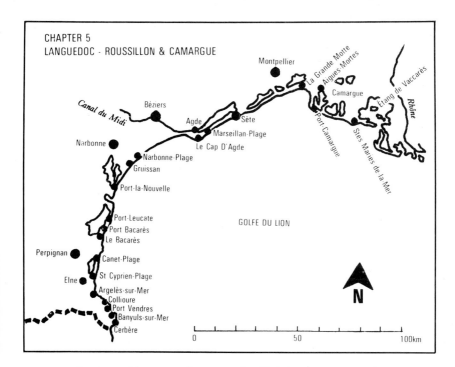

Montpellier

La Grande Motte
Aigues-Mortes

Camargue

Étang de Vaccarès

Rhône

Canal du Midi

Béziers

Agde

Sète

Marseillan-Plage

Narbonne

Le Cap D'Agde

Narbonne-Plage

Gruissan

Port-Camargue

Stes Maries de la Mer

Port-la-Nouvelle

Port-Leucate

GOLFE DU LION

Port Bacarès

Le Bacarès

Perpignan

Canet-Plage

Elne

St Cyprien-Plage

Argelès-sur-Mer

Collioure

Port Vendres

Banyuls-sur-Mer

Cerbère

N

0   50   100km

cargo vessels, along with a mass of pleasure boats, crowd its square harbour basin, surrounded by delightful quaysides.

In spite of modern apartment blocks, Collioure still justifies its title 'Pearl of the Côte Vermeille'. Considered to be the birthplace of Fauvism in 1905, it was visited regularly by Matisse, Derain and Vlamink, later by Dufy and Picasso. Many artists stayed at the Hostellerie des Templiers which has held onto paintings left as payment or souvenirs, as well as to a little of the original ambience. Like most towns associated with well-known artists of the past, Collioure attracts its complement of easel-painters touting for business.

When the town passed from Spanish to French hands in 1642, the great Templar Château Royal by the harbour, previously a defence against Saracen pirates, was rebuilt by Vauban. It is open to the public during summer exhibitions. Most visitors, however, will gravitate to the seventeenth-century fortified church and clocktower (once the lighthouse and predating the church by 300 years). Amongst other features, the dark, ornate interior contains nine magnificent gold-painted *retables*.

There are three beaches, colourful fishing boats and a host of bars where huge baroque ice-cream sundaes are served in the afternoon. The town's shady square is its social heart and a formidable *boules* arena; sunshine filters in dusty shafts onto the milieu below, dispersing into lyrical pools of light. No traveller to this southerly corner of France should miss Collioure.

Set against the profile of the Albères hills, outliers of the Pyrenees, Argelès-Plage boasts more than sixty campsites: it has been dubbed the 'camping capital of Europe'. Not surprisingly, its beaches, lined with pines and cork-oak, are enormous, stretching some 6km from Plage Nord to Racou-Plage and signifying the end of the rocky Côte Vermeille. There are innumerable diversions for holidaymakers, including

97

PLACES TO VISIT ON THE CÔTE
VERMEILLE

Cap Cerbère
Southernmost part of mainland
France with views south of Costa
Brava.

Banyuls-sur-Mer
Renowned for its wines and clear
inshore waters, ideal for diving.

Port-Vendres
Delightful harbour, with animated
quaysides.

Collioure
Popular 'Pearl of the Côte Vermeille',
haunt of many artists, seventeenth-
century church with fourteenth-
century clocktower, Templar's
Château, beaches and fishing boats,
shady village square.

a fairground, horse-riding, and dancing
in the village square at Argelès-sur-Mer,
now 2½km inland.

We are at the southern limit of an
extraordinary experiment in purpose-
built resort creation, extending as far as
the Rhône delta. Mosquitoes, breeding
in stagnant lagoons behind an empty,
sandy shoreline had deterred
exploitation until the French
government, anxious to divert tourists
away from the Spanish 'costas' into this
region, and at the same time to alleviate
overcrowding on the Riviera, decided on
a massive double-edged development
project for Languedoc-Roussillon.

It was to provide a comprehensive
new irrigation system to help
winegrowers (the coastal plain produces
40 per cent of all France's wine); and to
build eight brand new resorts — the
most ambitious state-sponsored
undertaking of its kind in history. Work
began in 1963 with the chemical
eradication of the mosquito and the
purification and dredging of the
lagoons. By allocating separate

Cap Cerbère, on
France's Mediterranean
frontier with Spain

architects to each coastal zone, the kind
of soul-less uniformity which afflicts so
many Mediterranean resorts has been
averted. We shall discover on our
journey whether the face of this 'New
California' is a universally accepted one.

Elne, on its low hill, was once 'by the
sea' but is now 5km inland. Hannibal
camped under its walls after crossing the
Pyrenees in 218BC and Emperor
Constantine named the town Helena
after his mother. The Cathédrale Ste
Eulalie dates back to the eleventh
century, with outstanding twelfth to
fourteenth-century cloisters, an
interesting archaeological museum and

Boules in the village
square at Collioure

good views of the River Tech.
    Elne's present-day seaside successor
and first of the new resorts to be
encountered, is a very different animal.
A still-untidy jumble of development, St
Cyprien-Plage is heavily committed to
sports such as golf (two courses), tennis,
swimming, riding and water sports.
Among several, there is one enormous
campsite, as well as an infrastructure of
bars, restaurants and shops.
    Excellent sandy beaches continue
uninterrupted along the coast,
disassociated from settlements,
untouched by development of the new
centres except for their freedom from
mosquitoes. Notices declare bathing to
be unsupervised and not unconditionally
safe, so discretion is needed.
    Curious old shacks line the shore of
Étang de Canet, most southerly of six
lagoons which suspend beach and coast
road between shimmering planes of
water.

    The customary scars of new building
and funfairs precede arrival at Canet-
Plage but do it no justice, for here is a
smart, lively holiday complex with nine
kilometres of superb, beach-tented
sands, a large yachting harbour and a
wide range of accommodation and
amenities. Built in the 1950s, Canet-
Plage, unlike the new resorts, has had
time to mellow and grow a heart. Noted
for its night-life, and partly due,
perhaps, to its proximity to Perpignan,
the town is hugely popular. There may
also be a sense in which this is due to
qualities frequently missing from more
recent development; reassuringly
familiar patterns of streets and
buildings, well-established residency, a
consolidated reputation.
    A warren of campsites, many with
swimming pools, connect at various
points with beaches at or between Ste
Marie-Plage and Torreilles-Plage. There
is a motor-drawn mini-train at the once

Art Nouveau on the streets of Collioure

unspoilt fishing village of Le Bacarès, in which tourists brave the heavy through-traffic to gaze out over unmade pavements, telegraph wires and advertising hoardings, en route for prettier locations. Sadly, it is not untypical of this emergent holiday-land, where, in the scheme of things, natural resources are often overridden by those whose very aim is to exploit them as attractions.

Northwards to Port-Bacarès, a dusty, incohate sprawl of villas, apartments and snack-bars leaves much to be desired. For the most part, the new resorts are thoughtfully planned — one either takes to their idiosynchratic styles or one doesn't — but in between them there is little evidence of planning policy, and faceless ribbon development is apparently allowed to proliferate.

Situated at the south end of the largest single lagoon — Étang de Leucate et de Salses — Port-Bacarès epitomises the more controversial face of resort modernism. Its amenities are above reproach, with a splendid marina, sailing and diving schools, water-skiing at nearby Port St Ange, tennis, riding, many restaurants and clubs. Its trump card is the Greek liner *Lydia*, beached in 1967 and converted into a night-club; a large car park caters for clients and sightseers.

For all this provision (and a reputation for lively entertainment), many aspects of the resort are grossly unappealing. Huge hoardings vie with tower-blocks whose fussy, ill-considered design is both visually jarring and lacks the homogeneity one would expect. At worst, the visual effect is ghetto-like, the vulgarity compounded by large-scale signboards for 'Zoomarin' and 'Teleski' amusement sites.

Sharing the same spit of land between lagoon and sea with the D627 coast road, Port-Leucate almost merges with Port-Bacarès, together one of the most extensive marina complexes in Europe, with over 700 mains-connected quayside berths and room for many more craft. There is, of course, a sailing school, a boatyard, also a water-sports instruction centre.

Avoiding the discordant excesses of Port-Bacarès, Port-Leucate's architectural style is a mix of little arched windows and balconies, its theme one of holiday villages rather than tower blocks.

The British-sponsored 'Ulysses' and 'Aphrodite' naturist villages, just to the north, symbolise the hedonistic ethos of this coast, where the elements conspire to provide an almost perfect environment for the acquisition of a healthy suntan. Naturism is by no means restricted to 'official' sectors, from which it inevitably over-spills; wide beaches stretch indefinitely in both directions and are never crowded.

By the shores of Étang de Leucate, the visual world is reduced to horizontals and endless, glittering water, the Pyrenees a receding silhouette to the south. It is often breezy on this coast — a stiff prevailing north-westerly — and wind-surfing is especially popular along the lagoon's east shore. There is dinghy sailing too, and the water is shallow enough for wading out in search of shellfish. A Centre d'Ostreiculture, at the Grau de Leucate, cultivates and sells oysters from a narrow creek lined with sheds and jetties.

Students of military fortifications should not miss the great castle of Salses, 10km away across the lagoon — marvellously preserved and spanning the historical gap between the days of the catapult and those of the cannon.

No commercial harbour other than Port-le-Nouvelle exists on the Golfe du Lion from Port-Vendres to Sète. Its year-round traffic of oil tankers and cargo vessels, some using the Canal de la Robine to Narbonne, connecting with the Canal du Midi, is conspicuous on a coast dedicated to leisure.

Though the railway threads across low-lying Ile Ste Lucie, there is no direct road link with our next port of call, so it is necessary to skirt the vast Étang de Bages et de Sigean, past tiny stone-walled terraces on parched hillsides, to the N9 or A9 Autoroute and thence to Gruissan.

(Despite being well inland, Narbonne's Cathédrale St Just rivals those of Chartres and Rouen, well deserving a visit, and there is an African Safari Park near Peyriac-de-Mer on the lagoon's west shore, with antelopes, lions, bears, alligators, rhinoceros and many birds.)

Begun in 1974, Gruissan is not only the newest of the Languedoc resorts but in many ways forms a bench-mark against which the others, more or less flambuoyant, might be assessed. Its western approaches are dominated by the old town's Tour Barberousse, across the Étang de Gruissan. Salt-pans extend south-west to the Étang de l'Ayrolle, and a chalet complex, raised on supports against high equinoctial tides, fronts a good beach at Gruissan-Plage.

Gruissan itself, in this era of second-home ownership, has not escaped the advertising hoardings, but they seem less obtrusive. Its architectural stamp is the little vaulted roof, a variation on a by-now familiar theme, repeated throughout the accommodation units surrounding a central port. In some lights the structures resemble plywood toys, their pink-brown rendering, or *crépi*, already stained and patchy: wear and tear from the elements, however, must be relatively slight.

Monoliths of grey stone have been used to break up space in paved courtyards — perhaps until the palm trees, as yet mere bushes, have had a chance to mature. Patronised by families, mixed age-groups and a plethora of pet dogs, the resort's shops

The beached liner *Lydia*, now a night-club at Port-Bacarès

and cafés, however well appointed, seem vaguely characterless. The conclusion could be drawn, perhaps unkindly, that for boat-and-apartment-owning dog lovers who value customised convenience above a traditional sense of place, this is Utopia!

There is more wind-surfing on the smaller Étang de Mateille, but the ubiquitous marshy scrubland and the occasional down-at-heel horse-riding 'ranch' paint a dismally unprepossessing picture. It is hardly relieved by an ugly mound of sand bearing an 'Aquajet' ride and fast-food stall, adjacent to new building a little farther north, though the nearby campsite appears to be an excellent one.

Narbonne-Plage has the open, airy feel of an Atlantic resort. Its vast beach is kept scrupulously clean, and a seafront market is held regularly on the

promenade. Montagne de la Clape
forms a picturesque hinterland of rocky
edges and mixed conifer forest, dotted
with road-side stalls inviting passers-by
to taste the exquisite local white honey
and wines of the region.

Sandy beaches sweep undiminished
past St Pierre-sur-Mer, with its Gouffre
de l'OEil (caves and a deep pool) to
Valras-Plage, a small bustling resort and
fishing harbour at the outlet of the River
Orb. As well as offering excellent
yachting in the river mouth, and a
number of good little restaurants,
Valras-Plage has adopted variations on
the bicycle as the principal means of
getting about.

Architecturally perhaps the most
interesting of the new resorts, le Cap
d'Agde dates from 1969 and is still
expanding. Small leafy squares link
pedestrianised streets lined with

Gruissan — one of the new generation resorts

shopping arcades, but most of the building is low-rise and harmoniously painted in traditional beiges, pinks, ochres and white, mimicking Languedocian styles like an elaborate but inoffensive stage-set.

There can be no doubt that le Cap d'Agde is prestigious and very popular — not least for Europe's largest naturist holiday town, complete with magnificent beach, supermarkets, night-clubs, casinos and accommodation for 20,000 people.

Small beaches east of the cape are of dark grey sand from the extinct volcano of Mt St Loop, just inland. From the rocky headland, there are good views to the Môle Richelieu, almost enclosing the port, and north along to Sète's distinctive hill.

The list of sporting amenities at le Cap d'Agde is formidable: tennis is a speciality, with seventy courts; there is squash, basketball, bowls, table-tennis,

Volcanic cliffs and beach at le Cap d'Agde

volley-ball, riding, a jogging track, go-karting, swimming pools, a shooting range, children's beach clubs, cyclo-cross, pony-riding and playgrounds. Add to this a sensational seven-acre 'Aqualand' park, every conceivable water-sport and a host of events, clubs and discos, and one's mind is left bemused at the scope and scale of provision!

Roads sweep traffic smoothly from outlying accommodation to the town and beach areas: there is, however, little chance to reach other destinations without becoming ensnared in the system. Like the resort itself, le Cap d'Agde's roads cater well for its residents but passers-through are left rather to their own devices.

First settled by the Phoenicians around 500BC, when it was known as Agathé, Agde's busy seaport trade with the eastern Mediterranean declined following the construction of Aigues-Mortes and Sète to the north. It was regularly raided by Saracens, or corsairs from the Barbary Coast, against which threat the Cathédrale St Étienne was systematically fortified. This great twelfth century edifice, its 3m-thick walls built from the same dark volcanic stone as many of the town's dwellings, is unusually sombre in a country whose old buildings are generally warm and mellow.

A fascinating little museum of local history (Musée agathois), containing Greek amorphae, may be found on Rue de la Fraternité, and, where the River Hérault runs through le Grau d'Agde, the original pre-1960s 'seaside', there are moorings for small boats and good angling.

A canal links the sea with the huge Bassin de Thau, on whose opposite shore are the small ports of Marseillan and Mèze, known for barrel-making, oysters and pleasure-boating. Marseillan-Plage, its funfair and numerous campsites, lie at the southern end of 14km of embanked corniche road (N112) which shares its spit of land with the railway and a fringe of beach.

Perhaps it is a small price to pay for increased personal space, but these long, gently-shelving sands tend to be litter-strewn and rather unkempt. And while a chain of small cafés selling frites, pizzas and *casses-croûte* may satisfy the inner man, the outer one has to contend with the roar produced by a constant stream of holiday traffic in the high season.

Built on and around Mt St Clair, from which there are outstanding views, Sète is France's largest Mediterranean port after Marseilles. It is a great wine-handling and fishing centre (mainly sardine and tuna), with vessels berthed right in the town alongside Quai de Bosc, and enjoys an enviable selection of seafood restaurants. (Try 'Sole Courbet', named after the city's founder, or *tielle*, a delicious fish-pie snack.)

Several waterways are spanned by the town, including the Canal de Sète, the final increment in a canal link between the Mediterranean and the Atlantic via Toulouse and the Garonne river. Sète's deep-water port receives oil tankers for the refinery at nearby Frontignan, as well as a diversity of cargoes from many parts of the world, notably North Africa with which it entered into an important trading relationship after the harbours at Narbonne and Aigues-Mortes silted up.

Ever since 1666, *joutes nautiques* (water jousting) has engaged local teams in colourful rivalry. In manoeuvres not without danger and requiring considerable skill, a lance-bearing representative from each side attempts to dislodge his counterpart from a perch on a sloping ramp at the stern of his boat rowed by ten oarsmen. An 'early bath' awaits the loser, though three opponents have thus to be dispatched in each round! The sport has developed its own

customs and traditions and is now an established tourist spectacle.

A museum to the poet Paul Valéry, who was born and is buried at Sète, can be found near the Cimitiere Matin, subject of his best-known poem. In addition it contains drawings and paintings by Renoir, Cézanne, Toulouse-Lautrec, Matisse and others.

An industrialised landscape reaches out past Frontignan but relents beyond, where low, wooded hills and vineyards clothe the slopes of Montagne de la Gardiole, home of Muscat wines. Vic-la-Gardiole and Villeneuve-les-Maguelonne are worthy villages, equipped with campsites, south of Montpelier's great conurbation.

Joutes nautiques are popular at Palavas-les-Flots, too, where stands the Ancienne Cathédrale de Maguelonne at the end of a thin road on a tongue of land. The town itself was destroyed in 737 and the Gothic Romanesque cathedral, restored in the nineteenth century, is all that remains. Palavas is developed but not recently so, its casino, funfair and eating places entertaining the inhabitants of Montpelier as much as visitors from further afield.

Exploitation of the coastal isthmus to the west is neither a visual blight nor innovatory: merely the anonymous ribbon of apartments and villas one grows to expect and mostly ignores. Carnon-Plage, another 'local' resort, sits opposite the conspicuous Aéroport de Fréjorgues. Dunes soften its beach outlook and the busy D62 road is set back near the Rhône-Sète canal, so the sands are well frequented throughout their length. For once, the inland lagoon, Étang de Mauguio, is an unattractive marshy alternative.

Irrefutably the most audacious and distinctive of the Languedoc 'New World' towns, la Grande Motte rises like a science-fiction city at the western edge of the Camargue. Its phalanx of white, stepped pyramids containing thousands of apartments, forms but one component in a highly integrated resort blueprint formulated by a team of engineers and architects in the mid-1960s. The result succeeded in subjugating the tyranny of the motor car in favour of pedestrians by providing almost unlimited free parking, broad streets and sensible connections to external road and rail networks.

At close quarters, la Grande Motte is a matrix of spacious, grassy concourses and shop-lined pedestrian arcades; innumerable bars and restaurants offer inexpensive menus and there is a lively night-life scene. In high season, the resort is crowded with youngsters for whom it clearly caters so well, and one is tempted to suggest that it addresses itself principally to this section of the market, though this is by no means exclusively the case.

There is a grand beach, some 4km long, with facilities for many water-sports on the Étang du Ponant, fishing in the Étang de l'or, moorings for nearly 2,000 craft, villas and holiday villages, and campsites in the vicinity capable of accommodating up to 15,000 people.

The pyramids and still less orthodox buildings, loved or despised, are conspicuous from near and far, their gaily coloured balconies and paintwork unequivocally modernistic: no lip-service here to traditional idioms. Yet, curiously, some street-level concrete structures, particularly on the seafront, seem grey and lifeless, devoid of intrinsic quality or merit — surely an opportunity lost.

For some, la Grande Motte, though clean and fashionable like others of its generation, will lack substance — that indefinable compounding of smells, unexpected little corners, the patina of old buildings, the hum of an indigenous population, the visual and social consequences of a longer history — all of which make browsing and discovery so absorbingly pleasurable when enough has been had of the beach.

Le Grau-du-Roi, a fishing village on a channel connecting salt-marsh with sea, has become a popular tourist spot,

---

THE NEW RESORTS OF LANGUEDOC-ROUSSILLON

St Cyprien-Plage
Dedicated to sports, especially golf.

Canet-Plage
More matured with 9km of superb beach, night-life and a pleasant ambience.

Port-Bacarès
Water sports, amusements, tower-blocks and a night-club in beached Greek liner *Lydia*.

Port-Leucate
One of Europe's greatest yachting marinas. Naturist holiday villages. Wind-surfing on Étang de Leucate.

Gruissan
Most recently constructed. Typical of new resorts with a harbour, accommodation units, and good beach.

Le Cap d'Agde
Prestigious, magnificently-appointed resort complex. Facilities for all sports and recreations. Huge naturist holiday town.

La Grande Motte
Futuristic pyramid apartment blocks. Lively, good beach and amenities for water sports.

Port-Camargue
Huge marina around beautiful villa-covered promontories on reclaimed marsh at edge of Camargue.

---

renowned for its *bouillabaisse* (fish stew) and its bullfights, an entertaining spectacle in which the bull is unharmed.

Port-Camargue, last of the new resorts on our journey east, ranks as one of the most beautiful. Its great marina complex, with moorings for over 3,000 pleasure craft amongst a maze of little villa-covered promontories, has been created from former marshland. Because the development is low-rise, there is little

La Grande Motte, one of the new Languedoc resorts

to interrupt the vast, watery spaciousness characteristic of the Camargue itself.

Other than at Stes Maries-de-la-Mer, the coast is inaccessible by road this side of the Grand Rhône. The littoral, in any case, is hard to define as the entire flat Plaine de la Camargue is an ambiguous interplay of land and water with few hard edges.

Aigues-Mortes looms up on the northern horizon, an unspoiled medieval fortress town with soaring bastions and ramparts which have stood untouched for seven centuries. Before it silted up and became stranded amidst saltflats, marsh and lagoons, the town and port thrived, with a population three times its present level. It has changed little in appearance since.

Two famous Crusades — those of 1248 and 1270 — set out from here under the leadership of King Louis IX, who eventually died of the plague in Tunis; his statue, by the sculptor Jacques Pradier, stands in the main square. Within the walls, the grid of town houses is of no great age or special interest, but containing shops and eating places to welcome the visitor (but only residents' cars are allowed in). Outside, however, the ramparts and battlements, up to 33m high with walls 7m thick, are immensely impressive, bearing ten gates and twenty watch-towers and culminating in the great Tour Constance, used as a prison for many years. There are marvellous views from the top.

Wasteland used for sports and fairs

Louis IX, when salt was virtually the only preserving and seasoning agent available.

Legend proclaims that sisters of the Virgin Mary and of Lazarus landed at Stes Maries-de-la-Mer in AD45, having fled persecution after the Crucifixion. An oratory was built commemorating the spot and the saints' tomb has attracted pilgrims since the Middle Ages. Gypsies and nomads particularly venerate Sarah, the black Egyptian maid of the two Marys, and on 24 and 25 May each year, Romany tribes congregate here from all over Europe for a Fair, night-long festivities and the ceremonial immersion in the sea of saintly effigies. Other pilgrimages take place on the penultimate Sunday in October, and the first Sunday in December.

The Romanesque fortified church, replacing earlier ones, forms a central attraction : walk round its ramparts or sit on the shallow-pitched roof for a spectacular vantage point over the town and surrounding countryside, especially at sunset. In the low crypt, warm and bright from candle flames, are the processional cross and a statue of Sarah, patron saint of gypsies. Views of the church are hard to come by in the densely built centre: a tower standing two streets nearer the sea provides the best of a few alternatives.

Stes Maries-de-la-Mer, with its long beach, tamarisk trees and harbour/marina, is a breezy, light resort, much loved in his time by Van Gogh, who immortalised its colourful fishing boats. Shops are unpretentious and relaxed, peddling the embodiment of regional themes in tourist-kitsch souvenirs — pink glass flamingoes, cowboy dolls, horse-paintings on leather — to a cosmopolitan influx of visitors. There is ample car parking to the west of the town.

Perhaps owing to its unique hold on this amorphous, shifting coast, Stes Maries does seem to possess special charm, encircled by water and aloof from the busy through-routes which

has largely replaced the moat, and the absence of any significant building on the south and east sides serves to preserve the town's original isolation and sense of historical context: turning a corner, one half expects to encounter Charlton Heston and a band of medieval knights!

The sun-baked, low-lying area to the south of Aigues-Mortes is a complex of salt-pans, Salins du Midi, repeatedly flooded with sea-water from May to September until huge deposits of salt have accumulated from progressive evaporation. These white hills, representing up to 500,000 tons of salt per year, shine mirage-like above purple lagoons, coloured by reaction with sunlight. The process of crystallization has remained unaltered since the days of

PLACES TO SEE IN AND AROUND THE
CAMARGUE

Aigues-Mortes

Sensational medieval fortress town
with intact surrounding ramparts and
great Tour Constance. Salins-du-
Midi salt-pans.

Stes Maries-de-la-Mer

Venue for Romany pilgrimage on
24-5 May. Climb to fortified Romanesque church ramparts for extensive
views over vast, flat landscape of
southern Camargue and coast.

Camargue

'Promenade à cheval', horseback
trips to see wildlife — flamingoes,
wild bulls and horses, flora — guided
by local *guardiens*. Boat trips up Petit
Rhône from Stes Maries and
Information Centre at Ginès, 5km
north.
Camargue Museum on D570 towards
Arles at Pont de Rousty.
See rice paddies; traditional
herdsmen's houses (*cabanes*), French
bullfights (bull unharmed).

Medieval ramparts at Aigues-Mortes

funnel the majority of pale, sun-starved
north Europeans to the beach and
amenity areas.

The Camargue, that wild, romantic
heartland of southern Provence cradled
between the Grand and Petit Rhône, is
renowned for its wild bulls, horses, bird-
life and flora. However, without going
to considerably more trouble than
driving along ribbons of tarmac in the
heat and bustle of high summer, the
eager visitor risks disappointment. For
at this time, the vegetation, less
colourful than in spring or even winter,
lies grey and dusty, the herds corralled
or dispersed, the flocks of flamingoes
limited mainly to the Réserve National
round the Étang de Vaccarès to which
only accredited naturalists and scientists
are granted access, by prior
arrangement. (It is an important staging
post for migratory birds such as egrets,
Egyptian ibis and Moroccan storks.)

Lest this discourages, it should be
added that even during the summer
season there is much to see, and
travelling on the roads that transect the
Camargue is rather more enjoyable than
on most in southern France. Everyone
appears to be travelling leisurely,
whether by car or bicycle, and the squeal
of tyre-rubber is blissfully absent!

Ranches advertising 'Promenade à
Cheval' line the roadsides, each with its
complement of permanently-saddled
white Camargue horses patiently waiting

Les Saintes-Maries-de- la-Mer, Camargue

Camargue ranch offering 'Promenade à Cheval'

for custom; some are left thoughtlessly
without shade. The local cowboys —
guardiens — guide parties of stetsoned
holidaymakers on sorties into the scrub
and salt-marsh during the season, where
there is an increased chance of spotting
wild-life (as there is on boat-trips up the
Petit Rhône).

Many *guardiens* are expert French
bullfighters. The nimble black
Camargue bull is small and intelligent,
ideally suited to the battle of wits as the
men involved brave its horns to remove
rosettes and tassels fixed there. It is all
good, spirited fun and a far cry from the
harrowing drama of a Spanish *corrida*.

For the Camargue Information
Centre and a view over the western
fringes of the Réserve Naturelle
Zoologique et Botanique, Ginès should
be visited, 5km north of Stes Maries-de-
la-Mer. Farther north still, on the D570

to Arles, a Camargue museum is housed
in the Mas du Pont de Rousty.

It may come as a surprise to discover
much of the Camargue under
cultivation, especially the western sector.
Rice has become an important crop,
supplying most of France's needs, but
others flourish too, including vines,
asparagus, oilseed rape and wheat. And
whereas the region as a whole is
epitomised by expansive, open horizons
dotted here and there with a farm or
cabane (a small thatched herdsman's
house curved at one end against the
winter mistral), in the north and west
there are stands of poplar and ash,
adding lushness and intimacy to a
landscape already richly endowed with
natural beauty.

Beyond the glittering salt-pans of
Salin-de-Giraud on the Grand Rhône, a
very different prospect awaits us...

6 Provence and the Côte d'Azur:

THE RHÔNE TO MENTON

East of the Rhône lies the Grande Cau, a stony, sun-browned plain thinly strewn with dark bushy trees and isolated buildings. Its southern fringes support the great new steel and petro-chemical complex of Fos.

Like the Languedoc resorts, this ambitious development is the result of public funding, though private enterprise is also involved. Due to world recession, it has never quite fulfilled its early promise but remains a formidable industrial site — a concentration of aluminium tanks and towers, smoking chimneys and gas flares, vast metal warehouses, concrete factories and office blocks.

In recent memory, tiny Fos-sur-Mer stood alone on its rock overlooking marshy flats. Today it is all but besieged by the new industry, its isolation more pronounced than ever. The beach, such as it is, runs along behind the new road's sea defences and must boast the least picturesque views on the entire Mediterranean coast!

At the turn of the century, Martigues was a small Provençal fishing village; the painters Corot and Ziem both worked here. But along with neighbouring Port-de-Bouc and Lavéra, it has been transformed by the expanding oil business. Happily, there are still numerous canals and quaysides, and a quality of light, which have earned it the title 'Venice of Provence'.

Martigues' face, at least, is able to turn east and north across a vast body of shallow water surrounded by limestone hills. The Berre lagoon has been dredged so that shallow-draft oil tankers may reach the open sea through the Canal de Caronte. There are good views over this flat and much used corner of Provence from Notre-Dame-des-Marins, north of Martigues, and, somewhat more fleetingly, from the A55 Autoroute carried over the Caronte Canal by a spectacular road bridge.

Cradling the Étang de Berre, an elevated arm of limestone links the Crau Plain to Marseille. These are the Chaine

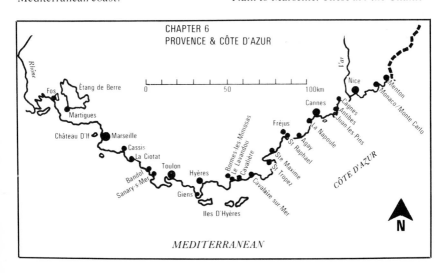

CHAPTER 6
PROVENCE & CÔTE D'AZUR

MEDITERRANEAN

de l'Estaque hills, arid and devoid of settlements for the most part, transected by the bold lines of through-roads. Yet tucked away in *calanques* (inlets) on the steep, wooded seaward edge is a string of pretty little fishing villages turned resorts, effectively hidden from the surrounding industry: lively Carro with a good beach, Sausset-les-Pins and its fine promenade, Carry-le-Rouet, le Rouet-Plage, Madrague-de-Gignac.

In the east between Niolon and l'Estaque's yacht harbour, the Rove underground canal begins its 7km bee-line, connecting the Marseille docks with the Étang de Berre. Built in 1920, it was in regular use until a serious roof-fall in 1963.

Marseille is France's second city and its largest, oldest port, established by Greek settlers in 600BC. It is a conurbation of intimidating proportions for the coastal traveller, famous amongst much else for some of the worst traffic jams in Europe.

There is curiously little to see in the way of true antiquities — Marseille has never been a respecter of its architectural heritage — but one can explore the Vieux Port, take a boat trip to the famous Château d'If, climb to the Notre-Dame-de-la-Garde Basilica on its limestone peak for superb panoramic views, visit numerous museums and art galleries, or wander along tree-lined boulevards.

La Canabière is one of the world's great streets, a stimulating kilometre of shops, cafés and hotels, generating the kind of energy and atmosphere associated with the best of city life. Away from tourist haunts, however, Marseille presents a different face. Groups of the poor, disaffected and unemployed congregate in bars and on street corners — a strongly Levantine milieu well known for its propensity for crime. It is a feverish, brassy place which some find threatening, but is also colourful, more typically a Mediterranean port than a French city.

In contrast to the expensive shops and restaurants of the city centre, Marseille's dockland is a largely unseen sprawl of gantries, warehouses and industrial estates, spanned by elevated roads. It is all a far cry from the serene beauty of the Camargue and, indeed, the genteel resorts of the Côte d'Azur ahead of us.

Marseille has, as one would expect, hotels of all grades and many restaurants, most of which will serve *bouillabaisse*, a fish stew for which the city is renowned. Someone once said, '*Bouillabaisse* is only good because it is cooked by the French who, if they cared to try, could produce an excellent and nutritious substitute out of cigar stumps and empty matchboxes!' Such scathing criticism, laced with a back-handed compliment to French cuisine, is not entirely without foundation, for the best, authentic *bouillabaisse* is neither universally available nor cheap.

For sightseeing, a car is almost a liability — there are buses, trams, taxis

Typical summer weather conditions on the Provence Coast and the Côte d'Azur						
	May	June	July	Aug	Sept	Oct
Average daytime air temperature °C	20.8	26.6	28.1	28.4	25.2	22.2
Typical daily sunshine hours	9	9.1	12.3	9.2	8.9	8
Days with some rainfall	7	5.5	-	8.5	3.5	5.5
Average sea temperature °C	16	19	21	23	23	19

Le Château d'If, Marseille

EXCURSIONS AROUND MARSEILLE

Drives or boat-trips to Étang de Berre, Martigues ('Venice of Provence') and views of huge petro-chemical complex at Fos. Visit *calanques* on south side of l'Estaque hills and small resorts of Carro, Sausset-les-Pins, Carry-le-Rouet and le Rouet-Plage.

Château d'If — 90-minute round trip all year from Quai des Belges, Vieux Port, Marseille.

Good rugged walking in Marseilleveyre and Puget massifs to east (GR98). Waterless in summer and can be very hot.

Rock-climbing on cliffs of *calanques*, fjord-like inlets reached on waymarked paths, 2-3 hours return. Best are En-Vau and Port-pin. Also make enjoyable boat-trips (from Marseille and Cassis) and good yacht anchorages.

France's highest cliffs on Cap Canaille, near Cassis — Grande Tête reaches 394m. Spectacular Corniche des Crêtes over high limestone upland to la Ciotat — wide views of *calanques* and coast.

and a new metro system. Excellent views of the old town and harbour may be gained from the terrace of a nineteenth-century château in the Parc du Pharo. Other worthwhile sights include the Musée de la Marine in the former Bourse (Stock Exchange) near the excavated remains of Greek harbour walls; and the Musée des Beaux-Arts in Palais Longchamp, containing works by many artists from the sixteenth to twentieth centuries; the well-known nineteenth-century political caricaturist and painter, Honoré Daumier, whose work is well represented, was himself a native of Marseille. Le Corbusier's tower of 'living units' was to be the precursor of tower-block domestic architecture everywhere and can be found on Boulevard Michelet.

City suburbs extend out untidily almost to Cap Croisette and the little harbour of Callelongue. There is a good, rugged walk (GR98) round this hilly bulge of coast, and a variant crosses the Marseilleveyre Massif at its highest point (432m). They are hot, waterless hikes in summer but enjoying magnificent scenery and opportunities for rock-climbing.

The Marseilleveyre and adjoining Puget range of bare dissected limestone hills form deep, fjord-like inlets called *calanques* where they meet the sea. None is accessible by road, but a car may be parked at Col de la Gardiole and the two most attractive *calanques* — En-Vau and Port-Pin — reached by foot on marked paths in two to three hours return.

Best of all is to enter the *calanques* by boat in calm seas, when the full beauty

The 'calanques' from the Corniche des Crêtes on France's highest cliffs

of their translucent water and precipitous limestone cliffs can be appreciated. In summer there are boat trips from Marseille and Cassis and these long indentations provide perfect anchorages for pleasure boats.

Mentioned by the poet Mistral and featured in paintings by Vlaminck, Matisse, Dufy and Kayser, Cassis is a busy little Provençal fishing port set back in a deep bay beneath France's highest cliff, Cap Canaille, which at la Grande Tête reaches a height of 394m.

Cassis is enormously popular with the Marseillais, many of whom have villas and flats here; it is not surprising to find a modern casino and good seafood restaurants where *bouillabaisse* and other dishes may be washed down with the local, heady, dry white wine.

For motorists, cyclists and even walkers, the Corniche des Crêtes is highly recommended. The tortuous road

climbs to a spectacular limestone upland, sparsely covered with scrub, wild herbs and beautiful flowers. On hot summer days it is strident with the washboard squeaking of cicadas, as they drift and flutter from bush to tree like huge hopping moths. Their song pervades Provence — sometimes a vapid background hiss, muted by undergrowth and the heavy air; at others, when you stop to listen, a curious, hypnotic counterpoint of individual pitches and rhythms rising to random, synchronised crescendoes.

Bizarre globular rock outcrops and natural arches bulge above terraced slopes of thin red soil, on which stand the blackened skeletons of aleppo pines, bearing witness to flash fires which threaten so much of Provence and the Côte d'Azur after prolonged dry spells. It is a quite remarkable landscape, with stunning viewpoints from the cliff tops, especially the Sémaphore.

Since the time of the early Greeks when it was an outpost of Marseille, la Ciotat has possessed a shipyard; it is now the most modern in France and constructs oil and gas tankers. The old port is preserved, teeming with pleasure craft and fishing vessels but visually dominated by the modern installations.

Boat trips leave from la Ciotat's quayside for the diminutive Ile Verte, and from its fort the rocky profile of Cap de l'Aigle (Eagle Cape) lives up to its name. To the west of the town lies the easily accessible Figuerolles Calanque, while to the north and east la Ciotat's harbour swings in a great semicircular arc from its dock gates to the beach and hotels of la Ciotat-Plage.

Les Lecques is a year-round family resort, backed by olives and vines and its fine sandy beach reaches to la Madrague. Here, built on the site of a Roman villa near the sea, the Musée Tauroentum exhibits many Roman mosaics and relics.

A steeper, wooded stretch of coast rounds the mostly inaccessible Pointe du Déffend to the outskirts of Bandol, a resort perhaps less well known to the British than those further east, yet with no less to offer the holidaymaker. The town is a compound of old and new. In its early undeveloped days, along with nearby Sanary-sur-Mer, it became the haunt of stage and literary figures, especially those from Germany in the 1930s — Bertholt Brecht, Arnold Zweig, Thomas Mann and others.

The intervening years have witnessed Bandol grow in size and sophistication, providing a wealth of sporting facilities, entertainment and many fine hotels. Sheltered from north winds, its three sandy beaches — Lido, Renecros and Casino — are justly popular and are backed by a long, palm-fringed promenade with numerous bars and shops.

Beyond a castle on the point lies Ile Bendor, served by a short seven-minute ferry crossing every half hour. Not long

ISLAND EXCURSIONS AROUND TOULON

Ile Bendor
7-minute crossing from Bandol. Reconstructed Provençal village, zoo, art gallery and theatre, exhibition of World Wines and Spirits.

Iles Embiez
Off Cap Sicié Peninsula. Aquarium and museum in Ricard Oceanographic Foundation. Remains of Sabran Château, marina, beaches, walks, fishing.

Presqu'ile de St Mandrier
Small resort linked to mainland. Boatyards and marina overlook Toulon's great harbour and roadstead.

Iles d'Hyères
Reached by boat from Toulon, Hyères-Plage, la Tour Fondue, Port de Mirimar, le Lavandou and Cavalaire-sur-Mer.
Porquerolles: walks through vineyards and woods of eucalyptus, pines and cork-oak.
Ile de Port-Cros: hilly and rugged, lush vegetation, delightful waymarked walks. Parc National where wild-life and flora are strictly protected.
Ile du Levant: mostly occupied by French navy, but Heliopolis (Sun City) naturist town in west very popular.

ago a deserted rock, it has been thoroughly exploited as a tourist attraction, with a reconstructed Provençal village, a zoo, an art gallery and theatre, a conference centre and a fascinating World Museum of Wines and Spirits. There is a good little beach and a selection of hotels and eating places.

Protected from the *mistral* by the wooded hill of le Gros Cerveau to the north, Sanary-sur-Mer is an equable, bustling place. Like much of the coast between Toulon and Marseille, it is

frequented more by locals from the two cities than by other French, even less by foreigners (though Aldous Huxley once lived here).

In many ways, Sanary is an agreeable surprise after the nondescript development strung along from Bandol. Its sizeable marina is backed by pretty, pastel-coloured houses and a lively waterfront with seafood stalls, fishing craft and a flower market. There are several good beaches, but its ambience owes more to quayside activity than to sun-worship.

Off the south-west tip of the Cap Sicié Peninsula lies a small group of islands in rich fishing waters, surely the delight of every enthusiast. The largest, Embiez, is a topographical pot-pourri of salt-marsh, coves, beaches, pine woods and vineyards and contains the celebrated Ricard Oceanographic Foundation's aquarium and museum. The marine biologist Alain Bombard, whose research has been based here, once crossed the Atlantic in a rubber dinghy to determine the effects on the human body of living almost exclusively off

food from the sea, including salt water.

Elsewhere on Embiez may be found the medieval ruins of Sabran château, a modern marina, sporting amenities and pleasant walks, all making the twelve-minute ferry trip from Port du Brusc eminently worthwhile.

In rough weather, the exposed Petit Gaou promontory is mildly reminiscent of the Brittany coast. Farther east, the highest ground on the Sicié Peninsula — Notre-Dame du Mai and the precipitous Cap Sicié itself (358m) — offers far-reaching views, from the *calanques* to the

Iles d'Hyères.

Apart from its fort, standing over 200m above the sea, Six-Fours-les-Plages has few redeeming features; a suburban hotch-potch lacking cohesion or direction except its outward occupation of available building land. At its eastern end, the little isthmus of Presqu'ile de St Mandrier is held to the mainland by a narrow spit of land from les Sablettes to Tamaris, where once lived the naval officers of Toulon and their wives.

Les Sablettes has a popular bathing beach facing the open sea, but views of the Toulon Roadstead are rather elusive and disappointing. Even from St Mandrier-sur-Mer's yachting anchorage and boatyard, Toulon's great natural harbour is incompletely seen, though naval vessels are frequently moored just offshore. Better glimpses can be caught from the steep residential lanes above St Mandrier, through gaps between trees, bushes and villas.

Like Marseille, Toulon will be hard-pressed to lure the coastal holidaymaker into its busy, traffic-choked metropolitan centre. While the city itself is not special, its position as a great naval base, land-locked on three sides by colourful mountain slopes, combines historical interest and strategic importance with an unusually beautiful setting. Louis XIV created Toulon's famous arsenal, and it was here in 1793 that the military career of Napoleon Bonaparte began with his successful skirmish against a British stronghold between la Seyne and Tamaris, nick-named 'Little Gibraltar'. Much later, this great naval city suffered heavy damage during World War II, though a section of the Vieille Ville escaped Allied bombing of the port.

In November 1942, Admiral Laborde, unable to escape the invading German's surprise advance, scuttled sixty ships of the French fleet in the Roadstead. It was not until August 1944 that the city was liberated, after the occupying forces had blown up the harbour installations, dockyards and the citadel.

For those interested in matters nautical, Pierre Puget's vigorously sculpted figures, 'Force' and 'Fatigue' guard entry to the Musée Naval, while the harbour and arsenal provide sights of both naval and merchant activity.

Covered fish, vegetable and fruit markets, shops and cafés along the Quai Stalingrad waterfront, the Musée des Beaux-Arts et Archaeologie, and the partly pedestrianised Vieille Ville are all worth seeing. There are boat trips both round the Inner Roadstead and across to the Iles d'Hyères, les Sablettes and St Mandrier.

Mont Faron's precipitous limestone ridge dominates Toulon's northern skyline. Near its summit stands the Mémorial National du Débarquement as a permanent tribute, with diorama and films, to the liberation of south-east France by the Allies in August 1944. There is an exceptionally fine panoramic view from the terrace and nearby, somewhat incongruously, a zoo and breeding centre for wild animals. Mont Faron is served by a scenic road running up through pine forest, and by a cable car from Super-Toulon.

Photography is an almost reflexive activity when visiting new places of visual interest, but it is officially frowned upon near to military or naval posts. Although the authorities do not actively harass tourists, discretion is preferable to the confiscation of one's film, or worse!

Hyères, well known to the British of the last two centuries, is the oldest Riviera resort; its illustrious visitors have included Napoleon, Queen Victoria, Tolstoy and Robert Louis Stevenson (who disliked the south of France and wrote, 'I was only happy once; that was at Hyères.')

The old town, some way inland, enjoys a particularly mild climate and an atmosphere that lingers enigmatically in the past. Avenues of palms, shady squares and exquisite gardens nudge the

hilltop castle ruins, and in Place Massillon, centre of the old town, a covered market is held each weekday.

Hyères relies as much on the cultivation of early fruit, vegetables, ornamental plants and its superlative vineyards as it does on tourism, and the surrounding land is intensively planted. Twentieth-century development being what it is, however, modern tower blocks, advertising hoardings and faceless industrial buildings swamp the greenhouses and market gardens.

The beach at Hyères-Plage lies cheek-by-jowl with a busy civil airport yet is still an immensely popular location for many land and water sports.

A narrow road (Route du Sel), closed to traffic in rough weather, traverses the length of a sandbar running from the mainland to the Gien Peninsula. This former island, fourth in the Hyères group, was again cut off by a great storm in 1811. Together with the D97 further east, the Route du Sel encloses les Pesquiers salt-pans. Still worked, they become a lagoon to the south, offering an ideal habitat for water-birds, including occasional flamingoes from the Camargue. Giens itself, no more than six hilly kilometres wide, has a small village resort with good views from the ruined château and from la Tour Fondue, whence boats sail for Porquerolles.

The Iles d'Hyères, also known as the Iles d'Or (Golden Isles), are a microcosm of southern Provençe and may be reached by boat from Toulon, Hyères-Plage, la Tour Fondue, Port de Mirimar, le Lavandou and Cavalaire-sur-Mer.

Ile de Porquerolles is the largest and nearest to the mainland, with tracks radiating from the tiny port through vineyards and woods of pine, eucalyptus and cork-oak. Its heather and pine fringed sandy beaches along the north shore, and the lighthouse standing 96m high on the southernmost point, are both marvellous two-hour return walks.

Ile de Port-Cros is altogether hillier

and more rugged, reaching over 200m above sea level. Numerous springs support dense woods and vegetation, and there are several waymarked walks of great charm. Together with neighbouring islands, Port-Cros has been designated a Parc National and a nature reserve, in which camping, lighting fires, shooting and even smoking are prohibited; needless to say, the flora and fauna, including marine life, are strictly protected.

Much of cliff-bound Ile du Levant is occupied by the French navy and is out of bounds to the public. In the extreme west, however, stands Heliopolis (Sun City), one of Europe's most famous naturist colonies, which attracts many summer visitors.

Beyond Cap Bénat's secluded little bays and rugged cliffs, a curtain rises on a richer level of picturesqueness, presaging the brilliant physical beauty of the Côte d'Azur east of Cannes.

Le Lavandou (from the lavender fields on the banks of the River Batailler) has managed to resist, to a large extent, the insidious encroachment of new development and is still, in spirit, very much the fishing port it has always been. At the turn of the century it was frequented by artists, writers and musicians and has lost little of its original charm in assimilating modern holidaymakers. There are excellent beaches, expecially Plage de la Favière, and la Lavandou is a good base from which to explore the Massif des Maures.

Too far inland to be just a coastal feature, the Massif des Maures (from *maouro*, Provençal for dark wood) nevertheless stamps its identity firmly upon the coast's topography from here to Fréjus and St Raphael. The N559 'Corniche des Maures' between Hyères and la Croix-Valmer, traces the steeply-sloping convolutions along the sea's edge, overhanging it at times like a good corniche should!

The grain of the hills runs east-west, rising to la Sauvette at 779m. They are deeply wooded with cork-oak, chestnut and pines along the coast; the southernmost chain is now all but submerged and forms the Iles d'Hyères. Cork-making and preserving sweet-chestnuts provide a living for the scattered indiginous population, though visiting tourists are being increasingly attracted by the profuse and very lovely wild flowers, shrubs and trees, bringing with them a demand for artefacts and souvenirs.

Devastating forest fires, such as the one north of Bormes-les-Mimosas in 1972, and others since, are a constant threat. Viewpoints, scenic drives and towns and villages of note within the massif are too numerous to list here, but an excursion or two would be amply rewarded.

Bormes-les-Mimosas, like le Lavandou, has remained aloof from the worst effects of tourist exploitation, but the little hilltop village is inescapably a tourist attraction. Happily for visitors and residents alike, car parking is, for the most part, discreetly out of sight underground and there is even a kind of one-way system.

In front of the sixteenth-century Chapelle St Francis stands a statue of Francesco di Paola, reputed to have saved Bormes from the plague in 1481. In the large, tree-lined village square opposite, locals playing *boules* mingle with onlookers; there are good views out to sea and across at the steep stack of old houses below the church, so typical of Provence.

Huge cacti sprout from rocks and walls beside the narrow lanes and, of course, there is an abundance of mimosa, eucalyptus and even camomile. Bormes' rather separated seafrontage, some 4km away, boasts three sandy beaches and marina accommodation for no less than 850 pleasure craft.

The span of coast eastwards to la Croix-Valmer yields a succession of small beach resorts, each distinctive and all very popular. Cavalière has trees growing on its sands, giving a desert-island image, and enjoys a pleasant

The harbour, St Tropez

southerly aspect over Cap Nègre to the Ile du Levant and Port-Cros. Rayol's beach lies well back in a narrow, terraced bay flanked by pinewoods, while on eastwards round Pointe de la Chappe are more wooded cliffs.

There is much new building at Cavalaire-sur-Mer; its 4km of east-facing sands, some of the loveliest on the Mediterranean, together with a busy port serving the Iles d'Hyères, are creating the all too familiar pressure to expand. In some contrast, la Croix-Valmer is best known as a health resort and rest centre! It was from these beaches — the Côte des Maures — that the Allied armies began their liberation of Provence in 1944.

The little D93 road curls and twists through the hills behind St Tropez, round the old villages of Gassin and Ramateulle in a landscape of cork-oaks, pines and stands of bamboo. It is odd that such places should remain almost untouched by the twentieth century, only a stone's throw from an internationally famous resort.

If not the oldest, the largest, or the most elegant port on the Riviera, St Tropez does have a reputation for attracting the wealthy and those in the public eye. However, when Guy de Maupassant came here in his yacht at the turn of the century, only a narrow-gauge railway and an old sailing boat from St Raphael, the *Lion de Mer*, connected it with the outside world. Even today, the main coast road by-passes the town, cutting south across the neck of the Camarat Peninsula. St Tropez is *en route* for nowhere!

After Maupassant, the neo-Impressionist Paul Signac became the first of many artists to spend their summers working in the area, some staying on permanently. Amongst them were Bonnard, Matisse, Marquet, Camoin, Dunoyer de Segonzac; the Musée l'Annonciade has a fine representative collection of their paintings and sculptures. The tradition of easel-painting lives on along the quaysides, but the work is almost all tourist-orientated — good natured enough, though at worst cynical and condescending.

Between the wars, St Tropez was discovered by Bohemia and the non-conformists of Europe and the USA. The great French novelist Collette settled here in 1923 and stayed for thirteen winters, but it was not until the era of Brigitte Bardot and Roger Vadim that the name St Tropez became synonymous with glamour, as celebrities from the theatre, cinema and television rubbed shoulders with each other and with an ogling public. Stars no longer flock here to be stared at, but the habit seems to have stuck: watching others and being scrutinised in return is almost *de rigueur*!

Surrounding its handsome green lifeboat in St Tropez's crowded harbour are yachts that make other pleasure craft on the Riviera look trifling by comparison — huge white hulls radiating light and opulence. Happily, the resort is a destination for common mortals too. Situated on an extremely beautiful gulf, it is well endowed with smart shops, bars, clubs and eating places, many in narrow, picturesque streets. In summer, a variety of fêtes, *nuits musicales* and folk festivals are staged.

Each year, on 16 and 17 May and again on 15 June, St Tropez honours its past in two processions and acts of self-assertion called *bravades*. The first commemorates the town's patron-saint, St Torpes, and the second an occasion in 1637 during the Thirty Years' War when a local militia drove the Spanish fleet from the harbour. Both festivals are colourful, noisy affairs with much music and firing of blank musket shot, hugely enjoyed by participants and spectators alike.

The legendary beaches, much loved by the British, of Plage des Salins, Plage de Tahiti and the vast Plage de Pampelonne, 5km of marvellous fine sand, lie 4km or so east of the town centre. Small sections of 'pay-beach' nearest the entrances are equipped with rows of coloured sunbeds and parasols, like open-air theatres looking out to a stage of cruisers and yachts moored in the bay. In high season, premier sections of beach are thick with prostrate suntanned bodies, but on Pampelonne in particular there is room for everyone. Caravan and campsites dot the entire Camarat Peninsula, many fringing the beaches themselves.

Port Grimaud, little more than a decade old, is the astonishing creation of Alsatian architect François Spoerry. Like a miniature, concrete Venice, it was conceived around the requirements of the boating fraternity and access is by foot or water only. There is room for 2,000 craft and shops, banks, cafés, hotels, a post office, even a church have also been provided. Guided tours and self-drive motorboat trips through the pretty canals reveal the village's decorative, quasi-Provençal style. Nowhere since Languedoc have we encountered the custom-built resort with its allusions to traditional architecture, its manicured quaintness. It is not to everyone's liking.

The N98, and Beauvallon-Plage which it bisects, are both heavily patronised in season. There are packed, dusty campsites and a funfair next to the beach; just inland, a nine-hole golf course.

Popular with families, Ste Maxime faces due south and is protected from the cold winter *mistral* by the Maures Massif. Unlike north-facing St Tropez, whose season virtually ends with September, Ste Maxime is a year-round resort, echoing St Tropez's liveliness with its own animated night-life. Good sandy beaches, especially north of Cap des Sardinaux at la Nartelle, are backed by low, round, wooded hills. Like many other communes along this coast, Ste Maxime prohibits informal overnight halts in caravans and caravettes; the signs are not universally respected but it is worth bearing in mind that accommodation is at a high premium during July and August.

Secluded villa settlements above rocky coves, such as Val d'Esquières, San-Peire-sur-Mer and les Issambres, give way to the alluvial Argens plain, where the hills step back for a few kilometres, to be replaced by marshy flats and good, wide sandy beaches along the Golfe de Fréjus. The area is renowned for its many campsites.

Away from clusters of population and amenity, car parking — the bane of the Riviera — is relatively easy, even in high season (though farther east this soon ceases to be the case). Roadside stalls go a long way towards serving the needs of campers and holidaymakers out for the day. There is a lagoon at St Aygulf, and enough inflatable plastic boats for sale to float an army!

Fréjus almost merges with St Raphael to form the largest urban centre since Hyères. Once a Roman harbour, it is now 2km from the sea and contains some notable restored ruins; its fifth-century Baptistry is one of France's most interesting early Christian buildings. Though incomplete, the Roman Arena north of the town is worth seeing (bullfights are held in it during July and August), along with other features on the compact site of the ancient city. There are guided tours of the Baptistry, Cloisters and Cathedral of Notre-Dame occupying the centre.

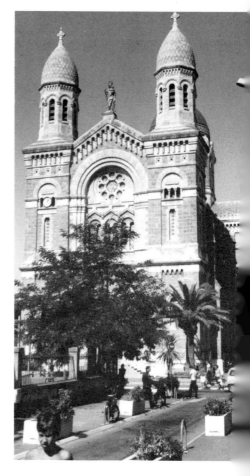

Notre-Dame-de-Victoire, St Raphael

Fréjus-Plage is not much of a seafront, though the long sands are pleasant enough. Holiday houses and apartments stretch to the airport, and the road is lined with shops and stalls selling basketware and ceramics. Just how the purchasers of huge earthenware urns get them home in one piece gives endless food for thought!

St Raphael shares Fréjus' Roman ancestry, but its emergence as a resort came about after the nineteenth-century journalist Alphonse Karr wrote glowing accounts of its beauty to friends in Paris. Writers, musicians and artists came to see for themselves — and stayed. Among the better known were Maupassant, Dumas and Berlioz. Gounod's 'Romeo and Juliet' was composed here in 1866.

A century earlier, marsh-fever had so debilitated the local fishermen and peasants that they were nick-named 'pale-faces', and even in Karr's day St Raphael was a sedate, somewhat sober place, dubbed 'Bournemouth of the Riviera'. Much of that has changed, though a flavour lingers on, here and there. Today it is a congenial, bustling town, neither expensive nor vulgar, and its clothing shops offer an especially good range of cheap holiday fashions.

At the heart of the old town stands the twelfth-century Church of the Knights Templar, which also provided safe refuge for the local population during attacks by pirates in those more perilous days. Next door is the Musée d'Archaeologie sous-marin; in and around St Raphael's busy marina-port can be found several diving clubs and it is largely their finds, notably of amorphae, which make up the museum's exhibitions.

Campsites hug the little beaches out towards Boulouris and le Dramont. Dusty and crowded in high season, one wonders how campers pitched without shade on scorched, iron-hard ground near incessant traffic on the busy N98 are able to tolerate such conditions; perhaps tents merely become shelters in which to sleep between long days spent in more agreeable surroundings.

Known as the Corniche de l'Esterel (or the Corniche d'Or), a delightful road runs east from St Raphael to la Napoule. Built in 1903 to open up a previously unknown coastline, and shadowed closely by the railway, it weaves sinuously along a platform in the steep hillsides high above the sea on the edge of the Massif de l'Esterel.

As old as the Maures Massif to the south, the Esterel is also of volcanic origin. Its rugged porphry rock, the colour of blood and Devon soil, is deeply fissured, often plunging precipitously to the sea, so that beaches are pebblier and harder to reach. Between settlements, snorkellers, scuba-divers and the more intrepid beachgoers will find clear and varied waters, leaving landlocked motorists on the Corniche to glance longingly down at the occasional yacht moored in an unfrequented cove. The land and the buildings upon it have the look and feel of unfired pottery — bone dry, all pinks and terracotta.

Inland, shrubs and bushes cover the hills where pine and cork-oak forests once thrived. Fire has always threatened the resinous forests of Provence, but the unprecedented conflagration of 1964 devastated the Esterel. Re-afforestation is hampered by disease affecting maritime pines, and by the sheer scale of the area involved, but a start has been made around Fréjus and St Raphael.

Elsewhere in this empty, rocky wilderness, many wild plants flourish and there are prehistoric remains, mines and quarries. The climb on foot to the summit of Mt Vinaigre (618m) is a worthwhile expedition.

Rocky headlands sprawl out to sea and little pebbly coves alternate with sandy beaches round to Cap Dramont, whose signal station provides a marvellous panoramic view. A short distance north lies the pleasant resort of Agay, tucked at the back of its magnificent bay between Cap Dramont and Pointe de Baumette, in the best natural anchorage on the Esterel coast. There are moorings, beaches of coarse sand and a refreshing sense of aloofness from commercialisation. An annual fête takes place at the end of July, with water-jousting.

Anthéor, facing the Ile des Vieilles and dominated by the Cap Roux range of hills, is followed by the vertical red cliffs of Pointe de l'Observatoire and a string of tiny bays, past le Trayas to Miramar. This last, elegant, resort is manageably crowded and car parking is surprisingly easy considering its proximity to the most congested stretch of coast in the whole of France, that from Cannes to the Italian border. Amongst its amenities can be counted an excellent swimming pool, but not all its beaches are free of charge.

Beyond Pointe de l'Esquillon, Port-la-Galère's honeycomb of futuristic villas down by the sea is daringly free of architectural cubiform orthodoxy: shades of la Grande Motte, though scale and setting are radically different.

Théoule-sur-Mer and la Napoule-Plage have sandy beaches; the latter also boasts a marina, fine restaurants, an eighteen-hole golf course and, above the shore itself, a massive castle-cum-stately home built on Roman and medieval remains. Before his death in 1937, the American sculptor and eccentric, Henry Clews, filled the castle and gardens with his extravagant and bizarre stone-carvings, which may be viewed, along with art exhibitions and concerts, during the summer.

The western end of the Golfe de Napoule, within sight of Cannes, is an unworthy prelude to one of the brightest jewels on the Côte d'Azur. Backed by the N98, railway and an industrial zone, a rocky beach straggles along past a giant fairground near the airport. Yet even here, many holidaymakers will have staked their claim by 9.30am on a warm morning and are already cooling off in the mellow Mediterranean.

Ever since Lord Brougham was prevented by a cholera outbreak from reaching Nice in 1834 and subsequently fell in love with what was then a small fishing village, Cannes has exercised a magnetic appeal. From being a venue for nineteenth-century English aristocracy, writers, poets and artists, it receives today a year-round influx of tourists and visitors participating in its world famous festivals: the International Film Festival in May, Drama and Music in July and August, an Amateur Film Festival in March, a Mimosa Festival in February, to name but a few.

It is easy to appreciate the reasons for its popularity. Beyond the square twelfth-century tower of le Suquet atop the old town, lies the port, thick with fishing and pleasure craft; it is flanked on the west by shops and restaurants, on the east by the minicipal casino. Rows of palm trees, beach tents and sunbeds swing round with a ribbon of sand to the Palm Beach casino and entertainments complex.

Above the beach runs the broad, flowery Boulevard de la Croisette, bordered by luxury hotels; behind it, the modern town, containing everything from morning markets to discotheques and cinemas, from sports centres to the smartest coutouriers. It is a ritzy, well-heeled, colourful place which some believe may nevertheless be losing its heart beneath the relentless pressure of motor traffic and mass tourism.

A small funicular railway from Boulevard Montfleury hoists visitors to the Observatoire at la Californie in Super-Cannes, and a lift completes the mechanical ascent to the tower, 325m above sea level. The truly immense panorama is said to rival the best anywhere on the Mediterranean coast.

The two Iles de Lérins, visible just offshore, provide pleasant wooded strolls past interesting historic buildings, and are reached in fifteen minutes by motor launch.

Vallauris stands 3km north from the sea, among mimosa and orange trees — a 'must' for those interested in crafts. It was a pottery town in decline after the war years, until Picasso returned to his beloved Mediterranean from Paris, rekindled the creative flame, and began working in the Madoura pottery. Today, Vallauris is an important centre for ceramic ware in France. Bowls and jugs made to Picasso's designs form just part of a prodigious output — sometimes blatantly commercial — from over a hundred potteries in the area; many use wood-fired kilns.

Other craftsmen and women produce olive-wood carvings and furniture, woven fabrics and glassware. There is a medieval chapel decorated by Picasso's 'War and Peace' paintings, and his bronze 'Man and Sheep' can be seen in the market square.

Juan-les-Pins is approached along the curve of sands by Golfe-Juan, leading the eye round to the toe of Cap d'Antibes. Dubbed the 'Funfair of Antibes', Juan-les-Pins was created by the American millionaire Frank Gould in the 1920s and owes nothing to an earlier history. Its night-life in a myriad of nightclubs, restaurants and open-air cafés, is magnetic; those disposed to fashionable dressing (the town is full of boutiques), bright lights and loud music gravitate here like moths round a flame. It is a fitting venue for the annual World Jazz Festival which is held each July in the Palais des Congrès, and sometimes outdoors beneath the pine trees.

Situated in an area well known for its exotic gardens and sub-tropical flora,

Antibes fosters the commercial production of roses, carnations, anemones and tulips. With 750 acres of greenhouses and frames — approaching a million square metres of glass — it is one of Europe's greatest horticultural centres.

On Cap d'Antibes, *pied-à-terre* of wealthy socialites, gentry and film-stars for almost a century, the Jardin Thuret has pioneered the acclimatisation of tropical trees and plants. Set up in 1856, the garden is now state-financed and contains many rare species.

Antibes itself has a fascinating Vieille Ville, full of atmosphere and colour — a labyrinth of narrow, cobbled and mostly pedestrianised streets lined with exellent little shops. In Cours Masséna, a covered market sells local produce from land and sea.

The Grimaldis have featured prominently in the history of this area

Agay, and the rocky edge of the Massif de l'Esterel

and it is in the medieval Château Grimaldi, for many years their own, that one of the finest collections of Pablo Picasso's work anywhere in the world may be found. There are drawings, paintings, lithographs, sculptures, etchings and ceramics, embracing, with vigorous inventiveness, so many of the Mediterranean's mythological motifs associated with this great artist: goats, bulls, centaurs, flautists, dancers and lovers.

North of Antibes and 4km inland at Biot, there is another impressive art collection, this time the work of Ferdnand Léger. There is also a developing craft centre which includes a glassworks.

The port of Antibes adds its complement of luxury yachts to the Côte d'Azur's tally. Good beaches of coarse sand are plied by swarthy vendors whose persistent calls tempt sunbathers to cool off with a '*boisson frais*' or a '*glace*'. Light aircraft drag slogans across the sky while heavier jets pass overhead to Nice's International Airport, but somehow the noise gets lost in the excitement of swimming, parascending and wind-surfing. Modern Antibes is not untypical of Côte d'Azur resorts — it has considerable *élan* and vies for popularity with St Tropez and the rest.

Fort Carrés severe grey walls herald 8km or so of unprepossessing coastline: an anonymous strip, a no-man's land, of narrow stony beach next to busy roads, railway and industrial estates. If you turn your back on the ugliness, as many do, putting up a sun umbrella and facing the anodyne Mediterranean, perhaps it is more bearable — out of sight, out of mind!

Half-way along at la Brague, near the D4 to Biot, is Marineland, Europe's first marine zoo, with performing dolphins, a killer whale, sea lions, turtles, penguins and sea birds.

Port-la-Galère and Port Grimaud pale into insignificance beside the mountainous, assymetrical apartment blocks at Baie des Anges. Like unfinished 'Lego' pyramids, they utterly dominate the landscape and are visible from Antibes to the Var. Andre Minangoy, their designer, incorporated swimming pools, cafés, shops and restaurants with a large marina to form a holiday complex as audacious and revolutionary as any in Languedoc. But unlike the architecture there, designed and built from scratch on a sparsely populated coast, grand gestures like Baie des Anges, however well they may express stylistic *joie de vivre* and confidence in the new prosperity, are jarring intrusions in such a densely settled area.

The beach at Cagnes-sur-Mer, no more than a narrow pebble bank, is backed by the Riviera's principal racecourse. The old upper town of Haut-de-Cagnes is very picturesque: its Château-Musée holds summer exhibitions of contemporary art and contains a Museum of the Olive Tree. There are superb views from the tower over hilly landscapes inland of the busy coastal fringe.

A little west at les Collettes, the studios, materials and some examples of work form an eloquent memorial to the painter Auguste Renoir; his house has been preserved just as it was during his lifetime.

We cross the Var and pass Nice's modern international airport, one of the world's most architecturally graceful, decorated with palm trees and flowering beet. Ahead lies Nice herself, Queen of the Riviera, City of Elegance evoking '*la Belle Epoque*' as few other places can. It is the largest and probably the oldest city between Marseille and Genoa.

Because its existence is independent of tourism (other industries include olive oil, perfume, cereal foods, clothing, flowers, as well as a university), Nice is all things to all men. With close on 350,000 permanent residents and a sheltered location, it is also a remarkably varied and beautiful city. Alternately Italian and French during the seventeenth and eighteenth

Bandol

Sanary-sur-Mer

Plage de Tahiti, St Tropez

St Jean-Cap-Ferrat from the Jardin Exotique, Èze

Jardin Exotique at Èze

centuries, its standing as a year-round resort was assured by the coming of the railway, and today it is the chief town of the Alpes-Maritimes, capital of Côte d'Azur.

Still strongly Italian in flavour, the old town should not be missed. Its polyglot population occupies a triangle formed by the Paillon torrent, Quai des États-Unis and Castle hill, and although its church buildings are mostly undistinguished Italian Baroque (Chapelle de la Miséricord is the exception), the warren of paved alleyways and narrow winding streets reward exploration.

Activity ceases for only a few short hours between the closing of late-night bars and restaurants and the early morning preparation of meat and fish in time for the first shoppers. The rattle of delivery vans and the heavy, repetitive thud of the butcher's knife punctuate the pre-dawn air. There is a good panoramic view right over the old town from a park near the summit of the château (Castle hill).

After a disasterous frost in 1822, which wiped out most of the local orange trees, the English colony of the time financed and organised the construction of a promenade along the Baie des Anges to provide paid work for local fruit-growers. Widened and extended several times since, the Promenade des Anglais now carries six lanes of frantic traffic between flower beds and palms for a distance of 7km.

129

PLACES TO VISIT FROM CANNES TO NICE

Cannes
Twelfth-century le Suquet tower atop old town; unsurpassed amenities, fashionable shops and entertainment, innumerable festivals throughout year, including famous Film Festival. Take funicular railway from Boulevard Montfleury to the Observatory in Super-Cannes for superlative panoramas.

Vallauris
Ceramics centre associated with Picasso — over 100 potteries and other crafts.

Antibes
Great horticultural area growing roses, carnations, anemones, tulips. Jardin Thuret on Cap d'Antibes has many rare trees and plants. Antibes' charming Vieille Ville with market, good shops in narrow streets. Château Grimaldi has best collection of Picasso's work in world. Fashionable, lively beach.

Marineland
Europe's first marine zoo, with performing dolphins, a killer whale, sea-lions, turtles, penguins and birds. At la Brague, near D4 to Biot.

Cagnes
Riviera's principal racecourse. Nearby picturesque Haut-de-Cagnes has museums to Renoir and the Olive Tree.

Nice
Narrow streets and alleys of Old Town, with flower market, shops and stalls. Promenade des Anglais sea-front. Numerous museums, galleries. Festivals and entertainment all year, including famous Battle of Flowers on day after Ash Wednesday. Excursions inland to hill villages of Beuil, Peille, Peillon, Aspremont. Walks in Alpes-Maritimes foothills. Boat trips/ferries to Corsica and along Riviera.

The seafront promenade is frequented by passers-by of every age, description and nationality, walking, jogging, roller-skating or simply taking in the view.

Nice is also a city of entertainment, renowned for its February Carnival and summer Flower Festivals. There are many events, too numerous to list here (but see under Further Information), events which include flower battles, open-air theatre, water sports, Fishermen's Festivals, an International Dog Festival, ballet, opera and concerts, an International Book Fair, folk festivals, street parades and much else all enjoyed by both visitors and locals.

The Marc Chagall and Matisse museums are just two of a liberal sprinkling within the city, dealing with a range of subjects from molluscs and crustacea to archaeology, natural

history to fine arts, while from the harbour, boat trips can be taken along the Riviera and farther afield to Corsica.

If there is a flaw in Nice's complexion, it is her beach — disappointingly pebbly by Riviera standards, but well patronised nevertheless and with all the usual amenities. The cleanest and clearest bathing lies further east in attractive rocky coves at the foot of Mont Baron.

Towards Italy, the Alpes-Maritimes foothills huddle close to the coast, forcing settlements, roads and railway onto natural south-facing terraces above the sea. At Nice, however, the hinterland still feels open and accessible and there are many worthwhile excursions north to the hill villages of Beuil, Peille, Peillon and Aspremont. Roads also lead into the Alpes-Maritimes proper, threading the great gorges of the Tinée and Vésubie rivers before their confluence in the Var. 'La Grande Traversée des Alpes', a 700km long-distance footpath (GR5), ends at Nice after its crossing of the French Alps from Geneva.

Villefranche, virtually a suburb of Nice, stands almost unchanged since the eighteenth century. Its covered streets of Italianate architecture lead down steps to broad quays, a few small beaches and a charming tree-lined promenade. From cafés round the little harbour, you can gaze across the deep roadstead to the luxury yachts and hanging gardens of Cap Ferrat. The tiny Romanesque fishermen's Chapelle St Pierre contains interesting modern frescoes by Jean Cocteau.

St Jean-Cap-Ferrat is another exclusive thumb of land — 3km of luxury villas all but concealed in dense vegetation. Illustrious residents have never been in short supply: Somerset Maugham lived, worked and entertained in his villa near the cape for forty years, and Villa des Cedres, near the sandy Plage de Passable and a lively zoo, once belonged to Leopold II of Belgium (its present occupant is Monsieur Marnier, of Grand Marnier fame). The only settlement as such is the former fishing village of St Jean, now host to pleasure craft.

Visitors to the peninsula should take in the Ile de France museum at Villa Ephrussi, a bequest by Baroness Ephrussi de Rothschild. As well as sumptuous displays of furniture, tapestries, paintings, sculptures, porcelain and costumes, seventeen acres of quite stunning grounds surround the buildings. Gardens characteristic of France, Spain, Italy, Japan and England combine typical flora with fountains, stepped cascades, statues and other formal features.

Between Nice and Cap Martin, the busiest and most built-upon coastline of the entire Riviera is kept alive and moving by three parallel roads and the A8 Autoroute. The N98 Corniche

---

PLACES TO VISIT BETWEEN NICE AND THE ITALIAN FRONTIER

Ile de France Museum
Villa Ephrussi, St Jean-Cap-Ferrat — sumptuous displays of furniture and Fine Arts, surrounded by gardens in national styles.

Èze
Medieval hill village on rock, 427m above sea. Jardin Exotique has spectacular cacti and fine views.

La Turbie
Trophée des Alpes monument and museum.

Monaco/Monte-Carlo
Famous skyscraper resort and principality with casino, palace, Jardin Exotique, caves and museum of prehistoric anthropology, oceanographic museum directed by Commander Jacques Cousteau.

Roquebrune
Tiny hilltop village, shops and houses hewn into rock. Tenth-century castle, oldest in France.

Menton
Pleasant, mild town, good amenities. Delightful Vieille Ville with International Chamber Music Festival during August in Italianate square by St Michel church.

Inferieure (Lower Corniche) runs a tortuous course along the sea's edge, often narrow and congested but providing access to harbours and beaches. The N7 Moyenne Corniche (Middle Corniche) and the D2564 Grande Corniche (Upper Corniche) link towns and villages of intermediate height and naturally offer the best views. All three roads are connected by many steep lateral lanes.

Set back above the busy local and tourist traffic, the A8 Autoroute penetrates rugged mountainsides up to

Monte-Carlo

500m above sea level in a great sweep of viaducts and tunnels to Nice Airport, and thence to Fréjus and cross-country to Marseille.

So sheltered as to be called 'Little Africa', Beaulieu has lured many a distinguished visitor: Queen Victoria, the Duke of Connaught, Lord Salisbury, Eugène Boudin, Maxim Gorki, to name but a few. The American journalist James Gordon Bennet, who despatched Stanley to find Dr Livingstone, died in his villa here in 1918. It is a quiet, year-round resort with a little port and luxuriant gardens.

Èze, on the Moyenne Corniche, is the most imposing medieval hill village on this coast, towering on a rock spire 427m above the sea, safe from the one-time malarious coastal fringe and sea-borne invaders. Though few live now in its steep streets, the pattern of life remains intimate, interdependent, unchanging.

There is no motor traffic and for the tourist it is a haven of quiet. Among concessions to visitors are a few boutiques, artists' studios and souvenir shops; donkeys are still used to transport heavy loads up to restaurants. Justifiably popular, and well worth a visit, its Jardin Exotique contains a splendid array of immense succulents — extravagant forms and textures, living abstract sculptures bursting into unlikely flowers. It is a quite extraordinary foreground for sensational views to Cap Ferrat and, in clear weather, Corsica.

At the junction of the Roman Via Aurelia and the Julian Way from Piedmont — through-routes still followed by today's roads and railways — stands la Turbie, on the Grande Corniche overlooking Monte-Carlo. A typical Provençal mountain village, backed by Mont Agel, its claim to fame is the great 'Trophée des Alpes' commemorating the Roman Emperor Augustus's subjugation of hostile alpine tribes who had disrupted communications between Rome and Gaul for so long.

The monument's original flambuoyance was lost through damage and neglect until an American, Edward Tuck, restored and rebuilt much of it in 1930, demolishing twenty-two private houses and a hotel in the process. It now stands over 30m high, with an accompanying museum.

In the mid-1800s, Monte-Carlo was a slope of stony fields and olive trees, a difficult image to invoke faced with today's mini-Manhattan below the limestone cliffs of Tête de Chien. The Principality of Monaco, 375 acres of cliff-bound peninsula, has a turbulent history, inextricably bound up with the Grimaldis: one of family feuds, political conflict and foreign occupation.

In 1861, Menton and Roquebrune, until then belonging to Monaco, were acquired for France by Napoleon III. The French government, in return, agreed to build a coast road from Nice, and by way of compensation for the loss of Monaco's citrus and olive revenue, an attempt was made to establish a Casino. It failed. Not until the coming of the railway in 1868 did Monte-Carlo's casino meet with success. Despite vigorous opposition from the British, it

Roquebrune from its tenth-century hilltop castle

went from strength to strength, taxes were abolished and building began in earnest.

Today, Monte-Carlo is synonymous with gambling, rich villas, palaces and luxury shops; it has been said that the strength of Monte-Carlo is the weakness of the world yet the fruits of its gambling revenue and materialism are equally well known. There is a prestigious Opera and National Orchestra, many festivals and events, including the Monaco Grand-Prix and the Monte-Carlo Rally, first held in 1911.

Cathedral, Palace and administrative buildings occupy the old site, Monaco-Ville. Just to the west at Fontvieille, an artificial peninsula is slowly growing out to accommodate new light industries, while the residential resort and casino of Monte-Carlo lies to the east. In between in the Principality's commercial centre of la Condamine, with shops, library, market and railway station.

Space may be at a premium (even the beach is imported!) but it is diligently used and there is much to see: the Changing of the Palace Guard at 11.55am each morning, the Jardin Exotique, containing over a thousand cacti clinging to a cliff face and criss-crossed by little paths and bridges, the neolithic Grotte de l'Observatoire caves and the museum of Prehistoric Anthropology.

The world-famous Musée Océanographique, part of a research institute directed by Jacques Cousteau, is endlessly fascinating. Other attractions include historic buildings, a zoo, a Museum of Dolls and Automata and, of course, the magnificent casino. Not everyone will choose to share in Monte-Carlo's concrete Utopia, but whichever of its qualities may be open to debate, uniqueness is not among them.

The diminutive, twisting streets and arched alleyways of ancient Roquebrune — where in deepest shade even the smells might be of a different age to our own — are constructed on such an intimate scale that they seem for a

Towards the Italian frontier, from Menton's Old Town

moment to be indoors, inside some strange, large house. The impression is soon dispelled by little dwellings and shops hewn back into the *rocca bruna*, a conglomerate of thickly embedded pebbles.

Craftsmen and women make and sell ceramics, wood sculpture, clothes, and even if the taste is at times unsophisticated, it is all refreshingly low-key compared with the pushy commercialism of larger resorts. Street names glazed onto bricks are set in stucco walls; it is an enchanting place.

The village clusters round a tenth-century castle established by Conrad, Count of Ventimiglia against the return of the feared Saracens, a centuries-long nightmare on this coast. Claimed to be the oldest in France, it is just what a castle should be with battlements, windows mere apertures in massively thick walls, an interior dimly lit and spartanly furnished as befitting the modest quarters of a feudal lord. Outside are views of tilting orange roofs and precipitous coastal hillsides. In the square below, nightingales sing from cages in windows, so perfectly you think at first it may be a recording.

The plague came to Roquebrune in the summer of 1467. A Passion of Thanksgiving for its ending has been held on 5 August every year since, with roles for local participants passed down from one generation to the next. Another religious procession takes place on Good Friday.

Royalty, peerage and wealthy businessmen gave Cap Martin its exclusive tag during the late 1800s, but its shore is too uncomfortably rocky for it to have earned full resort status. That could hardly have mattered less: it is now an up-market suburb of Menton, studded with millionaire luxury villas amongst olive groves, pine woods and banks of mimosa. Huge aleppo pines lean out over the rocky foreshore as if to share the cool breath of the sea.

Hill village, cape and the coast along to Menton are all rather wantonly lumped together under the name Roquebrune-Cap-Martin, as if they have much in common. However, hotels, restaurants, clubs and swimming pools line the approach to Menton, last town before the Italian frontier.

Protected from the *mistral* by grey limestone hills to the north and west, Menton's climate is exceptionally mild, so that lemon trees flower and fruit all year. Legend has it that Eve secreted a lemon in her bosom when she and Adam were expelled from Paradise. After a long search, they found an earthly

paradise where Menton now stands and lemons have thrived here ever since! A Lemon Festival and Golden Fruit Parade are held each February, the tons of fruit used in the floats going to hospitals or made into jam.

By the 1860s, Menton could be reached by train but it was still a small, mild Italian town. Fourteen years later, thanks largely to the efforts of a Dr Henry Bennett, it had become a winter health resort for those with chest complaints, especially the British. Cynics invented the slogan: 'Cannes is for living, Monte-Carlo for gambling, Menton for dying', but in fairness, other towns such as Hyères, Beaulieu and St Raphael deserved a similar label. Aubrey Beardsley came here in 1897 with advanced tuberculosis but died five months later aged twenty-six, a prodigious graphic talent lost forever.

By the 1930s, DDT had eradicated mosquitoes, and provision of 'proper facilities for sunbathing' gave Menton a summer clientele in addition to its winter trade. There are still tenuous traces of earlier British patronage — an Anglican church, an English club, library and estate agent.

The Promenade du Soleil is lined with palms shading outdoor bars and restaurants. Its beach is a mix of sand and pebbles, not wide but popular, and leads round east to the Musée Jean Cocteau (tapestries, gouaches and drawings) and the Quai-Napoleon. This delightful jetty affords a classic view of the Vieille Ville, beyond the masts of pleasure boats; it stands on a hill, houses stacked like tall, sand-coloured boxes with orange lids, tier upon tier to the belfry tower of St Michel.

Les Sablettes offers safe bathing in an artificial lagoon, extending eastwards to the marina and residential suburb of Garavan. In common with so many Mediterranean resorts, water sports abound — yachting, water-skiing, wind-surfing, pedalos, etc.

Menton's new town is cosmopolitan and business-like, without a sign of

Seafront gardens, Menton

pretension. Orange trees shade little squares off pedestrianised streets where you can sit with a drink, or browse in shops selling everything from clothes to the local speciality of glacé fruits. Jardin Biove, a long, flowery, ornamental garden, runs right through the town centre, and even parking seems a little easier than on much of the Côte d'Azur.

Menton's Vieille Ville, a maze of narrow, built-over alleys and curving flights of steps, is largely intact. Atop a double staircase from Quai Bonaparte lies a fine Italianate square, paved with a mosaic of the Grimaldi arms and

flanked by St Michel Parvis, the finest Baroque church in the region. The square forms the venue for an international Chamber Music Festival, and there are views of Italy between tall houses.

There is no more of France left to explore unless one goes inland. Excursions are possible to the 'villages perchés' of Castellar, Gorbio, Peille, and to Mont Agel, with many opportunities for walking tours in the high hills of the border massifs, but at the frontier post of Ponte San Ludovico our coastal journey reaches its conclusion.

136

Further Information

CROSS CHANNEL FERRIES

Brittany Ferries: Plymouth to St Malo and Roscoff. Portsmouth to St Malo. Cork to Roscoff.

Commodore Shipping Services: Jersey to St Malo.

Condor: Hydrofoil passenger-only from Channel Islands to St Malo.

Emeraude Ferries: Jersey to St Malo.

Hoverlloyd: Ramsgate to Calais hovercraft.

Irish Continental Line: Rosslare to Cherbourg and Le Havre.

DR Ferrries: Dunkirk to Ramsgate.

P & O Ferries: Dover and Southampton to Boulogne and Le Havre.

Sealink: Dover, Folkestone, Newhaven and Weymouth to Boulogne, Calais, Cherbourg, Dieppe and Dunkirk.

Seaspeed: Dover to Boulogne and Calais hovercraft.

Townsend Thoresen: Dover, Portsmouth and Southampton to Calais, Cherbourg and Le Havre.

For details of campsites and hotels, consult appropriate guides (eg Michelin); lists of Gîtes Ruraux (holiday homes) and Logis et Auberges (small hotels and inns), along with any other information on holidays and travel on the French coast may be obtained through the French Government Tourist Office, 178 Piccadilly, London W1V 0AL.

OPENING TIMES AND PUBLIC HOLIDAYS

State-run museums, art galleries and public monuments are usually open from 9.00 or 10.00am till noon, and 2.00pm to 7.00pm during the summer season, with shorter hours in winter. Tuesday is a common closing day, as are French public holidays: 1 Jan (New Year's Day); Easter Sunday and Monday; 1 May

(Labour Day); 8 May (VE Day); Ascension Day, Whit Sunday and Monday; 14 July (Bastille Day); 15 August (Assumption Day); 1 November (All Saints Day); 11 November (Rememberance Day); Christmas Day. Opening times and addresses are given for each establishment listed.

RESORT GUIDE

The resorts are listed in alphabetical order with their recreational and sporting amenities at or near each resort indicated by the following code and a description of the nature of the beach.

Y = Yachting, sailing school and/or pleasure-boat harbour
SP = Swimming pool
B = Boats for hire (sometimes motorised)
WS = Water-skiing
F = Footpaths (waymarked or especially numerous)
D = Diving (underwater, from shore or boat)
T = Tennis courts
R = Riding stables
C = Cycles for hire and/or good cycling area
A = Angling
G = Golf course(s)
RC = Racecourse
SY = Sand-yachting
X = Surfing (malibu board) particularly favourable
TO = Address of local Tourist Office (Office de Tourisme or Syndicat d'Initiative) for information on accommodation, amenities and events.
(N) = Naturist beach within reach, not necessarily at resort. (For further details consult with 'Guide l'Officiel du Littoral Nudiste, Plages Naturistes', available through Naturist Clubs or from 13 Place de Petit Bois, 44100 Nantes.) Petit Bois, 44100 Nantes.)

137

Beach Classification: sand, pebbles,
   shingle, rocky.

L'Aber-Wrac'h
Y, B, T, A, F — sand, pebbles and rocky

Agay
Y, B, WS, D, F, T, R — sand
TO: Boulevard de la Mer

Agde
Anciénne Cathédrale St Etienne, Rue
Louis-Bages — open all year.
Musée agathois, Rue de la Fraternité —
open daily except Tuesday. 'Joutes
Nautiques' (water-jousting) — first week
of August at Cap d'Agde.
TO: Rue Louis-Bages

Aigues-Mortes
Tour Constance and ramparts — guided
tours available, open daily except public
holidays.

L'Aiguillon-sur-Mer/La Faute-sur-Mer
Y, SP, B, T, R, C, A — sand (N)
TO: Rond-Point fleuri

Ile d'Aix
Sand and rocky
Musée Napoléonien, Maison de
l'Empereur — guided visits daily except
Tuesday, (free Wednesday). Musée africain
(Foundation Gourgaud) — guided visits
daily except Wednesday. Island reached
from Pointe de la Fumée, near Fouras.

Andernos-les-Bains
Y, SP, T, R, C, RC — sand
TO: 33 Avenue Général -de-Gaulle

Anthéor
Y, B WS, F, R — sand

Antibes
Y, SP, B, WS, D, F, T, R, C, G — sand and
rocky
Musée Picasso, Château Grimaldi, Vielle
Ville — guided tours daily; closed
Tuesday, 1 May and November.
Musée Archéologique, Bastion St André
— closed 1 May and November.
'Marineland' at Brague near D4 to Biot —
open daily all year, performances each
afternoon.
Sailors Festival and Procession — second
Sunday in July; Veteran Car Rally in May;

Flower Festival in June.
TO: 12 Place Général-de-Gaulle

Arcachon
Y, SP, B, WS, D, F, T, R, C, A, G, RC —
sand (N)
Aquarium and Musée. Boulevard de la
Plage — open daily Palm Sunday to first
Sunday in October.
Ferries to Cap Ferret, boat trips to Ile aux
Oiseaux and round the bay.
Fête de la Mer — 15 August.
TO: Quincouces de la gare

Argelès-Plage
SP, F, T, R — sand (N)
TO: Place Arènes

Arromanches-les-Bains
Y, SP, W, F, T, R — sand (N)
Musée du Débarquement — open daily all
year except Christmas

Audierne
Y, B, D, A, T — sand and rocky
La Chaumière (thatched cottage) Quai
Pellatan towards beach — guided tours
available daily, April to late September.
Boat trips to Ile de Sein.

Audresselles
Y, SY, F, T, C — sand and pebbles

Avranches
SP, F, T, R, A
Jardin des Plantes, Corniche St Michel —
open till 11pm June to September, 7.30pm
rest of year. Illuminations and recorded
commentary.
Musée d'Avranchin, Place St Avit — open
daily, Easter to September; closed
Tuesday.
TO: Place Littré

Bandol
Y, D, F, T, C — sand and pebbles
Boat trips to Ile de Bendor.

Banyuls-sur-Mer
Y, SP, D, F, T, R — pebbles and rocky
Aquarium — open daily.
Metairie Maillol, retreat and burial place
of sculptor Aristide Maillol — 4km south-
west on Baillaury valley road.
Wine Festival in August.
TO: Hôtel de Ville

Barfleur
Y, F, T, C, — sand and pebbles
Phare de la Pointe de Barfleur — open 9am
to sunset.
Saturday market.

Barneville-Carteret
Y, W, D, F, T, R, C, A — sand (N)
Phare — open daily in summer.
Regular sailings to Channel Islands.
Saturday market.

Base de Plein Air de Bombannes
Y, SP, T, F, etc
Open April to October.

Batz-sur-Mer
Y, T — sand
Église St Guénolé — belfry open mid-June
to mid-September.

La Baule
Y, SP, B, D, T, R, — sand
Concours d'Elegance (car parade) in
August.
TO: 8 Place Victoire and 5 Place Palmiers
(July/August)

Bayonne
SP, Y, T
Musée Basque, Rue Marengo — open daily
except Sunday and public holidays.
Musée Bonnat, Rue Jacques Laffite —
open daily from mid-June to mid-
September; weekday afternoons and
weekends the rest of the year; closed
Tuesday and public holidays.
Grandes Fêtes — corridas, pelota, folk-
dancing, etc — first week of August.
TO: Place Liberté

Beaulieu
Y, WS, D, T — pebbles
Villa 'Kerylos', Rue Eiffel —
reconstruction of a Greek villa, open
afternoons only; closed Monday and
November.

Beauvallon-Plage
B, WS, D, T, T, G — sand (N)

Belle Ile
Y, B, D, T, R — sand and rocky (N)
Citadels and Musée at le Palais — closed
Wednesday.
Grand Phare, Port Goulphar — open
daily, July to mid-September.

Ile de Bendor
SP, Y, B, D, F — sand
Musée Mondail des Vins et des Spiritueux

(Wines and Spirits of the World
Exhibition) — closed Wednesday.

Bénodet
Y, SP, B, D, T, R — sand (N)
Phare de la Pyramide — apply to the
keeper.
Boat trips to Quimper, Loctudy and the
Iles de Glénan.
TO: 51 Avenue Plage

Berk-Plage
Y, SP, B, W, SY, T, R, C, A, G, RC —
sand (N)
TO: Hall piscine, Esplanade Parmentier

Biarritz
SP, D, F, T, R, G, A, X — sand and rocky
(N)
Le Phare, Pointe St Martin — open June
to mid-September, afternoons.
Musée de la Mer, Esplanade de la Vierge
— open daily all year.
TO: Cité Administrative and Square
d'Ixelles

Bidart
T — sand and rocky
TO: Rue Grande-Plage (June to
September).

Biscarosse-Plage/Étang de Cazaux
Y, SP, T, R, C, A, F, RC — Sand (N)
TO: 19 Terrace-avenue Plage (closed)
October)

Blériot-Plage T — sand

Blonville-sur-Mer
SP, B, F, T, R — Sand

Bormes-les-Mimosas
Y, B, WS, D, F, T, R, G — sand
TO: Rue J-Aicard

Boulogne-sur-Mer
Y, SP, T, C, A, G — Sand
Basilica of Notre-Dame, Ville Haute, Rue
de Lille — crypt open daily, closed Sunday
morning and from Monday noon to
Tuesday noon.
Colonne de la Grande Armée, 3km north,
to left of Nl — closed Tuesday and
Wednesday and October.
Pilgrimage of Miracle of Notre-Dame and
Procession — last weekend August.
TO: Quai Chanzy

Boulouris
B, WS, F, G — sand

Bourgneuf-en-Retz
Musée du Pays de Retz. 6 Rue des Moines
— open daily except Tuesday; closed
January and February.

Ile de Bréhat
Y, D, F, A — sand and pebbles
Boat trips to island from Arcouest and
Port-Clos

Brest
Château and Musée Naval, near Cours
Dajot — closed Tuesday.
Tour Tanguy (museum of old Brest),
across River Penfeld from Château —
open daily except 1 May.
Musée, Place Carnot — closed Tuesday
and public holidays.
Palais des Arts et de la Culture — closed
Monday.

Brière (Parc Régional)
Waterways, lakes and marsh — sailing,
wind-surfing, fishing, observation of
wildlife.

Brignogan-Plage
SP, Y, T, F — sand, pebbles and rocky (N)
TO: Rue Général-de-Gaulle (July/August)

Cabourg/Dives-sur-Mer
Y, T, R, C, A, G, RC — sand (N)
International Tennis Tournament — first
fortnight in August.
Horse Show — first weekend in
September.
Daily market in summer.
TO: Jardins du Casino

Cagnes-sur-Mer
Y, SP, B, WS, D, F, T, R, C, RC — pebbles
Château-Musée, Haut-de-Cagnes — open
daily except Tuesday, 1 January, 1 May
and October to mid-November.
Exhibitions of contemporary art
June/July/August.
Musée Renoir, Avenue des Collettes —
open daily except Tuesday and mid-
October to mid-November.
Horse-racing at Hippodrome de la Côte
d'Azur — in August, September and
December to March.

Calais
Y, SP, W, SY, C, A — sand
Musée des Beaux-Arts et de la Dentelle —
closed Tuesday and public holidays.
Musée de la Guerre, Parc St Pierre — open
daily May to September.
International Music Parade — 1 July.

Camaret-sur-Mer
Y, B, D, T, A — sand, pebbles and rocky
Musée de la Marine, the Sillon — open
daily June to September; Wednesday,
Saturday and Sunday afternoons rest of
the year.
'Pardon' of Notre-Dame-de-Rocamadour
and Blessing of the Sea — first Sunday in
September.

Camargue
Réserve Nationale — access by special
permission only; contact la Capètiere,
13200 Arles.
Centre d'Information Ginès — closed
weekends October to March.
Pont de Gau Bird Sanctuary — open daily
till sunset.
Musée Camarguais, Pont de Rousty, 10km
south-west of Arles — closed Tuesday,
September to April and public holidays.
Boat trips on Petit Rhône — regular
service, Easter to October.

Cancale
Y, D, T, W, F — shingle and sand (N)
Église St Méen — ticket to climb tower
from Tourist Office.
Musée de Bois Sculptés, Place de la
République — open Easter to October.
TO: Rue du Port (Easter, Whitsun, June to
September)

Canet-Plage
Y, SP, T, R, C, D, WS — sand (N)
TO: Place Méditerranée

Cannes
Y, SP, B, WS, D, F, T, C, G — sand (N)
Musée la Castre, le Suquet — closed
Monday, November to mid-December and
public holidays.
Tour du Suquet — apply to keeper.
Observatoire de Super-Cannes, 3km north
open daily except November weekdays and
public holidays (reached by funicular
railway).
Boat trips to Iles Lérin.
Mimosa Festival — February;
Photography and amateur Film Festival —
March; International Film Festival —
May; Drama and Music Festival —
July/August; Fireworks Festival —
August; International Yachting Festival
and Royal Regatta, also Vintage Cars
Festival — September; International Golf
Tournaments — October/November.
TO: SNCF station and Palais Festivals et
des Congrès, la Croisette

Cap Breton/Hossegor
Y, SP, B, WS, D, F, T, R, C, A, G, X —
sand (N)
TO: Place Louis-Pasteur (closed October)
and Ave G. Pompidou

Le Cap d'Agde
SP, Y, B, WS, D, F, T, R, C, A, G — sand
(N)
'Joutes Nautiques' (water-jousting) — first
week of August.

Cap-Ferret
Y, B, WS, D, T, R, C, RC — sand (N)
Le Phare — open daily most of year.
Trains from Belisaire to La Plagne de
l'Océan — Sunday and public holidays
Easter to May; daily June to September.
Ferries and boat trips to Arcachon, Pyla-
sur-Mer, Ile aux Oiseaux.
TO: Place du Marché

Carantec
Y, F, T, A — sand and pebbles
'Pardons'; Notre-Dame-de-Callot — Whit
Sunday; St Carantec — 10am third Sunday
in July; Notre-Dame-de-Callot — Sunday
after 15 August.
TO: Rue A. Louppe (April to mid-
September)

Carnac
Y, B, T, R, F — sand
Musée Miln-le-Rouzic — open daily Easter
to September.
Tumulus St Michel, off D781 — guided
tours late March to September.
'Pardon' of St Cornély — second Sunday
in September.
TO: Avenue Druides

Carnon-Plage
SP, WS, D, T, C — sand

Carolles
F, T — sand

Carteret/Barneville
Y, W, D, F, T, R, C, A — sand (N)
Phare — open daily, summer only.
Regular sailings to Channel Islands.
Saturday market.

Cassis
D, R, T, F — sand and shingle (N)
Musée Archéologie — open Wednesday
and Friday mornings.
Boat trips to the *calanques*.

Cavalaire-sur-Mer
Y, B, WS, D, F, T, C — sand (N)
TO: Square de Lattre-se-Tassigny

Cavalaire
Y, B, WS, T — sand

Cayeaux-sur-Mer
B, SY, F, T, R, C, A — sand and pebbles

Cherbourg
Y, SP, T, R — sand
Musée des Beaux-Arts — new arts
complex.
Musée de la Libération, Fort du Roule —
open daily April to August; closed
Tuesday October to March.
Musée d'Histoire naturelle — open all
year, closed Tuesday and public holidays.
'Expo-nautique' Boat Show — late
May/early June.
TO: Rue du M. Foch

Ciboure
Y, D, T, G — sand and rocky

La Ciotat
SP, R, C, T, D — sand and rocky (N)
Musée d'Histoire locale, Rue des Poilus —
open Saturday evening, Sunday morning
and Wednesday afternoon. Église Notre-
Dame-de-l'Assomption — open daily July
to September. Midsummer Bonfire —
June; Michaelmas Fair and Fisherman's
Festival — September/October.
Boat trips to Ile Verte.
TO: 2 Quai Ganteaume

Collioure
Y, D, T, R — sand, pebbles and rocky
Église, Port d'Amont — open daily all
year. Château Royal — open daily (certain
rooms only) June to September.
Festival of Theâtre Midi — August;
Penitents Procession — Good Friday.
TO: Ave C. Pellatan

Concarneau
Y, SP, B, D, T, A — sand
Musée de la Pêche, Ville Close ramparts,
Rue Vauban, Ville Close — open daily
Easter to September; 9.30am to 8.30pm,
July and August.
Fête des Filets Bleus — middle weekend of
August.
TO: Quai d'Aiguillon

Le Conquet
Y, D, T — sand and rocky (N)
Boat trips for Ile d'Ouessant, Ile Molène
and Brest.
TO: (at Plougonvelin) Boulevard de la Mer
(July/August)

Contis-Plage
SP, T, R, A — sand (N)
View of Courant de Contis from Pont
Rose.

Courseulles
Y, SP, B, W, D, F, T, R, C, A, RC — sand
Musée d'Huitres (Oyster Museum) and
oyster beds (visits).
TO: 54 Rue Mer (June to September)

Coutainville
SP, B, W, D, T, R, C, A, G, RC — sand
(N)
Tuesday, Thursday and Saturday market;
Friday in Agon.
TO: Place du 28 Juillet

Le Croisic
Y, B, D, T — sand
Musée Naval, Hôtel de Ville — open
July/August.
Aquarium Côte d'Amour — open all year
except Tuesday, October to March.
TO: Place Gare

Croix-de-Vie/St Gilles
Y, SP, B, D, F, T, R, C, A — sand (N)
Boat trips to Ile d'Yeu.
TO: Place G. Kergoustin

La Croix-Valmer
SP, B, WS, F, T — sand (N)

Le Crotoy/St Valery-sur-Somme
Y, B, W, F, T, C, A — sand (N)
Chemin de fer de la baie de la Somme
(steam railway) — open weekends only,
early July to mid-September; departures
3pm and 5pm.
TO: Digue Jules Noiret

Crozon/Morgat
Y, B, D, T, R, A, F — sand and rocky (N)
Phare (Morgat) — apply to keeper.
Boat trips to Grandes Grottes.
TO: Boulevard Plage, Morgat (June to
mid-September)

Deauville
Y, SP, E, D, T, R, C, G, RC — sand
Grand-Prix horse-racing — last Sunday in
August; Antiques Festival — August; main
horse-racing season July to fourth Sunday
in August; World Polo Championships; air
trips; shooting range; daily morning
market; etc.
TO: Place Mairie

Dielette/Siouville-Hague
Y, D, F, T, R, A — sand (N)

Dieppe
Y, SP, W, F, T, R, C, A, G, RC, D — sand
and pebbles (N)
Château-musée, Square du Canada —
open daily, except Tuesday, mid-

September to June.
Musée de 19/8/1942, near Pourville —
open daily early April to mid-September.
Markets on mornings of Tuesday,
Wednesday, Thursday and all day
Saturday.
TO: Parc Jehan Ango

Dinard
Y, SP, W, F, T, R, C, A, G, B — sand and
rocky
Musée de la Mer, Promenade du Clair de
Lune — open Whitsun to mid-September.
TO: 2 Boulevard Feart

Dives-sur-Mer/Cabourg
Y, T, R, C, A, G, RC — sand (N)
International Tennis Tournament — first
fortnight in August. Horse Show — first
weekend in September.
Daily markets in summer, Wednesday and
Friday in winter.
TO: Jardins du Casino

Douarnenez/Tréboul
Y, SP, D, T, A — sand and rocky
Festival Mouez ar mor (Voice of the Sea)
— third Sunday in July and preceding
week.
TO: Rue Docteur Mével

Dunkerque
Sand
Musée des Beaux-Arts — closed Tuesday
and public holidays.
Departure of the Fishing Fleet — Shrove
Tuesday and preceding Sunday.
Fair of St Jean and International Folklore
Procession — last Sunday in June.
Pilgrimage to Nore-Dames des Dunes,
Blessing of the Sea, accompanied by
flotilla of boats — 15 August.
Collectors' Exchange Fair — early May.
TO: Beffroi, Rue Clemenceau

Elne
Cathédrale Ste Eulalie, Plateau de l'Église
— open daily; cloisters and musée closed
Tuesday and Sunday in winter.

Iles Embiez
A, D — sand and rocky
Aquarium and musée (Richard
Oceanographic Foundation) — open daily
all year except Wednesday morning in
winter; closed Christmas and New Year.
Islands reached by boat from Port du
Brusc.

Erquy
Y, F, T, R, A — sand and rocky (N)
TO: Boulevard Mer (May to September)

Étang d'Aureilhan
Y, SP, B, T, R, C, A — sand (N)
TO: Avenue M. Martin, Mimizan-Plage
(closed October)

Étang de Cazaux/Biscarosse-Plage
Y, SP, T, R, C, A, F, RC — sand (N)
TO: 19 Terrace-avenue Plage (closed
October)

Étang de Lacanau/Lacanau-Océan
Y, B, WS, T, R, C, A, G, F, X — sand (N)
Summer surfing fête.
TO: Place Europe

Étang de Léon
SP, B, F, T, C, A — sand
Boat trips down the Courant d'Huchet.

Étretat
B, F, T, G — pebbles (N)
Musée Nungesser et Coli, Falaise d'Amont
— open daily July/August; weekends only
Easter to mid-June.
Thursday morning market.
TO: Place Hôtel-de-Ville (June to mid-
September)

Èze
Ancien Château and Jardin Exotique —
open daily till sunset.
Frederick-Nietzche path — down through
pinewoods and olives to Èze-Bord-de-Mer.

La Faute-sur-Mer/L'Aiguillon
Y, SP, B, T, R, C, A — sand (N)
TO: Rond-Point fleuri (July/August)

Fécamp
Y, SP, D, F, T, R, C, A — pebbles
Musée de la Bénédictine, 110 Rue
Alexandre-le-Grand — guided tours
available Easter to mid-November.
Musée Municipal, Centre des Arts, Rue
Alexandre-Legros — guided tours daily
April to September; afternoons only rest of
year. Closed Tuesday.
Pilgrimages to Ste Trinité — Tuesday and
Thursday after Trinity Sunday.
TO: Place Bellet

Fort-Mahon-Plage
SY, T, R, C — sand
Sand-yachting races, Easter Saturday and
Sunday.

Forte la Latte
Near Cap Fréhel — guided tours available
Easter, Whitsun and June to late
September.

Fouras
Y, B, WS, D, T, C, A — sand

Château-musée, seafront — open daily
mid-June to mid-September; afternoons
only rest of year. Closed Sunday and
public holidays.
TO: Place Bugeau

Cap Fréhel
Lighthouse open daily Easter to mid-
September.

Fréjus/Fréjus-Plage
SP, Y, B, WS, D, F, T, R, C, G — sand (N)
Cité Episcopal (Cathedral Close) — guided
tours of cloisters, bapistry and museum —
daily except Tuesday and public hoildays.
Les Arènes (Roman Amphitheatre) —
open daily except Tuesdays and late
October to late November. Bullfights in
July and August.
Pagode Boudhique (Buddhist Pagoda),
2km north off N7 to Cannes — open June
to mid-September.
Parc Zoologique, 5km north— animals
and birds in natural enviroment — open all
year.
Safari de l'Esterel, near Parc Zoologique
— wild animals viewed from car — closed
Tuesdays and November to Easter.
'Bravade' — third Sunday after Easter.
TO: Place Calvini and Boulevard
Libération

Fromentine
Y, B, WS, D, F, T, R, C, A — sand (N).
Car ferry to Ile d'Yeu.

Frontignan-Plage
SP, Y, B, T, R, C — sand (N)

Giens
Y, D, R — sand and rocky.
Boat trips to Iles d'Hyères.

La Grande Motte
Y, B, WS, D, F, T, R, C, A — sand
International Festival of wind-surfing —
first fortnight of July.
Jazz Festival — end July.
TO: Place 1-Octobre-1974

Granville
Y, SP, W, D, F, T, R, C, A, G, RC — sand
and shingle (N)
Musée de vieux Granville, Grande Porte,
Haute Ville — open daily except Tuesdays
Whitsun to September; Wednesday
afternoons and weekends only the rest of
the year.
Historical granvillais (Waxworks museum)
79 Rue Couraye — guided tours available
daily mid-June to mid-September.

Pilgrimage of Seamen's Guilds,
processions — last Sunday in July.
'Pardon' of the Sea — early August.
TO: 15 Rue G. Clemenceau

Le Grau-du-Roi
SP, R, C, Y, A — sand (N)
TO: Boulevard Front-de-Mer

Gruissan
Y, SP, B, F, T, R, C — sand (N)
Musée militaire Roger Bosc, Route de
Port-la-Nouvelle — open daily; closed
November.
TO: Avenue Pech-Meynand

Guérande
St Michel gatehouse musée — open daily
Easter to September.
Église St Aubin — open all year; organ
concerts on summer Fridays.
TO: Tour St Michel (June to August)

Guéthary
D, F, T — sand

Guilvinec/St Guénolé/Lesconil
Y, D, T, R, A — sand and rocky (N)

Hardelot-Plage
SP, B, W, SY, F, T, R, C, G — sand

Le Havre
Y, SP, T, G, R, A, F — sand and pebbles
Église St Joseph, off Boulevard Francois I
— open daily.
André Malraux Musée des Beaux-Arts,
Boulevard Clemenceau — closed Tuesday
1 January, 1 May, 14 July, 11 November
and Christmas.
International Regatta — July; Festival of
the Sea — June/July; Flower parade —
August.
TO: Place de l'Hôtel de Ville

Hendaye
SP, Y, D, F, T, WS — sand
Église St Vincent, Hendaye-ville — open
all year.
TO: 12 Rue Aubépines

Honfleur
Y, SP, T, R, A — sand
Clocher de Ste Catherine, Rue des Logettes
— open daily Palm Sunday to September;
afternoons and weekend mornings
October to mid-November. Closed
Tuesdays and public holidays and mid-
November to Palm Sunday.
Musée Eugène Boudin, Place Erik Satie —
open as for Ste Catherine.
Musée de Vieux Honfleur, Rue de la Prison
— guided tours daily; closed Friday,

January, May and Christmas.
Seamen's Festival — Whit Sunday and
Monday.
TO: Chambre de Commerce, 3 Cours
Fossés

Hossegor/Capbreton
Y, SP, B, WS, D, F, T, R, C, A, G, X —
sand (N)
TO: Place Louis-Pasteur (closed October)

Houlgate
Y, SP, W, F, T, R, C, A, G — sand (N)
Fossil Museum. Music Festival.
TO: Rue Axbridge (mid-June to
September) and Boulevard Belges (closed
October)

Hourtin/Hourtin-Plage
Y, SP, B, WS, F, T, R, C, A — sand (N)
TO: Place Église, Hourtin (June to mid-
September)

Hyères/Hyères-Plage
Y, WS, D, T, R — sand (N)
Église Collégiale St Paul, Rue Ste
Catherine — open afternoons.
Musée Municipal, Place Lefevre — open
daily and weekend afternoons; closed
Tuesdays and public holidays;
experimental cinema — late August/early
September.
Gardeners' Festival — July; Flower
Parade — March.
Boat trips to Iles d'Hyères.
TO: Avenue J. Clotis

Iles d'Hyères
Y, F, T, D — sand and rocky (N)
Many waymarked walks. Boats from
Toulon, Hyères-Plage, la Tour Fondue,
Port de Mirimar, le Lavandou and
Cavalaire-sur-Mer.

Les Issambres
Y, B, WS, D, F, T, R, C — sand and rocky

Juan-les-Pins
Y, SP, B, WS, D, F, T, R, C, G — sand and
rocky
World Jazz Festival — July.
Classical Music Festival — April/May

Lac d'Hourtin — Carcans
Y, F, A

Lacanau-Océan/Étang de Lacanau
Y, B, WS, T, R, C, A, G, F, X — sand (N)
Summer surfing fête.
TO: Place Europe, Lacanau-Océan

Lancieux/St Briac-sur-Mer
Y, F, T, B, G — sand and rocky

Lannion
Brélévenez Church — open all year.
Église St Jean-du-Baly — closed Sunday
afternoons.
TO: Quai d'Aiguillon

Le Lavandou
Y, B, WS, D, T, C, G — sand (N)
Boat trips to Iles d'Hyères.
TO: Quai G. Péri

Les Lecques
Sand and rocky
Musée de Tauroentum — open 3-7pm
daily June to September; weekend
afternoons only the rest of the year.

Lesconil/Guilvinec/St Guénolé
Y, D, T, R, A — sand and rocky (N)
TO: Rue Pasteur, Lesconil

Lit-et-Mixe
SP, F, T, R

Locmariaquer
Y, B, T, F — sand

Locquirec/St Michel-en-Grève
Y, B, D, T, A — sand and rocky

Loctudy
Y, B — sand
Boat trips on River Odet and to Ile Tudy and
Iles de Glénan

Lorient
SP, T
Notre-Dame-de-Victoire, Place Alsace-
Lorraine — closed Sunday afternoons.
Boat trips for Ile de Groix and Port-Louis.
Inter-Celtic Festival — 3-12 August.

Luc-sur-Mer/Lion-sur-Mer
Y, SP, B, W, D, F, T, R, C, A, RC — sand

Madeleine, Plage de la
Sand
Utah Beach Landings Museum — open
daily except winter Sundays and public
holidays.
Commemoration of D-Day at Utah Beach
— 5-6 June.

Malo-les-Bains
Y, SP, W, SY, T, R — sand
Aquarium, Avenue du Casino — open
3-7pm, closed Tuesdays and public
holidays.
Carnival, with Gargantua and Dr
Piccolissimo — Shrove Tuesday and
preceding Sunday.

Marais-Poitevin (Parc Régional)
Coastal 'marais dessèché' and inland
'marais mouillé'; excursions in flat-
bottomed boats (*plattes*) arranged from
villages of Courçon, St Hilaire-le-Palud,
Sansais, Arçais, Damvix, la Garette,
Maillezais.
Good area for cycling.

Marennes
Y, SP, F, T, A — sand
Église St Pierre-de-Sales — belfry open
during season.

Marquenterre (Parc Ornithologique)
Waymarked footpaths; birdwatching and
photography hides amongst dunes and
marsh.

Marseillan-Plage
B, T, R, C — sand

Marseille
Y, SP, F, T, R, G, D
Musée de la Marine, Rue des Fabre —
open daily May to September; afternoons
only October to April; closed Tuesdays
and public holidays.
Musée de Vieux Marseille, Vieux Port
(north) — closed Tuesday, Wednesday
mornings and public holidays.
Musée Cantini (pottery), Rue Grignan —
closed Tuesday, Wednesday mornings.
Musée des Beaux-Arts, Palais Longchamp
— closed Tuesday, Wednesday mornings
and some public holidays.
Musée d'Histoire Naturelle, Palais
Longchamp — closed Tuesday,
Wednesday mornings. Zoo in park behind
palace — open daily.
Musée Grobet-Labadié, 140 Boulevard
Longchamp — closed Tuesday,
Wednesday mornings.
Musée des Docks Romains, 28 Place
Vivaux — closed Tuesday, Wednesday
mornings.
Château Borély, Avenue Clot-Bey —
museums closed Tuesday and Wednesday
mornings. Botanic gardens closed
weekends.
Château d'If — daily boat trips from Quai
des Belges, Vieux Port.
Boat trips to the *calanques*.
Santons Fair, La Canabière — two weeks
from first Sunday in November.
TO: 4 la Canabière

Martigues
SP, Y — sand and shingle (N)
Musée de Vieux Martigues — open daily
except Sunday morning July to September;
afternoons only October to June.
Musée des Beaux-Arts, Quartiers Ferrières

(old Customs House) — open afternoons all year, except Tuesdays.
Venetian Evening, procession of decorated boats — first Saturday in July.

Menton
Y, SP, B, WS, D, F, T, C — sand and pebbles
Musée Cocteau, Quai Napoléon — open daily except Monday, Tuesday and November.
Musée Carnolès, 3 Avenue de la Madone — old and modern paintings — closed Monday, Tuesday and public holidays.
Musée Municipal, Rue Lorédan-Larchey — open daily except Tuesday and November.
Hôtel de Ville, Rue de la République — guided tours of Jean Cocteau's murals — closed Tuesday and November.
Lemon Festival and Procession of the Golden Fruit — Shrove Tuesday week.
Festival Parade — June; Torchlight Procession — July; Lantern Parade — August; International Festival of Chamber Music, in floodlit Place de l'Église — first half of August.
TO: Palais de l'Europe, Avenue Boyer

Mers-les-Bains/Le Tréport
Y, SP, B, W, R, C, A — shingle and sand (N)

Merville-Franceville-Plage
Y, T, R, A — sand (N)
Battérie de Merville Landings Museum — open daily except Tuesday July to August.
TO: open Easter, Whitsun and mid-June to mid-September.

Meschers-sur-Gironde
Y, B, WS, T, R, C, A — sand
TO: Place Verdun (mid-June to mid-September)

Mimizan-Plage/Étang d'Aureilhan
Y, SP, B, T, R, C, A — sand (N)
Fête de la Mer — May.
TO: Avenue M. Martin (closed October)

Miramar
Y, SP, B, WS, D, G — sand

Monaco/Monte Carlo
Y, SP, B, WS, D, F, T, C, G — sand, pebbles and rocky
Musée Océanographique, Avenue St Martin — open daily.
Musée d'Anthropologie Préhistorique, Boulevard du Jardin Exotique — open daily.
Jardin Exotique and Grottes de

l'Observatoire — open daily to sunset.
Palais du Prince, including Musée Napoléon — guided tours of palace daily July to September; museum closed Monday and January.
Museum of Dolls and Automata, Musée National, Avenue Princess Grace — guided tours daily; closed public holidays.
Casino — open 10am-4am.
Feast of St Dévote — 27 January; Monte Carlo Rally — 27 January; Monaco Grand Prix — May; International TV Festival — February; International Tennis Championships — April; Fireworks Festival — July/August; World Amateur Theatre Festival — August/September; Monégasque National Fête — November; International Circus Festival — December.
TO: 2 Boulevard des Moulins

Mont-St-Michel
The Abbey — guided tours daily during summer; closed Tuesday during winter and public holidays.
Musée historical du Mont — open daily, guided tours available April to October.
Concerts of sixteenth- to twentieth-century music during July and August.
Festival of Archangel Gabriel, Mass — Sunday nearest 29 September.
Floodlighting every night July/August.
Religious Festival and Folk dancing — end of May.

Montalivet-les-Bains
T, R, C, A — sand (N)

Monte Carlo — see Monaco

Morbihan, Golfe du
Vast inland sea, dotted with islands, many inhabited. Sailing, windsurfing, fishing etc. Excursions of varying length arranged from Port-Navalo, Locmariaquer, Auray and Vannes. Roads also encircle the gulf.

Morgat/Crozon
Y, B, D, T, R, A, F — sand and rocky (N)
Phare, Morgat — open daily, apply to keeper.
Boat trips to Grandes Grottes from port.
TO: Boulevard Plage (June to mid-September)

Morlaix
Y, A
Musée, Place des Jacobins — open daily; closed Tuesday except August and some public holidays.

Les Moutiers
Église (eleventh-century) — open all year
except afternoons August.

La Napoule/Théoule-sur-Mer
Y, B, WS, D, F, G — sand and pebbles
Château de la Napoule, Henry Clews
Foundation — guided tours afternoons
except Tuesday; closed three weeks in
December.

Narbonne-Plage
Y, B, WS, D, T, R, C — sand
TO: Boulevard Méditerranée
(July/August)

Nauzan/Pontaillac/Royan
Y, SP, B, WS, D, T, R, C, A, RC — sand
and rocky

Nice
Y, SP, B, WS, D, F, T, R, C — pebbles
Musée Matisse, Arena Ville (including
adjacent Roman remains), 164 Avenue des
Arènes-de-Cimiez — guided tours, audio-
visual displays; closed Sunday mornings,
Monday, public holidays and November.
Musée National Marc Chagall, Avenue Dr
Ménard — open daily except Tuesday.
Musée Naval, Tour Bellanda, Parc du
Château — open daily except Tuesday,
public holidays and mid-November to
mid-December.
Musée d'Histoire Naturelle, 60 Boulevard
Risso — open daily except Tuesday, public
holidays and August.
Musée Masséna, 65 Rue de France —
closed Monday, public holidays and
November.
Musée de Malacologie (molluscs), 3 Cours
Saleya — closed Sunday, Monday and
some public holidays.
Musée des Beaux-Arts (Jules Cheret), 32
Avenue des Baumettes — open daily
except Monday, public holidays and
October.
Chapelle de la Miséricorde, Place Pierre
Gautier — apply to Tourist Office.
Musée Terra Amata, 25 Boulevard Carnot
(prehistoric man) — closed Monday;
English commentaires available.
Carnival, fireworks — Shrove Tuesday;
Battle of Flowers — day after Ash
Wednesday; International Book Fair and
Dog Show — April; Music Festival —
May; Grand Jazz Parade in Cimiez
Gardens — August; Autumn Music
Festival — October — and others!
Boat trips to many destinations on Riviera
and to Corsica.

TO: 32 Rue de l'Hôtel des Postes and 13
Place Masséna

Ile de Noirmoutier
Y, B, R, C, A — sand (N)
Château, Noirmoutier-en-l'Ile (musée) —
open February to October; closed
Tuesday.
Musée d'Art et de Tradition, la Guérinière
— open daily in season.

Notre-Dame-de-Mont
SP, F, T, C — sand (N)
TO: in town (mid-June to mid-September)

Ile d'Oléron
Y, B, WS, F, T, R, C — sand (N)
Musée de l'Ile d'Oléron, Rue Pierre-Loti,
St Pierre-d'Oléron — open Monday-
Saturday, mid-June to mid-September-
Lanterne des Morts, Place Camile-
Memain, St Pierre-d'Oléron.
TO: Place République, Château d'Oléron;
Place Gambetta, St Pierre-d'Oléron;
Carrefour du Port, St Trojan-les-Bains

Ouistreham/Riva-Bella
Y, SP, B, W, T, R, C — sand
Musée du No 4 Commando et 1st Special
Service Brigade — open weekends, April
to October.
TO: Jardins du Casino (June to mid-
September)

Paimpol
Y, SP, D, T, A — sand and rocky
'Pardon' of Notre-Dame-de-Bonne-
Nouvelle — second Sunday in December.

Palavas-les-Flots
Y, B, WS, D, T, R, C — sand
TO: Hôtel de Ville

La Palmyre
Zoo open daily all year

Paramé — see St Malo

Parc Ornithologique de Teich
Near Arcachon — open daily March to
September; weekends and public holidays
only the rest of the year.

Perros-Guirec
Y, SP, B, T, F, A — sand
Boat trips to Sept Iles from Trestraou
Beach, June to mid-September.
'Pardon' of Notre-Dame-de-la-Clarté —
15 August.
TO: 21 Place Hôtel-de-Ville

Piriac-sur-Mer
Y, SP, D, T, R — sand

Pont-Aven
A, F
Musée de la ville de Pont-Aven — open
daily mid-June to mid-September.
Chapelle de Trémalo, off D24 uphill to
right — key at farm out of season.
Festival of the Golden Gorse — third
Sunday in July
TO: Place Mairie (June to mid-September)

Pont-l'Abbé
Y, SP, T, R, A — sand
Musée Bigouden, Rue du Château — open
daily June to mid-September; closed
Sunday and public holidays.
'Pardon' of Notre-Dame-des-Carmes —
Sunday after 15 July; 'Pardon' of Notre-
Dame-de-Tréminou, 2km west — fourth
Sunday in September.
TO: Château

Pontaillac/Nauzan/Royan
Y, SP, B, WS, D, T, R, C, A, RC — sand
and rocky

Pornic
Y, SP, WS, F, T, R, C, A, G — sand
TO: Mairie (February to October)

Pornichet
Y, SP, B, D, T, R — sand
TO: Place A. Briand (closed December)

Port Bacarès/Port Leucate
Y, SP, T, R, C, D, WS — sand (N)
TO: Front de Mer, Port Bacarès

Port Camargue
WS, Y, T, R, A, B, D — sand

Port-en-Bessin
Y — sand

Port-Grimaud
Y — sand (N)

Port Leucate/Port Bacarès
Y, SP, T, R, C, D, WS — sand (N)
TO: Front de Mer, Port Bacarès

Port-Louis
Y, B, T — sand
Musée de la Marine — guided tours
available daily; closed Tuesday, public
holidays and November to mid-December.

Port-la-Nouvelle
Y, B, WS, D, T, R — sand (N)
Réserve africaine de Sigean, signposted off
N9 — open daily.

Port-Vendres
Y, D, — sand, pebbles and rocky (N)

Portbail
Y, SP, T, R, C — sand

St Cross Fair at Lessay — 9-12 September

Le Pouldu
Y, A, T — sand
TO: Boulevard Plages

Le Pouliguen
Y, D, T — sand and rocky
Église Ste Anne-et-St Julien, Place Mgr
Freppel — open June to October.

Préfailles
Y, F, T — sand and rocky (N)
TO: Grande-Rue

Pyla-sur-Mer
WS, D, F, T, C — sand (N)

Quend-Plage-les-Pins
W, SY, T, R, C, A — sand (N)
Parc Ornithologique du Marquenterre —
open daily April to early November.
TO: Pavillion d'accueil

Quiberon
Y, SP, B, D, T, R, F — sand and rocky (N)
Phare, Port Maria — open daily June to
August.
Boat trips for Belle-Ile, Ile de Houat and
Ile de Hoedic.
TO: 7 Rue de Verdun

Quimper
Cathédrale — open all year.
Musée des Beaux-Arts, Rue Élie Fréron —
open daily May to mid-September except
Tuesday and public holidays; afternoons
only mid-September to April.
Musée, adjacent to south side of cathedral
— open daily except Tuesday, mid-
September to June and public holidays.
Poterie, south-west of town — closed
Saturday afternoons, Sunday, public
holidays and last three weeks of August.
Great Festival of Cornouaille — fourth
Sunday in July and preseeding two days.
TO: 3 Rue du Rue-Gradlon

Rance Tidal Power Scheme
Between St Malo and Dinard — open
daily.

Rayol
B, T, C — sand (N)

Ile de Ré
Y, B, WS, D, F, T, R, C, A — sand (N)
Musée Naval et E. Cognacq, St Martin-de-
Ré — open daily mid-June to mid-
September; afternoons only rest of the
year. Closed alternate Tuesday in season,
Monday and Tuesday in winter; also
closed October and March and public
holidays.

Riva-Bella/Ouistreham — see Ouistreham

Rochefort
Y, T, A, RC
Maison de Loti, Rue Pierre Loti — guided
visits daily, afternoons only on Sunday and
public holidays; closed Sunday and
Monday mornings, also Tuesdays in
winter.
Musée Municipal des Beaux-Arts, Avenue
Général de Gaulle — closed Sunday,
Monday and public holidays.
Musée Naval, Hôtel de Cheusses — closed
public holidays.

La Rochelle
Y, SP, D, T, R, C, A — sand
L'aquarium R. Coutant, la Ville en Bois —
open daily.
Tour St Nicolas — open daily in summer,
afternoons in winter; closed Tuesday and
public holidays.
Tour de la Chaîne — tower itself not open
to public but model of Old la Rochelle in
Salon-de-Thé below.
Tour de la Lanterne — open daily in
summer, afternoons only in winter; closed
Tuesday and public holidays (combined
tickets available with Tour St Nicolas).
Hôtel de Ville, Grande-Rue des Merciers
— open daily Easter to September,
afternoons rest of the year.
Musée Lafaille, Rue Albert Premier —
open daily in summer, afternoons in
winter; closed Monday.
Musée du Nouveau Monde, off Rue
Gargoulleau — open daily except Tuesday.
Musée des Beaux-Arts, Rue Gargoulleau
— open daily except Tuesday and Sunday
morning.
Musée d'Orbigny, Rue St Côme — open
daily except Tuesday and Sunday morning.
Boat trips to Ile d'Aix, Ile de Ré, Ile
d'Oléron and along River Charente —
embark Quai du Carénage.
TO: 10 Rue Fleurian

Ronce-les-Bains
Y, WS, F, T, R, C — sand
TO: Place Brochard

Roquebrune-Cap-Martin
Y, SP, B, F, T, R — pebbles and rocky
Donjon (castle keep) — open daily; closed
November, and Friday in winter. Guided
tours available mid-July to August.
Procession of Entombment of Christ —
Good Friday evening.
Procession of the Passion — afternoon of 5
August.

Coastal path from Promenade Le
Corbusier, Cap-Martin to Monte-Carlo.

Roscoff
Y, A, T, R — sand, pebbles and rocky
Aquarium Charles Perez, Place Lacaze-
Duthiers, near port — open afternoons
April to May; daily June to mid-
September.
Boat trips to Ile de Batz from long jetty.

Rotheneuf
W, T, A, D, T, R — sand (N)
Aquarium — open daily.

Royan/Nauzan/Pontaillac
Y, SP, B, WS, D, T, R, C, A, RC — sand
and rocky
Église Notre-Dame, Place Notre-Dame —
open all year, music recitals July/August.
Fêtes-de-la-Mer — last weekend in June.
Car ferry (Bac) to Pointe de Grave —
frequent sailings from port.
TO: Palais des Congrès

Les Sables d'Olonne
Y, SP, B, WS, D, T, R, C, A, RC —
sand (N)
Musée de l'Abbaye Ste Croix, Rue de
Verdun — open daily mid-June to
September; afternoons only rest of the
year. Closed Monday and October.
TO: Place Navarin

Ste Anne d'Auray
Chartreuse d'Auray (Carthusian
Monastery), off D768 to Pontivy —
closed first two weeks in September.
Historial de Ste Anne (diorama) —
guided tours 9am-7pm May to
September.
'Grand Pardon' — 26 July.

Ste Anne-le-Palud
T — sand
'Grand Pardon' — last Sunday in
August.

St Aygulf
Y, B, WS, T, R — sand and pebbles (N)
TO: Place Poste

St Brévin-Les-Pins-l'Océan
Y, SP, B, W, D, F, T, R, C — sand
TO: 10 Rue Église

St Briac-sur-Mer/Lancieux
Y, F, T, B, G — sand and rocky
TO: 49 Grande Rue (Easter, Whitsun and
mid-June to mid-September)

St Brieuc/St Laurent-de-la-Mer
Y, W, F, T, A — sand and rocky (N)
Cathédrale St Etienne, Place Général de

Gaulle — open all year.
'Pardon' of Notre-Dame-de-l'Espérance
— 31 May.
Michaelmas Fair — 29 September.
TO: Gare Routière

St Cast-le-Guildo
Y, SP, W, F, T, R, C, A, B, D — sand
and rocky
TO: Place Général de Gaulle

St Cyprien-Plage
Y, SP, D, F, T, R, G — sand (N)
TO: Place Méditerranée

St George-de-Didonne
Y, B, WS, T, R, A — sand and rocky
TO Boulevard Michelet (February to
September)

St Gilles-Croix-de-Vie
Y, SP, B, D, F, T, R, C, A — sand (N)
Boat trips to Ile d'Yeu.
TO: Place G. Kergoustin

St Girons-Plage
R, C, SP, T, X — sand (N)

St Guénolé/Guilvinec/Lesconil
Y, D, T, R, A — sand and rocky (N)
Museum of Finistère Prehistory, St
Guénolé — open daily June to
September; rest of the year apply to
caretaker.
TO: Place des Écoles, St Guénolé (July/
August)

St Jean-Cap-Ferrat
Y, B, WS, F — sand, pebbles and rocky
Musée Ile de France, Fondation Ephrussi
de Rothschild, Boulevard Denis Séméria
— open afternoons only; closed Monday,
public holidays and November. Gardens
open mornings.
Zoo, Plage de Passable — open all year.
Promenade Maurice Rouvier and Pointe
St Hospice — walks on cape.
Venetian Festival — August.

St Jean-de-Luz/Ciboure
Y, D, T, G — sand and rocky
Église St Jean-Baptiste, Rue Garat —
open all year.
Maison Louis XIV, Quai de l'Enfant —
open daily July and August; closed
Sunday mornings June and September.
Closed during winter.
La Rhune mountain railway, from Col de
St Ignace — open Easter and May to
September. 1 hour return.
Festival of St John — June; Tuna

Festival — July; Music Festival — first
fortnight in September.
TO: Place du Maréchal-Foch, St Jean-de-
Luz

St Jean-de-Monts
Y, SP, B, WS, T, R, C, RC — sand
TO: Palais des Congrès, Avenue Forêt

St Malo/Paramé
Y, SP, T, A, G, D — sand
Aquarium, Porte St Thomas — open
9am-11pm July to mid-September, 10am-
6pm rest of the year.
Musée de St Malo, castle keep — open
daily, closed Tuesday in winter.
TO: Esplanade St Vincent

Stes Maries-de-la-Mer
SP, R, C, Y, A — sand (N)
Église — open daily all year; crypt closed
during services.
Gypsy Pilgrimages, religious ceremonies,
festivities — 23-4 May and penultimate
Sunday in October.
TO: Avenue Van Gogh

Ste Maxime
Y, B, D, T, R, C, G — sand
Museum of Mechanical Instruments and
Recording Machines, St Donat Park,
10km north — guided tours Easter and
May to September, daily except Tuesday.
Closed rest of the year.

St Michel-en-Grève/Locquirec
Y, B, D, T, A — sand and rocky

St Nazaire
SP, T, G — sand and rocky (N)
Terrasse Panoramique near port
submarine exit — open daily, June to
September.
TO: Place du Change

St Palais-sur-Mer
SP, Y, F, T, R, C, G, RC — sand (N)
TO: Residence St Palais (closed October)

St Pierre-sur-Mer
R, F — sand (N)

St Pol-de-Léon
Ancienne Cathédrale, Place Budes-de-
Guebriant — open all year.
Chapelle du Kreisker, Place Michel
Colombe — open afternoons Easter,
daily June-September.
TO: Place Evêche

St Quay-Portrieux
Y, SP, B, T, A — sand and rocky

Notre-Dame-de-l'Espérance, 2km south
— open every afternoon July/August;
Sunday afternoons only rest of year.
TO: Place Verdun

St Raphaël
SP, Y, B, WS, D, F, C, G — sand
Musée d'Archéologie Sous-Marine, Rue
des Templiers — open daily except
Tuesday mid-June to mid-September;
daily except Sunday rest of the year.
Église et Musée St Raphaël, Rue des
Templiers — open same times as
underwater archaeology museum next
door (see above).
Procession of the Sea — August
TO: Rue W. Rousseau

St Servan-sur-Mer
Y, SP, W, F, T, R, D — sand and rocky
Tour Solidor, Musée International du
Long-Cours Cap Hornier — guided tours
daily June to September; afternoons only
rest of the year. Closed Tuesday in
winter.
Parc des Corbières — open daily.

St Tropez
Y, SP, B, WS, D, T, C — sand (N)
Musée l'Annonciade, off Quai de l'Épi —
open daily except Tuesday, public
holidays and November.
Musée Naval, in citadel keep — open
daily except Thursday, public holidays
and mid-November to mid-December.
Boat trips to Port-Grimaud, Ste Maxime,
and (summer only) Iles d'Hyères and St
Raphael.
'Bravades' on 16-17 May and 15 June.

St Vaast-la-Hougue
Y, D, F, T, R, C, A — sand and pebbles
TO: Quai Vauban (mid-June to mid-
September)

St Valery-en-Caux
Y, SP, F, T, R, A — sand and pebbles
Friday market, also summer Sunday
mornings.
TO: Place Hôtel-de-Ville

St Valery-sur-Somme/Le Crotoy
Y, B, W, F, T, C, A — sand (N)
Chemin de fer de la baie de la Somme
(steam railway) — open weekends July to
mid-September. Departures 3pm and
5pm.
TO: 23 Rue Ferté (school holidays only)

Sables-d'Or-Les-Pins
T, F — sand and rocky (N)

Les Sablettes
Y, B — sand (N)

Salses
Le Fort — open daily (limited hours in
winter); closed Tuesday and public
holidays.

Sanary-sur-Mer
Y, D, T, C, A — sand and rocky
Chapelle de Notre-Dame-de-Beausset —
open afternoons July to early September;
Sunday afternoons only rest of the year.

Sète
Y, D, SP, T, A — sand and rocky
Musée Paul Valéry, Cimitière Marin,
Grand Rue Haute — open daily except
Tuesday and public holidays.
Festival du Theâtre — August.
Fêtes de St Louis — *joutes nautiques*,
fireworks, etc — last five days in August.
TO: 22 Quai d'Alger

Siouville-Hague/Dielette
Y, D, F, T, R, A — sand (N)

Six-Fours-Les-Plages
SP, Y, B, WS, D, F, T, R, C — sand
Ancienne Collégiale St Pierre — open
weekend afternoons.

Soulac-sur-Mer
SP, T, R, C, F — sand (N)
Basilica Notre-Dame-de-la-Fin-des-Terres
— open all'year.
TO: Place Marché (closed October)

Talmont-St Hilaire
Musée automobile de Vendée (vintage
cars), on D949 — open daily April to
September.

Taussat
Y, WS, D, T — sand

Toulon
Y, SP, T, G
Musée Naval, in Maritime Prefecture,
Quai Stalingrad — open daily except
Tuesday and public holidays.
Musée d'Art et Archéologie, Boulevard
du Maréchal Leclerc — closed Monday,
Thursday and public holidays.
Tour Royal, Pointe de la Mitre — guided
tours daily March-October; closed
Monday.
Musée d'Histoire Naturelle, Boulevard du
Maréchal Leclerc — open daily.

Mémorial National du Débarquement, Tour Beaumont, Mont Faron — open daily all year. Access by road or aerial cableway every 10 minutes.
Zoo, Mont Faron — open daily in season; closed mornings and Thursday in winter.
Boat trips to Iles d'Hyères, Porquerolles, Les Sablettes, St Mandrier, La Seyne, and round Inner Roadstead.
Festival of the Sea — June; Cartoon Film Festival and Veteran Car Rally — May; Flower Festival — April; International Dance Festival — July; Festival of Circus Artists — July/August; Santons Fair — November.
TO: Rue Léon Blum, la Seyne

Le Touquet-Paris-Plage
Y, SP, B, SY, F, T, R, G, RC — sand (N)
Phare — open daily.
Motorcycling weekend — mid-February; -Art, Crafts and Music Festivals — August; Flower Carnival — August; festivals and tournaments all year.
TO: Place de l'Hermitage

La Tranche-sur-Mer
Y, WS, T, R, C — sand (N)
Floral Displays — March and April
TO: Place Liberté

Trébeurden
Y, SP, D, T, R, A, F — sand and rocky (N)
TO: Place Crech Héry (closed November-December)

Tréboul/Douarnenez
Y, SP, D, T, A — sand and rocky
Festival Mouez ar mor (Voice of the Sea) — third Sunday in July and preceding week.
TO: Rue Docteur Mével, Douarnenez

La Tremblade
Y, F, T, R, C, A, RC — sand and rocky
TO: Place Ste Anne

Trégastel Plage
Y, B, D, T, R, F, A — sand and rocky
TO: Place Ste Anne

Tréguier
Y, SP, T, A
Cathédrale St Tugdual — open all year.
Maison de Renan, Rue Renan — open Easter to October.
Trégor hand-weaving workshop, Rue Renan — open mid-June to early September; visits available rest of the year except Sunday and 20 December to 10

January.
'Pardon' of St Yves — 19 May.

Le Tréport/Mers-Les-Bains
Y, SP, B, W, R, C, A — shingle and sand (N)
Daily markets except Sunday and Monday.
TO: Esplanade Plage

La Trinité-sur-Mer
Y, B, D, T, A — sand
Feast of the Trinity — 9-11 June.

Trouville
Y, SP, T, C, A, RC — sand
Daily markets Whitsun-September; Wednesday and Sunday in winter.
TO: Place du Maréchal Foch

La Turballe
Y, T — sand and pebbles (N)
TO: Place de Gaulle

La Turbie
Trophée des Alpes and Musée — open daily all year; guided tours mid-July to mid-September.

Le Val-André
Y, SP, B, F, T, R, A — sand and rocky (N)
TO: 1 Cours Winston Churchill

Vallauris
Musée National Picasso — open daily all year.
Galerie Madoura, ceramics workshop — closed weekends.
Musée Municipal, Château de Vallauris, Place de la Libération — exhibition of ceramics — open daily all year.

Valras-Plage
Y, B, WS, T, R, A, C — sand
TO: Place R. Cassin

Vannes
Cathédrale St Pierre, town centre — open all year; treasure open daily from mid-June to mid-September. Closed Sunday and public holidays.
Musée Archéologie, Château Gaillard — closed Sunday and public holidays.
Musée de l'Huitre, Rue Thiers — guided tours available daily; closed weekends and public holidays.
Boat trips for Golfe du Morbihan.
Festival of Arvor (in front of ramparts) — 15 August.

Viereville-sur-Mer
SP, W, D, T, R — sand
Musée Omaha — open Easter to September.

Veulettes-sur-Mer
SP, W, F, T — pebbles

Vieux-Boucau-Les-Bains
B, F, T, R, C — sand (N)
TO: Port d'Albret

Villefranche
Y, B, D, F, T — sand
Chapelle St Pierre, Port des Pêcheurs —
closed Friday from mid-November to mid-
December.
Musée Volti, scupltures — closed
November.

Villers-sur-Mer
Y, W, T, R, C — sand

Villerville
T, C — sand
TO: Rue Maréchal-Leclerc (closed
October)

Wimereux
Y, F, T, G — sand and pebbles

Ile d'Yeu
Y, WS, D, F, T, C — sand (N)
Musée-memorial Maréchal Petain, Port-
Joinville — open daily.
Grand-Phare, near Cadouere — guided
visits available except during storms or
maintenance work.
Festival of the Sea — May.
TO: tel: 58 32 58

BIBLIOGRAPHY

Ardagh, John, *France in the 80s* (Penguin
1982). Wide-ranging, authoritative
discussion of French society.

Shell Guide to France (Michael Joseph,
1984). Comprehensive gazetteer.

Titchmarsh, P. and H., *Exploring France*
(Jarrold, 1984). Illustrated pocket
companion.

Guide l'Officiel du Littoral Nudiste
(Éditions de Petit Bois, 1983). Guide to
European naturist beaches in French.

Baedeker's France (AA, Jarrold and
Baedeker, Stuttgart, 1984). Background
and gazetteer.

Michelin Camping Caravaning France
(1984). Handbook recommending
campsites.

Owen, Charles, *Just across the Channel*
(Cadogan Books, 1983). Guide to day-trips
and short holidays in northern France.

Michelin Green Guides to Nord de la
France, Normandy, Brittany, Côte de
l'Atlantique, Pyrénées, Causses, Provence
and Côte d'Azur.

Tingey, F., *The North of France* (Spurbooks,
1978). Picardy and Artois.

Helias, P.J., *Images of Brittany* (Éditions
Jos le Doare, 1983). Colour-illustrated
booklet.

Myhill, Henry, *Brittany* (Faber and Faber,
1969). Its history and people.

Lands, Neil, *The Visitor's Guide to Brittany*
(Moorland Publishing, 1984). Detailed
tourist guide.

Lands, Neil, *Languedoc-Roussillon*
(Spurbooks, 1976). History, people and
places.

Savage, George, *The Languedoc* (Barrie
and Jenkins, 1975). History, architecture.

Higham, Roger, *Provencal Sunshine* (Dent,
1969). A personal journey.

Brangham, Norman, *The Visitor's Guide to
the South of France* (Moorland Publishing,
1984). Detailed tourist and background
guide.

Howarth, Patrick, *When the Riviera was
ours* (Routledge & Kegan Paul, 1977).
Social and literary history.

Lyall, Archibald, *The Companion Guide to
the South of France* (Collins, 1978). Art and
architectural sites, history.

Index

(Page numbers in italics refer
to illustrations)

Aber Benoît, 44
Aber Ildut, 45
Aber Wrac'h, L', 44, 45, 138
Abers, the, 43-4, 45
Adour, River, 83, 90-1
Agay, 125, 127, 138
Agde, 105, 138
Agon, 29
Aigues-Mortes, 105-6, 108, 110, 138
Aiguillon-sur-Mer, L', 72, 73, 138
Aix, Ile d', 77-8, 138
Albères hills, 97
Alderney Race, 28
Alignements de Lagatjar, 48
Alignements, prehistoric, 58, 59
Alpes-Maritimes, 129-30
Ambès, 83
Ambleteuse, 14
American Military Cemetary, 25, 27
Andernos-les-Bains, 87, 138
Anglet, 91
Anse de Bénodet, 51
Anse de l'Aiguillon, 73, 75
Anse de Dinan, 48
Anse de Paimpol, 39
Anse de Vauville, 29
Anthéor, 125, 138
Antibes, 127-8, 130, 138
Aquitaine, 8, 9, 83-4
Arcachon, 83, 85, 87, 138
Arçais, 74
Arès, 85-6
Argelès-Plage, 97, 138
Argelès-sur-Mer, 98
Arles, 112
Armorique, Parc Régional de, 45, 49
Arromanches-les-Bains, 25-6, 138
Ars-en-Ré, 78
Aspremont, 130
Atlantic, 9-10, 20, 44, 46, 51, 54, 57, 63, 71, 74-5, 78-9, 83, 86, 92-3, 96, 106
Auberville plateau, 23
Audenge, 87
Audierne, 49, 138
Audinghen, 14
Audresselles, 14, 138
Auge, the, 25
Aulne, River, 47
Auray, 59-61

Avranches, 31-2, 138
Ay, River, 29

Bacarès, Le, 100
Baie d'Amour, 66
Baie des Anges, 44, 128
Baie d'Arguenon, 38
Baie d'Audierne, 50
Baie d'Authie, 17
Baie de Bourgneuf, 69
Baie de Douarnenez, 49
Baie d'Ecalgrain, 28, 32
Baie de la Frênaye, 38
Baie de Kernic, 44
Baie du Mont-St-Michel, 31, 35
Baie de Quiberon, 57
Baie de Somme, 18
Baie de St Brieuc, 39
Bandol, 117-18, 138
Bangor, 58
Banyuls-sur-Mer, 96, 98, 139
Barfleur, 27, 32, 139
Barneville-Carteret, 29, 30, 32, 139
Bassin d'Arcachon, 86-8
Bassin de Thau, 105
Batz, Ile de, 44, 63
Batz-sur-Mer, 65, 67, 139
Baule, La, 23, 62, 65, 67, 75, 139
Baule-les-Pins, La, 66
Bayonne, 90-1, 139
Beaulieu, 132, 135, 139
Beauvallon-Plage, 123, 139
Beauvoir-sur-Mer, 69
Beg-Meil, 51
Belisaire, 87
Belle-Ile, 57, 58, 69, 77, 139
Bélon, 55
Bendor, Ile de, 117, 139
Benerville, 23
Bénodet, 51, 55, 139
Berk-Plage, 17, 139
Bernerie-en-Retz, 69
Berneval, 18
Berre, Étang de, 113
Beuil, 130
Biarritz, 75, 85, 90, 91-2, 93, 95, 139
Bidart, 93, 139
Bidassoa, River, 95
Biganos, 87
Bigouden, costume, 51, 52
Billiers, 62
Biot, 128

Biscarosse,Plage, 85, 88, 139
Biscay, Bay of, 51
Blériot-Plage, 14, 139
Blonville-sur-Mer, 23, 139
Bonne Anse, 80
Bordeaux, 75, 81, 83, 86-7
Bormes-les-Mimosas, 121, 139
Boulogne-sur-Mer, 14, 15, 16, 55, 139
Boulouris, 125, 139
Bourgneuf-en-Retz, 69, 140
Brague, La, 128
Bray-Dunes, 11
Bréhat, Ile de, 40, 140
Bresle, River, 18
Brest, 9, 46-7, 55, 140
Brière, Parc Règional de, 63, 67, 140
Brighton, 18
Brignogan-Plage, 44, 140
Brittany, 8-9, 30, 33-5, 37-8, 43-5, 49, 55-6, 59, 62, 80

Cabo Higuer, 95
Cabourg, 24, 140
Caen Canal, 24
Cagnes-sur-Mer, 128, 130, 140
Cailland, La, 82
Calais, 12, 13, 15-16, 140
Calanques, the, 115, 116, 119
Callelongue, 115
Calvados Coast, 24, 26
Camaret-sur-Mer, 47, 48, 56, 140
Camargue, the, 29, 69, 97, 106-8, 110, 112, 114, 120, 140
Cambe, La, German War Cemetary, 26
Canal de Caronte, 113
Canal du Midi, 101
Cancale, 34-5, 140
Canche, River, 16
Canet-Plage, 99, 107, 140
Cannes, 9, 23, 26, 126, 130, 135, 140
Cap l'Abeille, 96
Cap de l'Aigle, 117
Cap d'Agde, Le, 103-4, 105, 107, 141
Cap d'Antifer, 20
Cap Béar, 96
Cap Balnc-Nez, 13, 14
Cap Bréhat, 39
Cap Canaille, 115-16

Cap Cerbère, 96, *98*
Cap de la Chèvre, 48
Cap Croisette, 115
Cap Ferrat, 131
Cap Ferret, 87-8, 141
Cap de Flamanville, 29
Cap Fréhel, 35, *38*, 39, 43, 143
Cap Gris-Nez, 13-14
Cap de la Hague, 28, 32
Cap de l'Homy-Plage, 90
Cap Hornu, 18
Cap Réderis, 96
Capbreton, 91, 141
Carantec, 43, 56, 141
Carentan, 26
Carac, 56, 58, *59*, 141
Carnac-Plage, 59
Carnon-Plage, 106, 141
Carolles-Plage, 31, 141
Carro, 114-15
Carteret, 29, *30*, 32, 139, 141
Cassis, 115-16, 141
Caux plateau, 19, 21
Cavalaire-sur-Mer, 117, 120, 122, 141
Cavalière, 121, 141
Cayeaux-sur-Mer, 18, 141
Champagné, 74
Channel Islands, 29, 36-7
Charente-Maritime, 79
Charente, River, 78
Château d'If, 114, *115*
Château d'Oléron, Le, 79
Chaume, La, 71-2
Chausey, Iles, 31
Cherbourg, 27-9, 32, 141
Cherrueix, 34
Ciboure, 93, 141
Ciotat, La, 115, 117, 141
Cognac, 82
Colleville, 25
Collioure, 97-8, *99-100*, 141
Concarneau, 53, *54*, 55-6, 141
Conquet, Le, 45, 141
Contis-Plage, 90, 141
Corniche Armorique, 43
Corniche Basque, 95
Corniche Bretonne, 42-3
Corniche des Crêtes, 115, *116*
Corniche Normande, 23
Corniche Vendéen, 71
Côte d'Albarte, 19, 21
Côte d'Argent, 85-6, 88, 91
Côte d'Azur, 8-10, 113-14, 116, 121, 126, 128-9, 136
Côte Basque, 93
Côte de Beauté, 81-2
Côte d'Emeraud, 35, 37, 39
Côte Fleurie, 23
Côte de Grace, 21
Côte de Jade, 68
Côte d'Opale, 14

Côte Vermeille, 96-8
Contentin Peninsula, 9, 24, 26-7, 29, 32, 39
Côtes-du-Nord, Department, 39, 43
Couarde-sur-Mer, 78
Courant de Contis, 90
Courant d'Huchet, 90
Courçon, 74
Courseulles-sur-Mer, 25, 142
Cousenon, River, 32-4
Coutainville, 29-30, 32, 142
Coutances, 29
Crach, River, 59
Cran-aux-Oeufs, 14
Crau plain, the, 113
Criel-Plage, 18
Criqueboeuf, 23
Croisic, Le, 63, 67, 142
Croix-de-Vie, 70, 141
Croix-Valmer, La, 121-2, 142
Crotoy, Le, 17-18, 21, 142
Crozon, 49, 142
Crozon Peninsula, 46-7

Damgan, 62
Damvix, 74
Dannery, 28
De Panne, 11
Deauville, 21, *22*, 23, 66, 142
Denneville, 29
Dielette, 29, 142
Dieppe, 18-21, 142
Dinan, 36-7
Dinard, 36-7, 39, 142
Dives, River, 24
Dives-sur-Mer, 23, 142
Doëlan, 55
Dol-de-Bretagne, 34
Dossen, River, 43
Douarnenez, 49, *50-1*, 56, 142
Douve, River, 26
Douville, 31
Douvres-la-Delivrande, 25
Dramont, Le, 125
Dune du Pilat, 88
Dunes-de-Varreville, Les, 27
Dunkerque, 11-12, 142

Elle, 74
Elne, 98-9, 142
Embiez, Iles, 117-18, 142
En-Vau-Calanque, 115
English Channel, 9, 13, 23, 28, 37
Erquy, 39, 142
Escalles, 14
Escoublac, 66
Estaque, L', 114
Estaque, Chaîne de, L', 114
Esterel, Massif de, L', 125
Étang d'Aureilhan, 89, 143
Étang d'Ayrolle, 101
Étang de Bages et de Sigean, 101

Étang de Berre, 113-14
Étang de Biscarosse et de Parentis, 89
Étang de Canet, 99
Étang de Cazaux et de Sanguinet, 89, 139, 143
Étang de Gruissan, 101
Étang de Lacanau, 86, 143
Étang de Léon, 90, 143
Étang de Leucate et de Salses, 100-1
Étang de Mateille, 102
Étang de l'Or, 107
Étang de Pinsolle, 90
Étang de Ponant, 107
Étang de Soustons, 90
Étang de Vaccarès, 110
Etaples, 17
Etier de Sud, 69
Étretat, 19-20, 142
Eyre, River, 87
Èze, *129*, 131-2, 142

Faou, Le, 47
Faute-sur-Mer, La, 73, 143
Fécamp, *19*, 143
Ferrat, Cap, 131
Ferret, Cap, 87-8, 141
Festival of Cornouaille, 53, 55
Figuerolles calanque, 117
Finistère, 43-4, 50-1, 55
Forêt de la Coubre, 80
Forêt de Longeville, 72
Forêt d'Olonne, 71
Forêt de la Tremblade, 79
Fort-Carrés, 128
Fort de la Hougue, 27
Fort la Latte, *38*, 143
Fort-Mahon-Plage, 17, 143
Fort National, 36
Fort de la Pierre-Levée, 69
Fort du Roule, 28
Fort St Nicolas, 72
Fort Suzac, 81
Fos, 12, 113
Fos-sur-Mer, 113
Fouras, 78, 143
Fréhel, Cap, 35, *38*, 39, 43, 143
Fréjus, 121, 124, 132, 143
Frémur, River, 37
Fret, Le, 47
Fromentine, 69-70, 77, 143
Frontignan-Plage, 106, 143
Fuenterrabia, 95
Fumee, La, 78

Garette, La, 74
Garonne, River, 106
Gassin, 122
Gave, River, 90
Genets, 31
Gerfleur, River, 29
Giens, 120, 143

Ginés, 112
Gironde, River, 9, 63, 80-3
Glénan, Iles de, 51, 55
Golfe du Lion, 9, 101
Golfe du Morbihan, 58-60,
　62, 146
Golfe, de Napoule, 126
Gorbio, 136
Gouédic, River, 39
Gouet, River, 39
Gougins, Les, 27
Goury, *28*
Grand Cau, 113
Grand Menhir, 58, 60
Grand Traict lagoon, 63
Grande Côte (Charente), 80,
　82
Grande Côte (Guérande), 65
Grande Motte, La, 106-7,
　108-9, 126, 143
Grande Rhône, 108, 110, 112
Grandchamp-Maisy, 26
Granville, 30, *31*, 32, 35, 143
Grau-du-Roi, Le, 107, 144
Gravelines, 12
Grayan-et-l'Hopital, 85
Grève de Goulven, 44
Gruissan, 101, *104*, 107, 144
Guérande, 62-3, *65*, 67, 80-3,
　144
Guérinière, 69
Guernsey, 29
Guéthary, 93, 144
Guilvinec, 51, 144
Guindy, River, 40
Guisseny, 44
Gujan-Mestras, 87

Hable d'Ault, 18
Hardelot-Plage, 16-17, 144
Harfluer, 20
Haut-de-Cagnes, 128
Havre, Le, 20-1, 144
Havre-Antifer port, 20
Hendaye, 83, 90, *94*, 95-6,
　144
Hermanville-sur-Mer, 25
Honfleur, 21-2, 144
Hossegor, 85, 90-1, 141, 144
Houlgate, 23, 144
Hourdel, 18
Hourtin, 144
Hyères, 120, 124, 135, 144
Hyères, Iles de, 117, 144

Ilbiarritz, 93
Ile d'Aix, 77-8, 138
Ile de Batz, 44, 63
Ile de Bendor, 117, 139
Ile de Bouin, 69
Ile de Bréhat, 40, 140
Ile Callot, 43
Ile du Grande Bé, 36
Ile de Groix, 56
Ile de Hoedic, 58

Ile de Houat, 58
Ile du Levant, 117, 121-2
Ile de Noirmoutier, 68-9, 77,
　147
Ile aux Oiseaux, 87
Ile d'Oléron, 77, 79, 147
Ile d'Ouessant, 45
Ile de Porquerolles, 120
Ile de Port-Cros, 117, 120
Ile de Ré, *73*, 77-8, 148
Ile de Sein, 49-50
Ile St Lucie, 101
Ile Tristan, 49
Ile-Tudy, 51
Ile Verte, 117
Ile des Vieilles, 125
Ile d'Yeu, 69, 71, 77, 153
Iles Chausey, 31
Iles Embiez, 117-18, 142
Iles de Glénan, 51, 55
Iles d'Hyères, 117, 119-22,
　144
Iles de Lérins, 126
Isigny-sur-Mer, 26
Issmabres, Les, 124, 144

Jaudy, River, 40
Jersey, 29, 31, 39
Jollouville, 31
Juan-les-Pins, 127, 144

Kerdruc, 55
Kerfany-les-Pins, 55
Kerlescan, Alignements de,
　58-9
Kermarguel, 44
Kermario, Alignements de,
　58-9

Lac d'Hossegor, 90
Lac d'Hourtin-Carcans, 85-
　6, 144
Lacanau-Océan, 85, *86*, 144
Lagatjar, Alignements de, 48
Laïta, River, 55
Lancieux, 37, 144
Lande de Fréhel, 39
Lande de Lessay, 29
Landes, the, 83, 85, *88-9*, 90-1
Landévennec, 47
Languedoc-Rousillon, 8-9, 96,
　107, 128
Lannilis, 44
Lannion, 43, 145
Lanton, 87
Lavandou, Le, 117, 120-1,
　145
Lavéra, 113
Lay, River, 73
Lechiagat, 51
Les Lecques, Les, 117, 145
Léguer, River, 42
Léon, 90
Lesconil, 51, 145
Lessay, 29

Levant, Ile du, 117, 121-2
Lézardrieux, 40
Lieu de Grève, 43
Lille, 11
Lit-et-Mixe, 89
Locmariaquer, 58-9, 60, 145
Locquirec, 43, 145
Locronan, 56
Loctudy, 51, 145
Loire, River, 62-3, 65-7
Lorient, 55-6, 67, 145
Luc-sur-Mer, 25, 145

Madelaine, Plage de la, 26,
　145
Madraque, La, 117
Madrague-de-Gignac, 114
Maillezais, 74
Malo-les-Bains, 11, 145
Mané-Lud, 58-9
Marais de Dol, 34
Marais de Machecoul, 69
Marais-Poitevin, Parc
　Régional de, 74-5, 145
Marais-Salants, 63, *65*, 67
Marais de la Vertonne, 71
Marans, 74
Marennes, 79, 145
Marineland, 128, 130
Marquenterre, Parc Ornitho
　-logique de, 17, 21, 145
Marseillan, 105
Marseillank-Plage, 106, 145
Marseille, 12, 20, 106, 113-
　17, 132, 145
Marseilleveyre Massif, 115
Martigues, 113, 115, 145
Massif de l'Esterel, 125, *127*
Maubisson, 85
Maures, Massif des, 121, 124
Mediterranean, 78, 89, 106,
　113, 122, 126, 128
Médoc, the, 82-3
Ménec, Alignements du, 58,
　59
Ménez-Hom, 49
Menton, 9, 113, 131, 133,
　134, 135, *136*, 146
Merlimont-Plage, 17
Mers-les-Bains, 18, 146
Merville-Franceville-Plage,
　24, 26, 146
Merschers-sur-Gironde, 81,
　146
Mesnil-Val, 18
Mèze, 106
Mimizan-Plage, 89, 146
Mindin Toll Bridge, 67
Minihy-Tréguier, 40, 56
Miramar, 125, 146
Monaco/Monte-Carlo, 131,
　132, 133-5, 146
Mont Agel, 133, 136
Mont Dol, 34
Mont Faron, 120

Mont St Clair, 106
Mont-St-Michel, 30-2, *33*, 34-5, 146
Mont Vinaigre, 125
Montague de la Clape, 103
Montagne de la Gardiole, 106
Montelivet-les-Bains, 85, 146
Montpelier, 106
Montreuil, 16
Morbihan, Golfe du, 55, 58-60, 62, 146
Morgat, 48, 146
Morlaix, 43, 146
Morlay, 18
Moulins, Les, 26
Moutiers, Les, 69, 147

Nantes, 67
Napoule, La, 125, 147
Napoule-Plage, La, 126
Narbonne, 101, 106
Narbonne-Plage, 102, 147
Nartelle, La, 124
Nauzan, 81, 147
Nez de Jobourg, 28, 32
Nice, 9, 126, 128, 130-1, 147
Niolon, 114
Niort, 73-5
Nivelle, River, 93
Noirmoutier, Ile de, 68-9, 77, 147
Normandy, 8, 18-19, 23-4, 33-4, 44, 86
Normandy Landings Beaches 24-7
Notre-Dame-de-Mont, 70, 147
Notre-Dame-de-Tronoën, 50, 56
Noyelles-sur-Mer, 18

Odet, River, 51, 55
Oiseaux, Ile aux, 87
Oléron, Ile d', 77, 79, 147
Orb, River, 103
Orne, River, 24
Ouessant, Ile de, 45
Ouistreham, 24, 26, 147
Oye-Plage, 13

Paimpol, 39, 147
Palais, Le, *57*, 58, 77
Palavas-les-Flots, 106, 147
Pallice, La, 75, 77
Palmyre, La, 80, 82, 147
Paramé, 35, 147
Parc Ornithologique du Marquenterre, 17, 21, 145
Parc Ornithologique du Teich, 87, 147
Parc Régional d'Armorique, 45, 49
Parc Régional de Brière, 63,

67, 140
Parc Régional du Marais-Poitevin, 74-5, 145
Pardons, Breton, 41, 56
Parentis-en-Born, 89
Pas de Calais, 14
Payré, River, 72
Pays Basque Coast, 90-2
Pays de la Loire, 59, 63-4
Peille, 130, 136
Peillon, 130
Penmarch Peninsula, 50, 55
Penzé, River, 43
Perpignan, 99
Perros-Guirec, *41*, 42, 56, 147
Petit Fort-Philippe, 12
Petit Grou promontory, 119
Petit Rhône, 110, 112
Petit Traict lagoon, 63
Peyriac-de-Mer, 101
Phare des Baleines, 77-8
Phare de Corduan, 80-1
Phare de la Coubre, 80, 82
Phare de Créac'h, 45
Phare d'Eckmühl, 51, 80
Phare de la Pointe de Barfleur, 27, 139
Phare de la Vieille, 49
Phare de la Vierge, 44
Pilat, Dune du, 88
Pink Granite Coast, *42*
Piriac-sur-Mer, 63, 147
Pléneuf-Val-André, 39
Plougastel-Daoulas, *47*
Plougastel Peninsula, 47
Plouguerneau, 56
Ploumanach, 42-3
Plozévet, 49
Pointe d'Arcachon, 88
Pointe d'Arcay, 73
Pointe de l'Arcouest, 39
Pointe de Baumette, 125
Pointe de Bihit, 42
Pointe de la Chape, 122
Pointe de Chémoulin, 67
Pointe du Chevet, 37
Pointe de la Coubre, 79
Pointe du Décollé, 37
Pointe du Déffend, 117
Pointe des Espagnols, 47
Pointe de l'Esquillon, 126
Pointe de Gâvres, 56
Pointe de la Garde, 38
Pointe de la Garde-Guérin, 37
Pointe de Grave, 80-3
Pointe du Grouin, 35
Pointe du Grouin du Cou, 72
Pointe du Hoc, *24*, 26
Pointe du Hock, 35
Pointe du Moulinet, 37
Pointe de Pen-Bron, 63
Pointe de Penhir, 48, 50
Pointe de Penmarch, 51

Pointe de Pléneuf, 39
Pointe de Primel, 43
Pointe du Raz, 49-50
Pointe du Roc, 30, *31*
Pointe du Roselier, 39
Pointe de St Cast, 38
Pointe de St Gildas, 68
Pointe de St Mathieu, 45, *46*
Pointe de Squewel, 42
Pointe de Suzac, 81
Poitou-Charentes, 63-4, 74
Pont l'Abbé, 51, 148
Pont-Aven, 55-6, 148
Pont-Croix, 49
Pont de Tancarville, 21
Pontaillac, 81, 148
Ponte San Ludovico, 136
Pornic, *66-8*, 69, 148
Pornichet, 66, 148
Porquerolles, Ile de, 117, 120
Port-d'Albret, 90
Port Bacarès, 100-1, *102-3*, 107, 148
Port-en-Bessin, 25
Port-Bloc, 83
Port-de-Bouc, 113
Port du Brusc, 119
Port-Camargue, 107, 148
Port-Cros, Ile de, 121-2
Port-la-Galère, 126, 128
Port Goulphar, 58, 77
Port-Grimaud, 123, 128
Port-Joinville, 69, 77
Port Leucate, 101, 107
Port-Lin, 65
Port-Louis, 56
Port-Manech, 55
Port Maria, 58
Port-de-la-Meule, 69
Port de Mirimar, 120
Port-Navalo, 59-60
Port-le-Nouvelle, 101, 148
Port-du-Pave, 75
Port-Pigeon, 58
Port-Pin Calanque, 115
Port-Rhu, River, 49, *50-1*
Port St Ange, 100
Port-Vendres, 96-8, 101, 148
Portbail, 29, 148
Portivy, 58
Portsall, 44
Portzic, Le, 48
Poterie, La, 20
Pouldu, Le, 55, 148
Pouliguen, Le, 65-6, 148
Poul-Rodon, 43
Pourville-sur-Mer, 19
Préfailles, 68, 148
Presqu'île de Quiberon, 57
Presqu'île de Rhuys, 62, 65
Presqu'île de St Mandrier, 117, 119
Provence, 9, 113, 116, 120-1
Puget, Massif de, 115
Puits d'Enfer, 72

Pyla-sur-Mer, 87, 148
Pyrenees, 93, 96, 98, 101

Quend-Plage-les-Pins, 17,
148
Quiberon, Presqu'île de, 57-
8, 77, 148
Quiberville-Plage, 19
Quimper, 51, *52-3*, 55-6, 61,
148
Quineville, 27

Rade de Brest, 47
Ramateulle, 122
Rance, River, 35-7, 148
Rayol, 122, 148
Raz de Sein, 49
Ré, Ile de, *73*, 77-8, 148
Renal, Le, 87
Réserve Naturelle Zoologique
et Botanique, Camargue,
112
Rhône, River, 9, 96, 98, 110,
113
Rhone-Sète Canal, 106
Rhune, La, 90, 93
Riva-Bella, 24, 26, 149
Rivière d'Etel, 56, *60*
Roche-Bernard, La, 34, 62-3
Rochefort, 78-9, 149
Rochelle, La, *74*, 75, *76*, 77-8,
149
Ronce-les-Bains, 79, 149
Roquebrune, 131, *133*, 134
Roquebrune-Cap-Martin,
135, 149
Rosaires, Les, 39
Roscoff, 44, 149
Rothéneuf Cove, 35, 149
Rouen, 17, 21, 101
Rouet-Plage, Le, 114-15
Royan, 80-3, 149
Rue, 16-17

Sables d'Olonne, Les, *70-1*,
149
Sables-d'Or-les-Pins, 39, 151
Sablettes, Les, 119-20, 151
St Aubin, 19
St Aubin-sur-Mer, 25
St Aygulf, 124, 149
St Benoît-des-Ondes, 34
St Brevin-les-Pins-l'Océan,
67, 149
St Briac-sur-Mer, 37, 149
St Brieuc, 39, 49, 149
St Cado, 56
St Cast-le-Guildo, 38, 150
St Cyprien-Plage, 99, 107,
150
St George-de-Didonne, *80*,
81-2, 150
St Germain-Plage, 29
St Gilles-Croix-de-Vie, 71,
150

St Girons-Plage, 90, 150
St Guénolé, 50, 150
St Hilaire-le-Palud, 74
St Jean-Cap-Ferrat, 131, 150
St Jean-de-Luz, 90, 93, *94-5*,
150
St Jean-de-Mont, 70, 150
St Jean-le-Thomas, 31
St Laurent-de-la-Mer, 39
St Laurent-sur-Mer, 25, 26
St Lunaire, 37
St Malo, 35, *36*, 37, 44, 150
St Mandrier-sur-Mer, 119-
20
St Martin-de-Ré, 77-8
St Michel-en-Grève, 43, 150
St Michel-en-Herm, 74
St Nazaire, 67, 150
St Pair, 31
St Palais-sur-Mer, 81, 150
St Pierre, 51
St Pierre-d'Oléron, 79
St Pierre-sur-Mer, 103, 150
St Pol-de-Léon, 43-4, 150
St Quay-Portrieux, 39, 150
St Raphaël, 121-2, *124*, 125,
135, 151
St Servan-sur-Mer, 37, 151
St Trojan-les-Bains, 79
St Tropez, *122*, 122-4, 128,
151
St Tugen, 49, 56
St Vaast-la-Hougue, 27, 32,
151
St Valery-en-Caux, 19, 151
St Valery-sur-Somme, 17-
18, 21, 23, 151
St Vincent-sur-Jard, 72
St Vivien-de-Médoc, 85
Ste Anne d'Auray, 56, 60-1,
149
Ste Anne-la-Palud, 49, 56,
149
Ste Marguerite, 18
Ste Marie, 68
Ste Marie-du-Mont, 26
Ste Marie-Plage, 99
Ste Maxime, 123, 150
Ste Mère-Église, 26-7
Stes Maries-de-la-Mer, 108-
10, *111*, 112, 150
Salins du Midi, 109-10
Salses, 101, 151
Sanary-sur-Mer, 117, *118-
19*, 151
Sangatte, 14
Sansais, 74
Sausset-les-Pins, 114-15
Sauzon, 58, 77
See, River, 31
Sein, Ile de, 49-50
Seine, River, 20-1
Selme, River, 32
Sept Iles, 42-3
Sète, 101, 104-6, 151

Seudre-Charente Canal, 79
Seudre, River, 79
Sion-sur-l'Océan, 70
Six-Fours-les-Plages, 119, 151
Slack, River, 14
Socoa, 93
Somme, River, 14, 17, 21
Sotterville-sur-Mer, 19
Soulac-sur-Mer, 83, 85, 151
Stella-Plage, 17
Surrain, 26
Surville, 29

Table des Marchands, 58, 60
Talmont, 81-2
Talmont-St Hilaire, 72, 151
Tamaris, 119
Tancarville, Pont de, 21
Taussat, 87, 151
Taute, River, 26
Tech, River, 99
Teich, Parc Ornithologique
du, 87, 147
Teste, La, 87
Tharon-Plage, 68
Théoule-sur-Mer, 126
Tinée, River, 131
Tombelaine, 32
Torreilles-Plage, 99
Toulon, 117, 119-20, 151
Touques, River, 23
Touquet-Paris-Plage, Le-,
16-17, 152
Tranche-sur-Mer, La, 72, 79,
152
Trayas, Le, 125
Trébeurden, 42, 152
Tréboul, 49, *50-1*, 152
Trégastel-Plage, *42*, 43, 152
Tréguier, *40*, 152
Trémazan, 44
Tremblade, La, 79, 152
Tréport, Le, 18, 21, 152
Trieux, River, 40
Trinité-sur-Mer, La, 59, 152
Trouville, 23, 152
Turballe, La, 63, 152
Turbie, La, 131, 133, 152

Val-André, Le, 39, 152
Val de Saire, 27
Vallauris, 126, 130, 152
Valras-Plage, 103, 152
Vanlee, River, 30
Vannes, 56, 59-60, *61-2*, 152
Var, River, 128, 131
Varengeville-sur-Mer, 19
Vendée, 8, 86
Vendée, River, 75
Verdon, Le, 83
Vers-sur-Mer, 25
Vésubie, River, 131
Veules-les-Roses, 19
Veulettes-sur-Mer, 19, 153
Vie, River, 70-1

Vierville-sur-Mer, 26, 152
Vieux-Boucau-les-Bains, 90, 152
Villaine, River, 63
Ville-Men, La, 39
Villefranche, 131, 153

Villeneuve-les-Maguelonne, 106
Villers-sur-Mer, 23, 153
Villerville, 23, 153
Vire, River, 26
Vivier-sur-Mer, Le, 34

Wimereux, 14, 153
Wissant, 14

Yeu, Ile d', 69, 71, 77, 153
Yport, 20

160